SPECIAL INTEREST TOURISM

Edited by

Betty Weiler and Colin Michael Hall

Belhaven Press
London

Halsted Press
an imprint of John Wiley & Sons, Inc.
New York Toronto

First published in Great Britain in 1992 by
Belhaven Press (a division of Pinter Publishers),
25 Floral Street, London WC2E 9DS

British Library Cataloguing in Publication Data
A CIP catalogue record for this book is available from the British Library

ISBN I 85293 072 1

Copublished in the Western Hemisphere
by Halsted Press, an Imprint of John Wiley & Sons, Inc. New York Toronto
[605 Third Avenue, New York, NY 10158–0012]

Library of Congress Cataloging-in-Publication Data
Weiler, B. (Betty)
Special interest tourism / B. Weiler, C. M. Hall.
p. cm.
Includes bibliographical references and index.
ISBN 1-85293-072-1 ; — ISBN 0-470-21843-6 (Halsted Press)
1. Tourist trade. I. Hall, C. M. (C. Michael) II. Title
G155.A1W37 1992
338.4'791—dc20 91-40465 CIP

Printed and bound in Great Britain

Contents

List of figures

List of tables

List of plates

List of contributors

Philip Dearden is an Associate Professor in the Department of Geography, University of Victoria, British Columbia, Canada.

C. Michael Hall is a Senior Lecturer in Tourism and Heritage Management in the Department of Management Systems, and Senior Research Fellow, New Zealand Natural Heritage Foundation, Massey University, Palmerston North, New Zealand.

Sylvia Harron is a graduate of the Department of Geography, University of Victoria, British Columbia, Canada.

John M. Jenkins is undertaking postgraduate research in the Department of Geography and Planning, University of New England, Armidale, New South Wales, Australia.

Margaret E. Johnston is an Assistant Professor in the Centre for Northern Studies, Lakehead University, Thunder Bay, Ontario, Canada.

Katherine M. Kalinowski is a graduate of the Department of Recreation and Leisure Studies at the University of Alberta, Edmonton, Alberta, Canada.

Harold Richins is a Senior Lecturer in Tourism Management in the Department of Management at the University of Newcastle, Newcastle, New South Wales, Australia.

Raymond S. Tabata is the Marine Extension Agent with the University of Hawaii Sea Grant Extension Service, Honolulu, Hawaii, United States of America.

Peter S. Valentine is a Senior Lecturer in the Department of Geography, James Cook University, Townsville, Queensland, Australia.

Betty Weiler is a Senior Lecturer in Tourism and Marketing in the Department of Management at the University of Newcastle, Newcastle, New South Wales, Australia.

Christopher Wood is the Director of Australians Studying Abroad, an educational travel company based in Melbourne, Victoria, Australia.

Heather Zeppel is undertaking postgraduate research at James Cook University of North Queensland, Townsville, Queensland, Australia.

Preface

Many people helped to provide stimulus for researching and writing *Special Interest Tourism*, including friends, colleagues, and advisers Patrick Armstrong, Tim Burton, Graham Castledine, Dave Crag, Jenny Craik, Ian Elliot, David Mercer, Peter Murphy, David Press, Gerry Redmond, Dennis Rumley, and Michael Wood. The present volume was conceived at the 1988 Christchurch meeting of the International Geographical Union Commission on Leisure and Recreation organized by Doug Pearce. Since that meeting, the ideas for the book were encouraged and supported by our former colleagues at the University of New England, including, but not limited to, Bill Boyd, Claire Campbell, Derrin Davis, Ian Dutton, Steve Hapgood, Jenny Kinny, Cliff Ollier, Tim Pedrazinni, John Pigram, Jeremy Smith, Margot Sweeny, Jim Walmsley, and many of the tourism students at the Northern Rivers campus. Our present colleagues in the Department of Management Systems, Massey University, New Zealand, and the Department of Management, University of Newcastle, Australia, also provided invaluable assistance and understanding in the completion of this project.

When the book was adopted by Belhaven Press, Iain Stevenson played a particularly patient and understanding role as Editorial Director. Others who have contributed to its development and maturation by assisting in research and commenting on drafts include David Estreich, Tracey Johnson, Peter Kennedy, Neil Leiper, Simon McArthur, Andrea McIlroy, Ian Mitchell, and Kathy Richins. The authors of the individual chapters also acknowledge the cooperation of respondents, institutions, and organizations in facilitating their research.

Nurturing and moral support were provided by many individuals, including Mariella Bates, Nicole Beasley, Christine Collister, Anne-Louise Crotty, Clive Gregson, Bill Faulkner, Jacqui Pinkava, Penny Spoelder, Brian Springett, Delyse Springett, Ivan Surridge, Josette Wells, David Whitson, Len Zell, and the staff of Options at Massey University. Financial assistance was gratefully received by the authors from the Massey University Research Fund and the University of New England for research into special interest tourism. The institutional support provided by the New Zealand Natural Heritage Foundation is gratefully acknowledged, as is the help of Linda Coop, Linda Macnamara, Stephanie Pearson, and Tony Vitalis of the Department of Management Systems, Massey University.

A final word of thanks goes to all those directly involved in special interest tourism, as hosts, managers, employees and participants. Your enthusiasm and dedication to the pursuit of special interest tourism has made this book possible.

C. Michael Hall,
Massey University and New Zealand Natural Heritage Foundation, New Zealand

Betty Weiler,
University of Newcastle, Australia

1 INTRODUCTION

What's Special about Special Interest Tourism?

C. Michael Hall and Betty Weiler

> New kinds of life-style and a new realization of the importance of relations between people and between people and nature are features of the 1980s. Gaining in importance are participation in outdoor activities, awareness of ecological problems, educational advances, aesthetic judgement and improvement of self and society. The search for these new values in the exercise of tourism is reflected in organized recreation and the new products that have emerged, such as active holidays and special interest tourism (World Tourism Organization, 1985, p.3).

Introduction: The Changing Tourism Marketplace

The international travel market is changing. Increased spending power per capita, greater leisure time, a better travelled and more discerning public, and major socio-demographic changes in the developed world, point to a substantially different travel market in the 1990s to that which existed during the 1970s and early 1980s (Chew, 1987; Lickorish, 1987; Martin and Mason, 1987; Shackleford, 1987). Sociodemographic changes marked by an active aging population, later marriage, two-income families, childless couples, and a rising population of single adults, have led to substantial changes in travel and leisure demand. 'The overriding result of these social changes will be ever greater variety – variety in tourist types, needs and patterns' (Martin and Mason, 1987, p.113). While travel costs will remain a significant determinant of travel decisions, tourist satisfaction is increasing in importance. Value for money is important in this context, rather than cheapness or bargain-basement offers. As Lickorish (1987, p.94) noted, 'There are many places (which vary with the individual) that one would not go for free. The true tourism product is a visit to an appealing destination for some deeply satisfying purpose (business or pleasure)'. Similarly, Krippendorf (1987a, p.174), observed that 'people are becoming more determined to derive satisfaction from all areas of life, and travel must provide something extra to attract the potential tourist away from a fulfilling job and pleasurable home life'.

Krippendorf (1987a, b) has argued that fundamental changes are occurring in the tourism market with the development of new patterns of tourism consumption (Table 1.1). According to Krippendorf (1987a), the year 2000 will witness substantial declines in those tourists for whom hedonism is a dominant travel

Table 1.1 The changing composition of the western tourist market

Market Segment	Travel Motivations	% of market 1986	% of market 2000
Work-oriented (live for work)	• recover – rest, doing nothing, passivity, being served, switching off; and • liberation – no duties, no worries, no problems.	10–20	≈10
Hedonistic lifestyle (one works in order to live)	• experience something different, explore, have a change; • have fun, enjoy oneself, play; • being active, together with others; • relaxation without stress, do as one pleases; and • nature, enjoying proximity with nature, and intact environment.	≈60	45–60
'New unity of everyday life' (reduced polarity between work and leisure)	• broaden one's horizon, learn something; • introspection and communication with other people; • come back to simpler things and nature; • creativity, open-mindedness; and • readiness for experiments.	20–30	30–45

Source: Krippendorf, 1987a, pp.174–175.

motivation and for whom tourism is seen purely as a mechanism for recovery and liberation to then pursue work activities. Instead, the travel market will place emphasis on the environmental and social context within which tourism occurs and the humanization of travel (Krippendorf, 1987a, b).

Substantial evidence exists for Krippendorf's (1987a) analysis of changing tourism consumption patterns and their implications for the marketplace. The emergence of satisfaction as the principal criterion of vacation selection has led to a marked shift towards 'active' holidays. 'Changing social patterns have given rise to new patterns in holiday-taking; special interest holidays to cater for the expanding range of interests of a leisure society, e.g. activity holidays for those whose sedentary occupations encourage more energetic forms of travel' (Holloway, 1985, p.39). Similarly, Helber (1988, p.21) reported a trend towards 'experience oriented' holidays with an emphasis on action, adventure, fantasy, nostalgia, and exotic experiences. In the Australian context, Frew (1989) reported: 'Today's sophisticated travellers no longer want to spend their time sunbaking by the side of five-star hotel pools, or whittling away their wealth in glitzy shopping malls. People want to "experience" a holiday, whether it be learning to milk cows on a farm, rafting down white-water rapids, or crossing Kakadu by light aircraft'.

Table 1.2 The motivations associated with special interest activities

Setting	Special Interest Activities	Related Motivations
urban	museums	novelty, diversity, discovery, authenticity, uniqueness, education.
	art galleries	emotion, beauty, exclusiveness, uniqueness, authenticity, education.
	heritage	atmosphere, ambience, perceived authenticity, discovery, education.
	arts and community festivals	authenticity, emotion, escape.
	performing arts	emotion, escape.
	cultural (ethnic) travel	authenticity, uniqueness, social contact, novelty, education.
	sports tourism	spectating, improved physical well-being, social contact.
rural	cultural (ethnic) travel	authenticity, uniqueness, social contact, novelty, education.
	arts and community festivals	authenticity, emotion, escape.
	heritage	atmosphere, ambience, perceived authenticity, discovery, education.
	adventure travel	risk seeking, self-discovery, self actualization, contact with nature, social contact.
	health tourism	improved physical well-being.
	sports tourism	improved physical well-being, social contact.
	farm and ranch tourism	contact with nature and the rural environment, social contact, discovery
natural	nature-based tourism	contact with nature, discovery, knowledge, education, scientific curiosity.
	adventure travel	risk seeking, self-discovery, self actualization, contact with nature, social contact.

Sources: Young and Crandall, 1984; Hall, 1989; Tabata, 1989; Hall and Zeppel, 1990; Zeppel and Hall, 1991; Hall (Chapter 11), Harron and Weiler (Chapter 7), Kalinowski and Weiler (Chapter 2); Valentine (Chapter 9); and Zeppel and Hall (Chapter 5).

Profiling the Special Interest Traveller

The western leisure and travel market has become increasingly segmented and specialized with the development of new styles of leisure and tourism (Hendee, Gale, and Catton, 1971; Mercer, 1981; Kellert, 1985; Crompton and Richardson, 1986; World Tourism Organization 1985; Hall, 1989, 1991). However, the limited studies of specialization within the tourism market reflect the difficulties encountered in classifying travellers on the basis of motivations or psychographic profiles (Hall, 1989). Nevertheless, several studies have identified a number of motivations which may be associated with specific special interest activities (see Table 1.2).

Although only a limited profile exists of special interest tourists, it would appear that many, though not all, broadly correspond to the allocentric category of Plog's (1974) psychographic continuum. Allocentrics focus on life's varied activities and prefer unfamiliar, novel trips. A further dimension of the motivations of the special interest market was provided in the research of Crompton (1979, p.419) who, in a study of tourist motivations, noted 'that many respondents did not receive sociopsychological satisfactions, but received almost exclusively cultural benefits. Two primary cultural motives were expressed. They were novelty and education'. Cultural, educational, and historical travel motivations have also been given prominence in the work of Ritchie and Zins (1978), Smith (1989), Hall and Zeppel (1990), Zeppel and Hall (1991), and O'Rourke (1990), and are reviewed in the chapters on educational travel, ethnic tourism, and arts and heritage tourism (Chapters 2, 7 and 5).

Snepenger's (1987) segmentation of the Alaskan vacation market paid specific attention to the novelty-seeking role. Based on the typology of tourist roles proposed by Cohen (1972), Snepenger's study indicates that the characteristics of the novelty seeking or 'explorer' tourist segment, either through the pursuit of new activities or the conduct of familiar activities within unfamiliar surroundings, has substantial implications for the nature of tourism marketing and management, and the provision of the tourist experience, a point also taken up in the research of Harron and Weiler (Chapter 7), Tabata (1989, and Chapter 13), and Valentine (Chapter 9).

REAL Travel

Despite difficulties in neatly categorizing the special interest traveller, several authors have suggested that special interest tourism may be characterized by the tourist's search for novel, authentic, and quality tourist experiences; and by the tourism industry's provision of such experiences (Read, 1980; Snepenger, 1987; Hall, 1989, 1991; Hall and Zeppel, 1990). As Tabata (1989, p.70) observed: 'The special interest traveller wants to experience something new, whether it is history, food, sports, customs or the outdoors. Many wish to appreciate the new sights, sounds, smells and tastes and to understand the place and its people'. Indeed, Read (1980, p.202) suggested that the term of special interest travel be discarded and replaced by the notion of REAL travel: 'Travel with only four additives. That travel would be REWARDING; it would be ENRICHING; it would be ADVENTURESOME; and it would be a LEARNING experience' (see concluding chapter). However, as the following chapters indicate, the basis for segmenting and targeting the special interest market is not just the motivations or the demographic and psychographic profile of participants but also the nature of the interest they are pursuing.

The Scope and Definition of Special Interest Tourism

In 1980, Read argued that special interest travel would be a 'prime force in the expansion of tourism' and would 'dominate the industry in the next decade and be responsible for an unprecedented rise in visitor satisfaction' (1980, p.195). According to Read (1980, p.195): 'special interest travel is travel for people who are going somewhere because they have a particular interest that can be pursued in a particular region or at a particular destination. It is the *hub* around which the *total* travel experience is planned and developed'. Special interest travel is sometimes equated with the term 'active' tourism. According to Heywood (1990, p.46), the increased active component of travel is illustrated by the trends in tourism 'towards conservation, scholarship, science and environmental awareness'. The active involvement of travellers in the cultural and/or physical environment they are visiting is regarded as a key element of special interest travel (Read, 1980; Hall, 1989; Tabata, 1989; Hall and Zeppel, 1990; Wood, 1990). According to the World Tourism Organization (1985, p.3):

> Active holidays could be defined as holidays during which a person engages in a cultural, artisanal or leisure activity or sport with a view to fulfilling himself and developing his personality. Special interest tourism, meanwhile, is specialized tourism involving group or individual tours by people who wish to develop certain interests and visit sites and places connected with a specific subject. Generally speaking, the people concerned exercise the same profession or have a common hobby.

A critical element of active and specialty tourism is the realization that transport and accommodation considerations alone do not provide the tourism product. Instead, the tourism experience can be enriched 'by allowing greater integration with the place visited and fuller involvement in the social and cultural life of the holiday destination' (World Tourism Organization, 1985, p.3). As Pearce (1988, p.219) suggested 'The future trends for tourism seem to suggest that travellers will be especially concerned not with just being "there", but with participating, learning and experiencing the "there" they visit'. For the purpose of this book, special

interest tourism can be said to occur when the traveller's motivation and decision-making are primarily determined by a particular special interest. Therefore, the term special interest tourism or travel as used in this book implies 'active' or 'experiential' travel. Special interest tourism is often regarded as synonymous with 'ethical travel' and 'social tourism' (Frommer, 1988), 'secondary tourism' (World Tourism Organization, 1988); 'eco-tourism' (Boo, 1990), 'educational travel' (O'Rourke, 1990), and 'alternative', 'appropriate', 'environmental', 'nature-based', and 'sustainable' tourism (Gonsalves, 1987; Richter, 1987, 1989; Kutay, 1989). However, while the pursuit of quality travel experiences is common to all forms of special interest tourism it is not always the case that special interest tourism *is* quality travel.

Size of the Market

The exact size of the special interest tourism market is unclear. However, it is generally regarded to be a growing segment of international travel and western domestic markets (Read, 1980; World Tourism Organization, 1985; Frommer, 1988; Hall, 1989, 1991; O'Rourke, 1990). For instance, the Australian National Tourism Committee (1988, p. 27) has placed considerable emphasis on special interest tourism as 'a growth area of travel with potential for much further development' and noted 'a worldwide trend towards "travel with a purpose"' (1988, p. 25). The World Tourism Organization (1985) estimated that the special interest market contributed about two to three per cent of total domestic or international travellers in the 1970s and early 1980s. In contrast, Tabata (1989, p.69) reported that, 'a survey of U.S. travel agents revealed that about 15% of bookings involved special interest travel. One agent said that "people are tired of doing the same old thing, and are interested in action-packed trips such as hiking, biking and rafting"'. Similarly, Alpine (1986) observed that special interest travel is booming, a substantial proportion of the market being composed of high-income earners who are going on longer and more expensive holidays characterized by their challenge and diversity.

The development of the special interest tourism market is illustrated in the growth of magazines and periodicals such as the *Specialty Travel Index* which provides a comprehensive coverage of 'thousands of unusual travel opportunities worldwide' (Hall, 1989, p.81). Activities which the *Index* advertises are extremely diverse and include such special interests as archeology, ballooning, bicycle touring, bed and breakfast, brewery tours, canal cruising, goat trekking, golf, gourmet travel, health and fitness, opera, photography, river rafting, safaris, scuba diving, tennis, trains, and wineries. The range of special interest activities is also indicated in travel guidebooks. For instance, Fodor's 1990 guide to South America described the continent as largely a special interest destination, and noted the following activities as being part of the specialty travel activities available in South America: hiking and trekking, river running, fishing, archaeology, architecture, art, black culture, Club Med, and flora and fauna.

Settings, Activities and Motivations

As the above discussion of special interest activities illustrates, special interest tourism can occur in both urban and non-urban settings and may encompass a number of motivations (Table 1.2). Special interest travellers can be delineated according to whether the primary focus of their interest is on an activity or activities, and/or the destination or setting (Table 1.3). For instance, the focus on

Table 1.3 Market niches based on primary trip focus and setting

Primary Motive	Setting: Urban	Non-urban/rural
Activity	art and heritage tourism e.g. performing arts	sport tourism e.g. scuba diving
		adventure travel e.g. white-water rafting
	educational travel e.g. French language study	health and fitness tourism e.g. health cruises
		nature-based e.g. birding
Destination	art and heritage tourism e.g. museums and art galleries	ethnic travel e.g. hilltribe trekking
	educational travel e.g. architectural tour of Europe	nature-based e.g. Galapagos Island tours
	sport tourism e.g. spectating at the Olympic Games	adventure travel e.g. trekking in Nepal
		health tourism e.g. European spa tourism

learning as an activity provides the distinguishing factor for educational travellers who may pursue their interest in a variety of settings (O'Rourke, 1990; Kalinowski and Weiler, Chapter 2). In contrast, the substantial educational motivations of nature-based or ethnic tourists are in addition to other motivations such as contact with nature or indigenous populations (Harron and Weiler, Chapter 7; Valentine, Chapter 9). In the case of nature-based tourism the environmental setting will sometimes be more important a determinant of the travel product than a specific participant motivation or the pursuit of a particular activity. In other cases, such as birdwatching, the activity is of primary importance. While the products offered to the different market segments may have certain commonalities, it is important to recognize that commercial success may be dependent on distinguishing between specialty groups established through a common activity or focus and groups with an interest in a particular destination or setting. However, it should be noted that as activity-oriented special interest travellers develop higher levels of experience and expertise, then destination choice may play a greater role in the selection of travel opportunities (Hall and McArthur, forthcoming).

The contributions to the present volume show commonalities at three levels of increased complexity. First, and most simply, industry publications such as *Specialty Travel Index* unite the subject matter of the book from a product marketing perspective. The active and experiential nature of special interest tourism present relatively specific target markets to tourist operators and wholesalers which are reflected in advertising and product development. Second, as discussed above and illustrated in the following chapters, special interest tourists exhibit a common desire for authenticity, immersion in the cultural and/or physical environment, and the pursuit of environmental and experiential quality. These characteristics may be distinguished by educational and cultural motivations, and by a desire to experience novelty and uniqueness as part of the travel experience. Third, participants in special interest tourism activities exhibit the tendency to develop their own social world marked by specialized communication channels (Shibutani, 1955) in which 'amorphous, diffuse constellations of actors, organizations, events and practices... have coalesced into spheres of interest and involvement for participants' (Unruh, 1980, p.277). The first two have already been outlined in detail, the third will be illustrated below.

Devall (1973) noted that leisure social worlds, such as those derived from specialized activities such as mountaineering and surfing, offered major sources of orientation and reward from members, in a similar way to how the workplace meets the needs of those who are work-oriented (Krippendorf, 1987b). As Bryan (1977) noted, 'What may well be significant about these groups is that they not only serve as standards of reference for leisure behaviours, but may revolve around and influence central life interests and most other areas of life activity'. Clearly, not all or even most participants in a given recreational or touristic activity will be members of a social world segment. However, it can be hypothesized that special interest tourists will be more likely to exhibit preferences and behaviour associated with a particular leisure social world.

Stebbins (1982) has examined the development of leisure social worlds in his study of 'serious leisure'. The notion of serious leisure is closely related to Krippendorf's (1987a) identification of the 'new-unity-of-everyday-life' market segment (Table 1.1), which exhibits a reduced polarity between work and leisure. Indeed, both writers see the development of serious leisure as a phenomenon of postindustrial society. According to Stebbins (1982, p.253):

> leisure in postindustrial society is no longer seen as chiefly a means of recuperating from the travail of the job... If leisure is to become, for many, an improvement over work as a way of finding personal fulfillment, identity enhancement, self-expression, and the like, then people must be careful to adopt those forms with the greatest payoff. The theme here is that we reach this goal through engaging in serious rather than casual or unserious leisure.

Special interest tourism may be regarded as a form of serious leisure given that it exhibits several of the characteristics of serious leisure. First, special interest tourists tend to be seeking durable benefits such as 'self-actualization, self-enrichment, recreation or renewal of self, self-expression, social interaction and belongingness, and lasting physical products of the activity' (Stebbins, 1982, p.257). (See also Zeppel and Hall, Chapter 5; Johnston, Chapter 12; Kalinowski and Weiler, Chapter 2; and Harron and Weiler, Chapter 7, for examples within this volume.) Second, participants often require a special knowledge, training, or skill in order to pursue a special interest tourism activity (see Johnston, Chapter 12, and Tabata, Chapter 13). Third, there is a tendency for amateurs, hobbyists and specialty travellers to have a 'career path' in pursuing their interests which may also incorporate a degree of perseverance against adversity (Devall, 1973; Bryan, 1977; Stebbins, 1982; Mitchell, 1983; Kellert, 1985; Andressen and Hall, 1988/89). Fourth, special interest tourists tend to exhibit a unique ethos which is represented by a specific social world 'composed of special beliefs, values, moral principles, norms, and performance standards' (Stebbins, 1982, p.257). (See also Mitchell, 1983, for a discussion of this phenomenon within the context of mountain climbing.) Finally, participants of special interest travel tend to identify strongly with their chosen activity or pursuit (Stebbins, 1979; 1982), for example, in the case of international travel by American conservation groups and professional societies, to promote education and professional development of members (Laarman, Stewart, and Prestemon, 1989).

The last two characteristics may help explain the relationship between special interest tourism and 'ethical' or 'appropriate tourism'. The identification process and the establishment of specific life worlds by cultural and nature-oriented tourists would assist in the development of a symbiotic relationship with the social and physical environment which they visit. One potential outcome of this relationship is the development of codes of ethics, management and protection which would assist in ensuring that the tourism resource (either social or natural) is preserved for future visitors and for the benefit of the resource itself. This point is addressed further in the concluding chapter of this book.

Special Interest Tourism as Ethical Tourism

As noted above, special interest tourism has been variously described as 'appropriate', 'ethical', or 'alternative travel'. Frommer (1988, p.v) describes 'alternative travel' as 'a new kind of vacation that improves upon the stale and tired variety'. The essence of alternative travel is the active, conscious involvement of the visitor with the host in a manner which does not degrade the quality of the destination's socio-cultural or natural environment. Cultural tourism, in particular, is seen as a mechanism by which tourists can learn from the host society and experience a different culture in a non-exploitative manner (Dearden and Harron, Chapter 8; Harron and Weiler, Chapter 7; Wood, Chapter 4). As Read (1980, p. 199) stated:

> The local people must be involved – be a part of the tourism experience – and recognize that the 'special interest' tour group is not merely a group of people coming to gawk at zoo-like culture. Our experience has shown that the kind of traveler who is attracted by a 'special interest' is indeed looking for [a] rewarding, enriching, adventuresome, learning experience...

The search for a more socially aware tourism is not isolated to cultural tourism. In the case of adventure recreation, Raines (1988–89, p.5) noted that 'adventure education has evolved from society's militaristic need to promote hardiness in the population and the basic human need for stimulation driven by curiosity and the quest for knowledge'. For adventure, cultural, and educational travellers, self-actualization has become a major travel motivation. However, the tourist experience should not to be gained at the expense of damaging the qualities of a society which made the experience possible (Krippendorf, 1987a, b; Richter, 1989).

The Greening of the Tourism Industry

The emergence of special interest travel and the subsequent 'greening' of the tourism industry has substantial implications for tourism management and marketing. If Krippendorf's (1987a, p.175) assertion, that 'the market is shifting from manipulated, uncritical "old tourists" to mature, critical and emancipated "new tourists", is true, then tourism marketing will, of necessity, become more socially responsible and environmentally oriented. Venth (1985) has identified three main components of this new form of tourism marketing which specifically caters to the environmentally-conscious market segment:

- The marketer puts an accent on what he is doing himself in favour of the preservation of nature and environment.
- The marketer appeals directly to the sense of responsibility of these environmentally-conscious people and asks them to participate actively in keeping nature unspoiled (behaviour code). He takes them at their own word.
- The environment is scarce and thus a luxury good, and consumption must be restricted. This extracts a price in self-discipline, respect – and money. The marketer and the consumers have to be ready to pay this price. The marketer has to prove that he is willing to pay the price (Venth, 1985, in Krippendorf, 1987a).

The implications of the development of the environmental tourism market for tourist management and product development can be seen in the promotion of ecotourism at a national level in Costa Rica (Fennell and Eagles, 1990) and Ecuador (Wilson and Laarman, 1987), and the activities of tourist operators and non-profit organizations in the marketplace. For example, non-profit organizations have been established, such as the Eco-Tourism Society in the United States and the New Zealand Natural Heritage Foundation, which act as brokers between commercial operators and the traveller, and as operators of educational and environmental tours in their own right. (See Valentine, Chapter 9, for a further discussion of nature-based tour operators and Harron and Weiler, Chapter 7, for a discussion of ethnic tour operators.)

Heywood (1990, p.45) argued that tourism has the potential to be a relatively clean industry as it relies upon the environment for its continuing existence and success: 'It is because tourism is based on very high cultural values – spirit of enquiry, love of beauty, search for knowledge, and respect for nature – that it tends to be self-correcting in its impact on the physical and cultural environments in ways that none of the more material industries are'. The environmental dependence of tourism is clearly illustrated in Valentine's chapter on nature-based tourism (Chapter 9). However, the relationship is also apparent in Jenkins' study of fossicking in northern New South Wales (Chapter 10), Johnston's research on risk recreation in New Zealand (Chapter 12), Tabata's examination of scuba-diving in Hawaii (Chapter 13), and Hall's review of adventure tourism (Chapter 11).

The implications of the ethical orientation of special interest travel are immense. In the short-term, they will require the development of new attitudes by tourist operators, marketers, and managers who wish to tap into this market. In the long-term special interest tourism may offer opportunities to develop sustainable forms of tourism that do not degrade social or natural resources.

A Beginning

The present book examines special interest activities from the perspectives of both activities and destinations (see Tables 1.2 and 1.3). Authors were asked to provide their own interpretation of special interest tourism within the scope of their particular studies or reviews. The combination of review chapters and case studies hopefully provides the reader with a useful introduction to the manner in which special interest tourism has itself developed. Nevertheless, the unification of a range of specialized touristic activities which this book attempts under the banner of 'special interest tourism' presents a challenge, particularly when relatively little systematic research has previously been conducted on the subject. The review chapters on educational travel (Kalinowski and Weiler, Chapter 2), arts and heritage tourism (Hall and Zeppel, Chapter 5), ethnic tourism (Harron and Weiler, Chapter 7), nature-based tourism (Valentine, Chapter 9), and adventure, sport, and health tourism (Hall, Chapter 11), provide an overview of the literature discussing the development of particular market segments. The series of case studies on study tours (Kalinowski, Chapter 3; Wood, Chapter 4), cultural festivals (Zeppel, Chapter 6), hill-tribe trekking (Dearden and Harron, Chapter 8), fossicking (Jenkins, Chapter 10), yachting holidays (Richins, Chapter 14), and mountain recreation (Johnston, Chapter 12), places the market segments within a particular regional context or discusses a particular product and provides a further illustration of some of the trends and issues identified in the review chapters.

This book is intended as a timely examination of a rapidly developing pattern of touristic activity. The following chapters share a number of commonalities which indicate that the subject special interest tourism can, to some extent, be treated as a coherent entity. The growth of special interest tourism not only has implications for the way in which tourism is perceived but also in the way in which it will develop in the future, a point returned to in the concluding chapter. However, of most interest, in view of the contemporary debate over the ability of tourism to become a sustainable industry, is the extent to which special interest tourism may offer a new opportunity to establish a form of tourism which is compatible with the socio-cultural and natural environments, a point also returned to in the concluding chapter. Special interest travellers have the potential to become visitors who contribute to the well-being of the host and the destination, and are welcome to return. This book is designed as one contribution to such a development.

References

Alpine, L., 1986, Trends in special interest travel, *Specialty Travel Index*, Fall/Winter: 83–84

Andressen, B., Hall, C.M., 1988/89, The importance of intense negative outdoor experiences, *Recreation Australia*, 9 (1): 6–8

Australian National Tourism Committee, 1988, *Tourism*, Australian Tourism Commission, Canberra

Boo, E., 1990, *Ecotourism: the potentials and pitfalls*, 2 Vols., World Wildlife Fund, Washington D.C.

Bryan, H., 1977, Leisure value systems and recreational specialisation: the case of trout fishermen, *Journal of Leisure Research*, 9: 174–187

Chew, J., 1987, Transport and tourism in the year 2000, *Tourism Management*, June: 83–85

Cohen, E., 1972, Towards a sociology of international tourism, *Social Research*, 39: 164–182

Crompton, J.L., 1979, Motivations for pleasure travel, Annals of Tourism Research, 6: 408–424

Crompton, J.L., Richardson, S.L., 1986, The tourism connection: where public and private leisure services merge, *Parks and Recreation*, October: 38–44, 67

Devall, B., 1973, The development of leisure social worlds, *Humboldt Journal of Social Relations*, 1 (Fall): 53–59

Fennell, D.A., Eagles, P.F.J., 1990, Ecotourism in Costa Rica: a conceptual framework, *Journal of Park and Recreation Administration*, 8 (1): 23–34

Fodor's Travel Publications, 1990, *Fodor's 90 South America*, Fodor's Travel Publications, New York

Frew, W., 1989, On the trail of adventure travel, *Australian Financial Review*, 17 May.

Frommer, A., 1988, *The new world of travel 1988*, A Frommer Book published by Prentice Hall Press, New York

Gonsalves, P.S., 1987, Alternative tourism – the evolution of a concept and establishment of a network, *Tourism Recreation Research*, 12 (2): 9–12

Hall, C.M., 1989, Special interest travel: A prime force in the expansion of tourism?, 81–89 in R. Welch, ed., *Geography in action*, University of Otago, Dunedin

Hall, C.M., 1991, *Introduction to tourism in Australia: impacts, planning, and development*, Longman Cheshire, South Melbourne

Hall, C.M., McArthur, S., forthcoming, Commercial whitewater rafting in Australia, *Leisure Options: Australian Journal of Leisure and Recreation*, 1 (4).

Hall, C.M., Zeppel, H., 1990, Cultural and heritage tourism: the new grand tour?, *Historic Environment*, 7 (3/4): 86–98

Helber, L.E., 1988, The roles of government in planning in tourism with special regard for the cultural and environmental impact of tourism, pp.17–23 in D. McSwan, ed., *The roles of government in the development of tourism as an economic resource*, Seminar Series No.1, Centre for Studies in Travel and Tourism, James Cook University, Townsville

Hendee, J.C., Gale, R.P., Catton, W.R., Jr., 1971, A typology of outdoor recreation activity preferences, *Journal of Environmental Education*, 3: 28–34

Heywood, P., 1990, Truth and beauty in landscape – trends in landscape & leisure. *Landscape Australia*, 12 (1): 43–47

Holloway, J.C., 1985, *The business of tourism*, Pitman, London.

Kellert, S.R., 1985, Birdwatching in American society, *Leisure Sciences*, 7: 343–360

Krippendorf, J., 1987a, Tourism in Asia and the Pacific, *Tourism Management*, June: 137–139

Krippendorf, J., 1987b, *The holiday makers: understanding the impact of leisure and travel*, Heinemann Professional Publishing, Oxford

Kutay, K., 1989, The new ethic in adventure travel, *Buzzworm: The Environmental Journal*, 1 (4): 31–36

Laarman, J.G., Stewart, T.P., Prestemon, J.P., 1989, International travel by U.S. conservation groups and professional societies, *Journal of Travel Research*, 28 (1): 12–17

Lickorish, L., 1987, Trends in industrialised countries, *Tourism Management*, June: 92–95

Martin, W.H., Mason, S., 1987, Social trends and tourism futures, *Tourism Management*, June: 112–114

Mathieson, A., Wall, G., 1982, *Tourism: economic, physical and social impacts*, Longman, New York

Mercer, D., 1981, Trends in recreation participation, 24–44 in D. Mercer, ed., *Outdoor recreation: Australian perspectives*, Sorrett Publishing, Malvern

Mitchell, R.G., 1983, *Mountain experience: the psychology and sociology of adventure*, The University of Chicago Press, Chicago

O'Rourke, B., ed., 1990, *The global classroom: an international symposium on educational tourism*, Department of Continuing Education, University of Canterbury, Christchurch

Pearce, P.L., 1988, *The Ulysses factor: evaluating visitors in tourist settings*, Springer-Verlag, New York

Plog, S.C., 1974, Why destination areas rise and fall in popularity, *The Cornell Hotel and Restaurant Administration Quarterly*, 15: 55–58

Raines, J.T., 1988–89, Foundations of adventure programs. *Leisure Information Quarterly*, 15 (4): 1–6

Read S.E., 1980, A prime force in the expansion of tourism in the next decade: special interest travel, 193–202 in D.E. Hawkins, E.L. Shafer, J.M. Rovelstad, eds, *Tourism marketing and management issues*, George Washington University, Washington D.C.

Richter, L.K., 1987, The search for appropriate tourism, *Tourism Recreation Research*, 12 (2): 5–7

Richter, L.K., 1989, *The politics of tourism in Asia*, University of Hawaii Press, Honolulu

Ritchie, J.R.B., Zins, M., 1978, Culture as a determinant of the attractiveness of a tourist region, *Annals of Tourism Research*, 5: 252–267

Shackleford, P., 1987, Global tourism trends, *Tourism Management*, June: 98–101

Shibutani, T., 1955, Reference groups as perspectives, *American Journal of Sociology*, 60: 562–569

Smith, V., ed., 1989, *Hosts and guests: the anthropology of tourism*, 2nd. ed., University of Pennsylvania Press, Philadelphia

Snepenger, D., 1987, Segmenting the vacation market by novelty-seeking role, *Journal of Travel Research*, 27 (2): 8–14

Stebbins, R.A., 1979, *Amateurs: on the margin between work and leisure*, Sage Publications, Beverly Hills

Stebbins, R.A., 1982, Serious leisure: a conceptual statement, *Pacific Sociological Review*, 25: 251–272

Tabata, R., 1989, Implications of special interest tourism for interpretation and resource conservation, 68–77 in D. Uzzell, ed., *Heritage interpretation*, Vol.2, *The visitor experience*, Belhaven Press, London

Unruh, D.R., 1980, The nature of social worlds, *Pacific Sociological Review*, 23: 271–296

Venth, O., 1985, *Umweltsensiblät und konsequenzen für das tourismusmarketing*, Gesellschaftliches Wertesystem, Berlin

Wilson, M.A., Laarman, J.G., 1987, *Nature tourism and enterprise development in Ecuador*, Southeastern Center for Forest Economics Research, Research Triangle Park (North Carolina)

Wood, C., 1990, Educational tourism and the future, 227–244 in B. O'Rourke, ed., *The global classroom: an international symposium on educational tourism*, Department of Continuing Education, University of Canterbury, Christchurch

World Tourism Organization, 1985, *The role of recreation management in the development of active holidays and special interest tourism and consequent enrichment of the holiday experience*, World Tourism Organization, Madrid

World Tourism Organization, 1988, *Secondary tourism activity development in Fiji: opportunity, policies and control*, United Nations Development Program/World Tourism Organization, Madrid

Young, R.A., Crandall, R., 1984, Wilderness use and self-actualization, *Journal of Leisure Research*, 16: 149–160

Zeppel, H., Hall, C.M., 1991, Selling art and history: cultural heritage and tourism, *Journal of Tourism Studies*, 2(1): 29–45

2 REVIEW

Educational Travel

Katherine M. Kalinowski and Betty Weiler

Introduction

'Travel is fatal to prejudice, bigotry and narrow-mindedness' (Mark Twain). Although we might wish for this to be the case in all forms of travel, only a small fraction of travel experiences are designed with learning as their primary objective. Educational travel includes those special interest tourism experiences motivated primarily by interest in learning. This chapter focuses on forms of travel which are distinctly educational with respect to their origins and reasons for development, the experience that they provide, the traveller's motivations, and the characteristics of the travel experience. Current opportunities for educational travel are discussed with respect to the providers and their destinations, and future prospects for this type of special interest tourism are explored.

The Origins and Emergence of Educational Travel

Travel for education is not a new concept. Many of the world's learned citizens, since the beginning of recorded history, have recognized and endorsed travel as a means of education. For the most part, the British are credited with instituting the 'travel as a means of education' phenomenon (Brodsky-Porges, 1981, p.177). In the seventeenth century whoever wanted to be 'in the fashion' had to take part in a 'gentleman's' tour of Europe. Known more commonly as the 'The Grand Tour', this form of travel became an important part of the education of a person of the landed gentry or ruling class (Loschburg, 1979, p.59).

This tradition of the educational value of travel facilitated the development of study abroad as a legitimate component of tertiary education in Europe and later in the United States. The modern-day 'learning vacation' concept seems to have originated at Chautauqua, a residential institution in New York. Initiated in 1874 by a Methodist minister and an Ohio businessman, Chautauqua blends the concepts of an outdoor recreation setting with social activities and learning opportunities (Eisenberg, 1989, p.ix).

One of the most distinctive aspects of the origins of educational travel is the influence of the adult education movement of the late twentieth century in North America. This movement, together with the ageing North American population, has caused educational travel to expand rapidly in recent decades, particularly among non-school age segments of the population (Weiler and Kalinowski, 1990). A major component has been the Elderhostel movement of the late 1970s, which has played a large part in the rapid growth in educational travel for older adults (Eisenberg, 1989, p.ix).

Educational travel today is a sophisticated and competitive industry quite independent of mass tourism, with opportunities marketed through numerous handbooks and guides generally obtained from non-tourism outlets. For example, language study courses throughout Europe are described in the Institute of International Education's (IIE) annual *Study Holidays* guide. IIE also publishes an annual guide entitled *Vacation Study Abroad*, which in 1990 described some 1,300 summer study programs in over sixty countries. *Learning Vacations* is into its sixth edition (1989), and lists four hundred educational travel opportunities offered by universities, colleges, religious institutions, non-profit organizations, museums and private companies. Adult study vacations sponsored by tertiary institutions and other non-profit organizations are described for the American market in *The Guide to Academic Travel* (first edition, 1990) and for the Canadian market in the *Educational Travel Planner* (first edition, 1990). Some guides limit themselves mainly to identifying resources for studying overseas (for example, *Transitions Abroad: The Guide to Learning, Living and Working Overseas* and *Work, Study, Travel Abroad: The Whole World Handbook*) while others endeavour to list actual study tours (for example, Kaye Evelyn's *Travel and Learn: The New Guide to Educational Travel* lists over one thou-sand study trips around the world). The variety of opportunities for learning while travelling described in these guides is nothing short of remarkable.

The development of educational travel in countries with less of a tradition of 'study abroad' has been less apparent. In Australia, for example, the tourism industry and government tourism authorities appear to view educational tourism as marginal to Australia's tourism industry. Australia has a smaller and less significant non-profit sector than North America, and has therefore had to rely on initiatives by tertiary institutions and by individuals working within or in conjunction with these institutions. More recently, the private sector has recognized the opportunities that this tourism market segment has to offer. (A good example is provided in the case study by Wood in Chapter 4.)

The 'Education' in Educational Travel

A perusal of any one of the guides listed above reveals the breadth of educational travel today. Educational travel is a chance to explore a chosen site firsthand, to experience an unfamiliar environment through interaction with qualified instruction without the pressure of formal homework or test requirements. It can involve touring or visiting a single destination. It can last a few days or several months. It may be relatively formal or very loose and unstructured.

Educational travel can serve a wide variety of purposes, such as satisfying curiosity about other people and their language and culture; stimulating interest in art, music, architecture or folklore; inspiring concern for natural environments, landscapes, flora and fauna; or, deepening the fascination of cultural heritage and historic places. It is important to reiterate, however, that educational travel goes beyond a curiosity, interest or fascination for a particular topic. It involves a travel experience in which there is organized learning, whether that be formal or experiential.

Education can be defined as 'the organized, systematic effort to foster learning, to establish the conditions, and to provide the activities through which learning can occur' (Smith, 1982, p.37). The key word in this definition is 'learning'; the way in which it is defined, implicitly or explicitly, will determine the type of educational travel experience to be offered. Kulich (1987, p.171) distinguishes between learning and education. Learning is a natural process, occurring throughout life and mostly incidental. Education, however, is a conscious, planned, sequential and systematic process, based on defined learning objectives and using specific learning procedures.

Kidd (1973, p.23) writes that there is no answer to 'what is learning', but learning can be observed, noted and characterized, and the steps and effects can be described. There is debate, according to Smith (1982, p.34), between psychologists and educators on what exactly is human learning. Nevertheless, there is general agreement that it is a very complex process that involves the emotions, the mind, and the total self. Smith continues that it has been suggested that the term 'learning' eludes universal definition, as it is used to describe a product, a process, or a function. When used to describe a product, the emphasis is on the outcome of the learning experience. When used to describe a process, an attempt is made to clarify what happens when the learning experience takes place. When used to describe a function, the emphasis is on certain organized steps and intentional aspects believed to assist the production of learning.

Educational travel can offer learning as a product, as a process, as a function, or some combination of these. In the first definition, learning as a product, the focus is on the end; in the second and third definitions, learning as a process or function, the focus is on the means to an end. The type of definition used will affect the educational travel experience to be provided. If learning is defined as an end, then the focus of the experience will be on the facilitation of the acquisition or mastery of what is already known about something, such as a trip to a marine biology station to study marine life. If learning is defined as a means to an end, then the focus of the experience is to promote the extension and clarification of meanings for each individual involved, such as a trip to an ancient monument after a period of indirect study using books and slides.

Within each definition of learning, the commonality is that there is *newness*; something that did not exist or was not previously retained has been grasped (Smith, 1982, p.35). Cohen (1974) points out that tourism is typically characterized as having expectations of pleasure from novelty and change. The unifying feature here regarding learning and tourism is this concept of newness or novelty, simply because it involves experiences that are unfamiliar to the person (see discussion of 'novelty' in Chapter 1).

St. Augustine once wrote 'the world is a book and those who stay at home read only one page' (Eisenberg, 1989). Perhaps it is from this basis that St. Augustine and other famous writers have deduced that travel should be equated with learning. At the very least, learning and travel are mutually compatible, and the educational travel industry therefore endeavours to provide opportunities where both can be enjoyed simultaneously.

Motivations for Educational Travel

As discussed in the introductory chapter, special interest travel motives go beyond the pleasure realm. The reasons, many and varied, are often cultural, historical and educational. In the case of educational travel, the primary motive ostensibly is education or learning. Although some learning probably goes on in most forms of travel, the educational traveller chooses to travel, as well as makes other decisions such as when and where to journey, based on the interest in learning (Richins and Weiler, 1990).

Historically, travelling for pleasure, pure and simple, was not considered a fully legitimate reason for travel and even today 'the suspicion still endures that travel for its own sake is an idle pleasure' (Cohen, 1974, p.541). In the past, more legitimate purposes were sought to rationalize a journey by combining the seeking of pleasure with such things as education, culture, or health, to justify the trip.

Today, an educational guided tour may serve as a legitimizing mechanism for leisure (Schmidt, 1979, p.444). This is based on the premise that for certain people, certain types of leisure activities are more socially sanctioned and more individually rewarding than are others. Therefore, for those who value educational types of leisure, the guided study tour serves as a legitimate type of leisure. Schmidt (1979) adds that all tours may not be intellectually challenging, but the form and structure in which these activities take place are seen as credible. Furthermore, many individuals do not want to 'waste time' during their vacation, as they want to have something to 'show for it'. By stating that they were on a study tour, these people provide a legitimate and succinct account for themselves and their audience on how the vacation was spent.

Characteristics of the Educational Travel Experience: The Tour Guide

In addition to its historical origins and to travellers' motivations, another unique characteristic of educational travel that distinguishes it from other

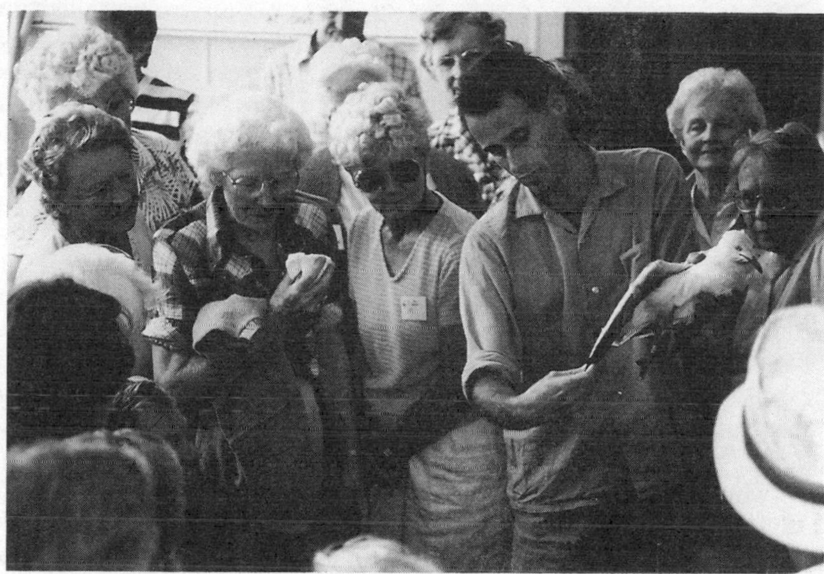

Plate 2.1 Ornithologist explaining the finer details of flight during a University of Queensland Field School (courtesy of TraveLearn)

forms of group travel is that the tourist is accompanied by a 'teacher', referred to variously as a resource person, tutor, professor, leader or guide. There are both similarities and differences between the educational travel guide and the 'normal' or mainstream tour guide (Schuchat, 1983).

The role of the modern tour guide can be traced as far back as the Grand Tour of the seventeenth and eighteenth century. Cohen (1985) writes that the modern-day tourist guide has developed from two diverse antecedents: the pathfinder and the mentor. The pathfinder's function of leader is outer-directed; the mentor's function of mediator is inner-directed. It is in the function of mediator that Cohen discusses education of the tourist. Based on his review of literature, Cohen sees the dissemination of correct and precise information as the main role of a guide. S/he is an 'information giver and fount of knowledge' and a 'teacher and instructor' (Cohen, 1985, p.15).

Guiding involves elements of both teaching and acting according to Holloway (1981). Holloway conducted an exploratory study on tourist guides and found that most guides perceive the sub-role of information-giver as being their most important function. Other sub-roles include:

- teacher or instructor;
- motivator or initiator into the rites of the tourism experience;
- missionary or ambassador for one's country;
- entertainer or catalyst for the group;
- confidant, shepherd, or ministering angel; and,
- group leader and disciplinarian.

In an effort to satisfy their customers of the quest for a unique tourism experience, guides have developed a set of manipulative and dramaturgical skills. Guides are expected to disseminate a wide variety of knowledge relating to tourist sights and attractions and also relating to the whole spectrum of the host destination. Consequently, a characteristic of professional status for guiding is the acquisition of knowledge and delivery of accurate information to their customers (see plate 2.1). Acting as a catalyst, the guide also endeavours to stimulate social interaction within the group, which is perceived as an essential component of the total tourism experience.

The 'teacher' or guide in an educational travel experience differs from a tour guide on a 'normal' tour (Weiler and Richins, 1990). First, a guide on a 'normal' tour is likely to spend more time in the pathfinder role, acting as an escort, an entertainer, a tour manager and an organizer of group events. In an educational travel experience, the 'teacher' is not usually relied upon to conduct these tasks.

As for the mentor role, there are differences in terms of the style and content of the guide's 'information-giving'. The 'normal' guide may have been instructed to impart information which the official tourist authorities consider appropriate to maintain the desired 'tourist image' of the host setting. However, the 'teacher' in the educational travel experience is more likely to be objective and neutral in his/her delivery of information, and not as concerned with maintaining a desirable host image (Weiler and Richins, 1990).

Finally, the leader or guide in the educational travel experience is of much more importance to the overall quality of and satisfaction with the total educational travel experience than with a more typical group travel experience. Research has found that organizers and participants of educational travel put a very strong emphasis on the tour guide in promoting tours, and in evaluating the quality and success of tours (Weiler and Richins, 1990).

Characteristics of the Travel Experience: The Stages of Travel

Yet another distinguishing characteristic of educational travel can be illustrated using temporal models, developed in both the recreation and education fields, to describe the 'recreation experience' and the 'learning process'. Clawson and Knetsch (1966, p.33) have outlined five stages of the recreation experience:

- anticipation and planning,
- travel to the site,
- on-site experiences,
- travel back, and
- recollection.

A recreation experience begins with a person anticipating a particular event. If the feeling from this anticipation is positive, then planning will occur and the recreational experience goes further. This first phase includes such

Table 2.1 Stages of the educational travel experience

Clawson and Knetsch (1966)	Apps (1978)	Educational Travel Experience
anticipation and planning	planning	anticipation and planning
travel to the site		travel to the destination
on-site experiences	carrying out	on-site behaviour
travel back		travel back
recollection	evaluation	recollection and evaluation

aspects as perceived images and expectations, and trip preparation. The next major stage of the experience is travel to the destination, and this leads to the third part of the total recreation occurrence, on-site activities and experiences. The occurrences of the fourth phase, travel back, are usually different to the travel to the site. In the final stage of recollection, impressions are recollected and perceptions turn to memories. Achievements and shortfalls are evaluated and this judgement often provides the starting point for anticipation of a new recreational experience.

Apps (1978, p.18), an adult educator, describes another temporal model. This model consists of a three-stage learning process:

- planning,
- carrying out, and
- evaluating.

Essentially these broad phases include:

- determining and identifying learning objectives;
- completing the task decided upon;
- determining if the learning objectives have been met, making necessary adjustments and deciding on follow-up activities.

By placing these models side-by-side, as shown in Table 2.1, it can be seen that they parallel each other and may be combined to illustrate the stages of the educational travel experience:

- anticipation and planning;
- travel to the destination;
- on-site behaviour;
- travel back; and,
- recollection and evaluation.

This further illustrates the commonalities between the educational experience and the travel experience. The model is particularly useful as a basis for examining the educational component of the travel experience. Clearly, learning experiences in educational travel need to be planned and evaluated. Furthermore, if all five stages are important to the travel experience, then the facilitation of learning should occur at *each* of the five stages.

With respect to style of learning, Brookfield (1986) writes on the facilitation of adult learning and presents principles to be considered in the provision of effective learning. According to Brookfield, 'praxis' is at the heart of effective facilitation. This is a process in which the educator and learners are continuously engaged in an alternating process of exploration, followed by action based on this exploration, reflection on this action, and further exploration, and so on. This continuous cycle of exploration, action, and reflection reinforces the need for provision of learning throughout the entire educational travel experience.

Current Opportunities for Educational Travel: Providers and their Destinations

Clearly, the provision of a quality learning experience is at the heart of educational travel. Who can, and who are, providing such experiences?

Providers of educational travel opportunities can include religious organizations, non-profit organizations, private institutions, private and public-sector educational institutions, and private industry, to name a few. The relatively small role played by the private sector is yet another important feature of educational travel that distinguishes it from mainstream tourism.

An example of an educational travel program provided by a religious organization is the Chautauqua Institution mentioned earlier, which offers programs at its residential site located on Lake Chautauqua in the State of New York (Eisenberg, 1989). Programs ranging from one day to nine weeks in length are offered annually in the fine and applied arts, targeting children, adults and older adults.

Elderhostel is an example of the second type, a non-profit organization that combines the idea of providing 'hostel' accommodation for travellers of sixty years of age and older with access to university campuses. The participants enjoy short-term (usually one week) inexpensive academic programs. This concept started in 1975 in the United States with two hundred students (Burrow, 1985, p.356). By the late 1980s there were 190,000 people enrolled in close to 1,000 different colleges, universities and other educational institutions found in over forty different countries (Welcome to Elderhostel, 1990, p.2).

As an example of a private institution's efforts to meet the public's diverse interests, the Smithsonian Institution in the United States sponsors three types of learning adventures: study tours, seminars and research expeditions. In 1990, about 6,000 people participated in some two hundred learning adventures that lasted from three to thirty days (Brownell, 1990, p.118).

Private language schools, colleges and universities are typical examples of educational institutions. The case study by Kalinowski (Chapter 3) illustrates the role played by one public-sector institution, the Faculty of Extension at the University of Alberta. The second case study by Wood (Chapter 4) describes the growth of an educational travel business, Australians Studying Abroad (ASA), operating in the private sector.

The destinations of educational travel programs are as diverse as the organizations who offer them. They involve both domestic and overseas destinations, both to developed and developing countries, and may involve a single country or a tour of several countries. Richins and Weiler (1990) examined tertiary institution providers and programs in Canada and Australia and discovered some interesting differences. In Canada nearly eighty per cent of the educational travel programs were to destinations overseas; in comparison, only thirty-three per cent of the Australian programs journeyed outside of Australia. Canadian tours were most likely to go to Europe, followed by Asia (Japan and the Soviet Union) and the South Pacific. On the other hand, Australian tours were most likely to travel within Australia, followed by Asia (mainly China) and the South Pacific. At present, there is very little travel by either the Canadian or Australian tertiary educational travel markets to the continents of South America and Africa.

The Future of Educational Travel

Where does educational travel go from here? According to some, the present western world is gradually moving away from traditional values which have survived for over seventy-five years to new or alternative values that are being adopted on an ever-widening scale. A large number of people in developed western nations, explains Plummer (1989), are in the midst of a change in the basic value structure, perhaps even a 'paradigm shift' or reordering of the way they see the world around them. More people are seeking self-actualization as opposed to traditionally defined sets of goals for success. There is a greater value on experience, which in turn is prompting the growth of travel, lifelong education, the arts and sport (Plummer, 1989, p.13).

Fay, McCune and Begin (1987) write that providers of education must prepare for upcoming value changes in the population by the year 2000, changes which include a rejection of authority, an increased concern for autonomy and creativity, the placement of self-expression over status, a quest for pleasure-seeking together with a desire for new experiences, an emphasis on community, a desire for participation in decision-making, a hunger for adventure, and a need for inner growth and self-expression.

Cross (1981, p.9) states that industrialization has created a pronounced tendency to separate education, work and leisure. This has resulted in a linear life plan in which education is for the young, work is for the middle-aged and leisure for the elderly. She claims that many people are opting for an alternative 'blended life plan' in which the periods of leisure, work and education are redistributed across the entire life span. Cross finds, however, that upwardly mobile workers are adding education to their work schedules which are already full and, in effect, they are using their leisure time for education.

This general tendency toward an ever greater diversity in lifestyle has implications for special interest tourism in general and for educational travel in particular. Schwaninger (1989, p.501) summarizes the ramifications as follows: further increasing pluralization and differentiation of demand; a decrease of physically and culturally passive forms of vacations in favour of more active pastimes; a shift towards custom-made holidays packages; and, an emergence of new specialized markets and market segments.

Changes of particular significance affecting the marketing of tourism products, according to Martin and Mason (1987), can be grouped into three factors: people, attitudes and leisure time. Related to the people factor:

- the population is growing older;
- lifestyles are becoming more diverse; and,
- educational standards are slowly and steadily rising producing tourists who have higher levels of ability and knowledge.

Related to the attitude factor:

- there is increased concern for quality in the tourist experience related to all aspects; and,
- there is growing awareness of the range of choices available for tourists, and also an increased demand for better service standards and 'value for my money' from providers of tourism products.

Related to leisure time, the key issue is increased flexibility in work patterns in such aspects as:

- hours worked in full-time employment;
- growth in part-time and shared time employment; and,
- more time periods away from formal work, e.g. sabbaticals and unemployment.

The literature has stressed that what is required of tourism products is to satisfy new market demands through a shift away from traditional types of tours toward product specialization. Chovanec (1987, p.51), upon examining the present-day package tour product, concludes that traditional holiday packages no longer suffice. Chovanec (1987) indicates that although special interest tours, by their very nature, may not produce the large profits per tour desired, in the long run they are the more viable and therefore profitable alternative.

In summary, planning for the future of educational travel includes taking into account value changes as well as demographic, economic and technological changes. The future of educational travel and other tourist products involves more than a change of scenery or weather. With a growing desire to gain firsthand experience, to engage in active pastimes and to learn more about foreign cultures (Schwaninger, 1989), providers in tourism must rethink their strategies to accommodate the growing sophistication of travellers.

One component of such planning must be increased emphasis on quality. This may mean a reduced emphasis on quantity in terms of distance covered or number of sites visited. It will certainly mean more attention to how adults learn, providing opportunities for praxis as discussed earlier. It will also mean more attention to all five stages of the educational travel experience. The individual responsible for facilitating learning, whether a 'teacher' or a tour leader, will need to be present and actively contributing through all five stages of the travel experience.

Avenues for future research, as with most types of special interest tourism, are numerous. Research investigating the relationships between learning as a travel motive, measures of perceived or actual learning that occurs, and travel satisfaction would be extremely valuable. Relationships between the distribution of educational travel destinations and Butler's (1980) tourist destination life cycle model might also be useful to explore in future research. There has been some evidence that the stage of development of the destination and the type of tourist that visits the destination are closely related (Keller, 1987), so it seems likely that educational tourists will be attracted to destinations at particular stages of the destination's life cycle. More research and planning will no doubt contribute to the increase in quantity, and also, hopefully, to the continued improvement in the quality of these important sectors of special interest tourism.

References

Apps, J., 1978, *Study skills for those adults returning to school*, McGraw-Hill, Toronto

Brodsky-Porges, E., 1981, The grand tour: travel as an educational device, *Annals of Tourism Research*, 8 (2): 171–186

Brookfield, S., 1986, *Understanding and facilitating adult learning*, Jossey-Bass Publishers, London

Brownell, B., 1990, Studying with the Smithsonian, *National Geographic Traveler*, 7 (5): 118–120

Burrow, M., 1985, Elderhostels – for people on the move in mind and body, *Adult Education*, 57(4): 356–358

Butler, R. W., 1980, The concept of a tourist area cycle of evolution: implications for management of resources, *The Canadian Geographer*, 24 (1): 5–12

Chovanec, C. A., 1987, *Package tours: new trends and socio-economic environmental influences*, Unpublished master's thesis, University of Carleton, Ottawa

Clawson, M., Knetsch, J.K., 1966, *Economics of outdoor recreation*, John Hopkins, Baltimore

Clemmer, J., 1990, *Firing on all cylinders*, Macmillan of Canada, Toronto

Cohen, E., 1974, Who is a tourist: a conceptual clarification, *The Sociological Review*, 22 (Nov.): 527–555

Cohen, E., 1985, The tourist guide: the origins, structure and dynamics of a role, *Annals of Tourism Research*, 12 (1): 5–29

Cross, K.P., 1981, *Adults as learners*, Jossey-Boss Publishers, San Francisco
Eisenberg, G., 1989, *Learning vacations*, 6th Ed., Peterson's Guides, Princeton, N.J.
Fay, C.H., McCune, J.T., Begin, J.P., 1987, The setting for continuing education in the year 2000, *New directions for continuing education*, 36 (Winter): 15–27
Hamilton-Smith, E., 1987, Four kinds of tourism? *Annals of Tourism Research*, 14 (3): 332–344
Holloway, C., 1981, The guided tour: a sociological approach, *Annals of Tourism Research*, 8 (3): 377–402
Kalinowski, K.M., 1989, *Educational travel: a case study, University of Alberta Faculty of Extension, 1984–1988*, Unpublished master's thesis, University of Alberta, Edmonton
Keller, C. P., 1987, Stages of peripheral tourism development – Canada's Northwest Territories, *Tourism Management,* 8 (1):20–32
Kidd, J.R., 1973, *How adults learn*, Follett Publishing, Chicago
Kulich, J., 1987, The university and adult education: the newest role and responsibility of the university, 170–190 in W. Leirman, J. Kulich, eds, *Adult education and the challenges of the 1990s*, Croom Helm, New York
Loschburg, W., 1979, *History of travel*, George Prior Associated Publishers, London
Mackay, K.J., 1989, Tourism quality, 549–552 in S. F. Witt, L. Mountinho, eds., *Tourism marketing and management handbook*, Prentice Hall, New York
Martin, W.H., Mason, S., 1987, Social trends and tourism futures, *Tourism Management,* 8 (2): 112–114
Plummer, J.T., 1989, Changing values, *The Futurist,* 23 (1): 8–13
Richins, H., Weiler, B., 1990, The distribution of educational travel programmes in Australia and New Zealand, 246–76 in B. O'Rourke, ed., *The global classroom: an international symposium on educational tourism*, University of Canterbury, Christchurch
Schmidt, C., 1979, The guided tour: insulated adventure, *Urban Life*, 17 (4): 441–467
Schuchat, M., 1983, The comforts of group tours, *Annals of Tourism Research*, 10 (4): 465–477
Schwaninger, M., 1989, Trends in leisure and tourism for 2000–2010: scenario with consequences for planners, 599–605 in S. F. Witt, L. Moutinho, eds. *Tourism marketing and management handbook*, Prentice Hall, New York
Smith, R.M., 1982, *Learning how to learn*, Follett Publishing, Chicago
Smith, V., 1977, Introduction, in V. Smith, ed., *Hosts and guests: the anthropology of tourism,* The University of Pennsylvania Press, Pennsylvania
Weiler, B., Kalinowski, K.M., 1990, Participants of educational travel: a Canadian case study, *The Journal of Tourism Studies,* 1 (2): 43–50
Weiler B., Richins, H., 1990, Escort or expert? Entertainer or enabler? The role of the resource person on educational tours, 84–94 in B. O'Rourke, ed., *The global classroom: an international symposium on educational tourism*, University of Canterbury, Christchurch
Welcome to Elderhostel, 1990, *Elderhostel Catalog,* 12 (6): 2

3 CASE STUDY

Universities and Educational Travel Programs: The University of Alberta

Katherine M. Kalinowski

Introduction

A common provider of learning for adults within all nations is the university. Traditionally, a university has been seen as a place where students go to increase their level of understanding, realize their intellectual abilities, learn to become responsible people, and basically add to their quality of life. More specifically, the university has been invested with degree-granting power. However, many universities have recently seen the number of adults enrolled in university non-degree programs reach and often exceed the number of registered full-time students. Such extension programs, also known at some institutes of higher learning as extra-mural studies, continuing education, further education and adult education, are designed to provide adults within the surrounding community with non-degree educational opportunities. One form of extension learning is educational travel.

Within Canada, there are over sixty universities, each offering both degree programs and non-degree continuing education programs. This case study will examine the educational travel opportunities offered by the extension division of one of the major universities within the country, that being the University of Alberta. Located in Edmonton, Alberta, this university has been providing educational travel opportunities for adults for over twenty years. Within recent years, there has been a steady increase in the number of educational travel tours offered by the University's Faculty of Extension. Furthermore, as will be described in this case study, the potential for offering such tours in the future is even more significant.

The phenomenon of educational travel at a case study level can be viewed from the supplier or the consumer perspective. This chapter explores the aspect of educational travel from the perspective of the supplier, the University of Alberta (a more detailed version can be found in Kalinowski, 1989). The consumer perspective is presented in Weiler and Kalinowski (1991).

For this case study, educational travel is defined as those organized learning opportunities delivered to adult students not actively seeking a degree, and involving journeys outside the province of Alberta for a duration of more than 24 hours and less than a year. It is also important to note that only those trips which actually took place were analysed; cancelled trips were not included.

The time period selected for investigation was from 1984 to 1988. This particular interval was chosen for two reasons:

(a) in 1984, educational travel was seen by the University as having enough merit to be offered on an annual basis; and,
(b) documentation of educational travel prior to 1984 was sketchy.

For this case study all data were collected during the spring of 1989.

The purpose of this Chapter is to present some insights that illustrate the dimensions of university-based educational travel. Discussion topics include the supplier of educational travel and the tours that were offered. This is followed by a review of the characteristics of the people who participated in educational travel. Since these are educational tours the provision for planned learning will also be examined. Finally, the implications of the findings in this case study will be presented.

The Supplier of Educational Travel

According to the mission statement of the Faculty of Extension, its main purpose is to serve as a link between the University and the people of the province who require access to the information and expertise of the University, in order to solve practical problems and to further personal and professional growth. The Faculty offers a variety of courses in the areas of business, fine arts, the humanities, the social and physical sciences, and the professions. The annual registration for non-credit courses in these subject areas exceeds 20,000 students. From 1984 to 1988, three of the thirteen administrative units within the Faculty of Extension offered non-credit educational travel opportunities. The units known as Fine Arts, Science and Technology, and Liberal Studies offered a variety of educational travel opportunities ranging from art history to marine biology.

The Fine Arts Unit offered learning opportunities in areas such as art history, music appreciation and printmaking. The main goal of the Fine Arts Unit has been to develop an informed public awareness in the visual and performing arts through provision of a university-level non-credit programme. The Science and Technology Unit offered courses on topics concerning biology, geography and general sciences. The goal of this Unit has been mainly to provide the working professional practitioners with opportunities to keep in touch with the latest in technology, upgrade or improve existing skills, and interact with other professionals working in allied fields. The main objective of the Liberal Studies Unit was adopted from a model which views learning as being engaged in for its own sake. The subject areas in the courses provided by this Unit stem from the Humanities and the Social Sciences, such as anthropology, natural history and literature. They are intended to facilitate the development of a stronger mind among the general public and special groups (e.g. seniors), and become a part of the richer life these people have earned.

Characteristics of the Educational Travel Tours

The number of successful educational travel tours increased from three in 1984 to ten in 1988. A grand total of 29 tours were offered to 529 participants. The Fine Arts Unit offered six Art History Tours to destinations in Central America, South America and Europe. This Unit also offered two Music Tours to the United States. The Science and Technology Unit offered five Historical/Cultural Tours to destinations in Europe and Asia. As well, this Unit offered four Marine Biology Tours to the Bamfield Marine Station located on Canada's west coast. Finally, the Liberal Studies Unit offered a total of twelve Natural History Tours to the west coast of Canada, with nine to the Queen Charlotte Islands and three to Vancouver Island.

All of the educational travel tours offered from 1984 to 1988 operated on a cost-recovery basis, and for the majority of tours a profit was made. In the case of Science and Technology's historical/cultural educational travel tours, it was required that each tour generate a certain amount of profit. Revenue came from tuition fees, and a tour budget was based on a minimum enrollment number. This number was usually 14 registrants. If the minimum enrollment was not met, then the tour was either cancelled or modified in some way to cover all expenses. A direct correlation was generally found between revenue and enrollment. Tours with maximum enrollments generated high profits, and tours with low enrollments broke even.

With respect to the human resources, a relatively high percentage of permanent academic staff members were directly involved in educational travel (4 out of the total Faculty number of 23.5). It appears that because of the nature of educational travel, a tremendous amount of time was spent by both the academic and non-academic staff in their organization and administration. However, there did not seem to be a great amount of coordination of these tours between the units. This may be due in part to the flat, less centralized organizational structure of the Faculty of Extension. An advantage of this structure has been that it allowed considerable latitude for staff members to perform their duties. The disadvantage is that this decentralized structure does not require the units to work together on administering the educational travel tours. Evidence of teamwork among the units was found in the early years, 1984 and 1985; information evenings for the upcoming educational travel tours were jointly organized by these three units. Little evidence of such coordination could be found in the more recent years, 1986 to 1988.

For the most part, experience in providing these educational travel opportunities was acquired on-the-job. It appears that none of these staff members had received previous training in the travel and tourism field. Nevertheless, they clearly possessed expertise in adult education programming, and apparently, had acquired the capabilities necessary to offer educational travel tours.

Set within the academic environment, the Faculty of Extension had access to other human resources, giving it a definite advantage. For example, it could use the expertise of members of other faculties and departments on campus, and also members of staff from other universities. Of the twenty-three resource people (tour leaders) employed for the educational travel opportunities, ten were affiliated with the University of Alberta and two had been with other western Canadian Universities. Also, the Faculty had the advantage of a positive reputation and image through being associated with a very large, mature and well-respected post-secondary educational institution in the form of the University of Alberta.

The cost of the tours ranged from Cdn.$225 to $4,750, with the average cost being Cdn.$1,946. Of that fee, a portion of the total cost was tax deductible. The tax deductible amount was calculated by determining the cost of the educational component of the tour. An important point should be mentioned concerning Canadian income tax laws. During the studied time period, the usual rule was that the fee for any educational course taken by an adult at a recognized learning institution was tax deductible provided this fee was paid by the individual who took the course. In other words, the chosen study tour did not have to relate directly to the individual's occupation. Therefore, all participants of the educational travel tours were eligible to receive a tax deduction from a portion of the total course fee.

The number of participants in each tour ranged from 2 to 41, with an average of 18 participants per educational travel opportunity. The length of the trips ranged from 4 to 30 days, with the average being 13 days. An overview of the entire educational travel program revealed that tours with domestic or within Canada destinations were less costly, shorter in duration and had fewer participants than tours with international destinations. Relatively speaking, the educational travel program at the Faculty of Extension is small; between 1984 and 1988, registrations for these courses made up two per cent of the total number of registrations in the Fine Arts, Science and Technology, and Liberal Studies Units.

Characteristics of the Participants

Knowledge about who takes educational travel tours is essential in effective program planning, design and implementation. For this reason an analysis of the University of Alberta's Faculty of Extension educational travel participants was conducted.

The yearly participation rate in the educational travel program increased from 72 in 1984 to 172 in 1988. Of this total, data on 21 individuals on two Queen Charlotte Tours were not available. Unfortunately, profile data on the total sample of 508 participants were limited to the information that existed in the files. Of the total number of participants, 229 (48 per cent) took part in educational travel tours which had an international destination and were of at least two weeks in duration. An in-depth analysis was conducted of these international tour participants including gender, age, place of residence, occupation and repeat users.

The female:male ratio of the international tour participants was 66:34. The range in age of the participants on the international tours was 14 to 84 years, with 53 years being the mean. The proportion of participants whose place of residence was Greater Edmonton was 86 per cent. The participants of international tours came from a number of occupations; the majority (70 per cent) were employed. The various positions and percentages included: professional or senior managerial (27 per cent); middle or low management (12 per cent); technical (15 per cent);

homemakers (8 per cent); trade or semi-skilled (6 per cent); other (2 per cent); and, retired (30 per cent).

The typical participant of an international educational travel tour can be described as follows: female, between 55 and 69 years of age, living in Greater Edmonton, and either retired or employed in a professional or senior managerial occupation. Of the 229 international tour registrations, 46 individuals or 25 per cent of this subgroup were repeat clients. The overall profile of the typical international tour repeat user is as follows: female, elderly (between the age of 65 and 69) living in Greater Edmonton and retired. It seems that these people have both the time and money to repeatedly attend educational travel tours.

Educational Tours as Planned Learning

In Chapter 2 educational travel was distinguished from other forms of special interest tourism by the primary motive for travel, that being a keen interest in learning. Learning was described as occurring naturally and incidentally. Education, on the other hand, was described as a consciously planned process using specific learning procedures. Consequently, one significant feature of an educational travel experience is the provision of planned learning. It becomes the supplier's responsibility to provide these planned opportunities. Also introduced in Chapter 2 was a five-stage framework of the educational travel experience consisting of anticipation and planning, travel to the destination, on-site behaviour, travel back, and recollection and evaluation. This framework may be used to examine the planned learning activities organized by the staff of the Faculty of Extension for the educational travel tours.

Provision for planned learning begins with supplying a 'teacher', more commonly known as the resource person and also called the tour leader. Having the appropriate resource person was described by some staff as one of the most important aspects of a successful educational travel experience. A resource person of high quality was sought, including one who had both the knowledge-base in the subject matter and the ability to 'teach' adults. For one unit, the importance of a capable resource person was such that if an appropriate candidate could not be found, the educational tour would be cancelled.

Participants of the tours also felt that the resource person was a valuable part of the total experience. From the responses found on the mail-back questionnaires distributed to each participant when he/she returned home (return rate of 63 per cent!) all the resource people used by the Faculty received a high rating for ability. Those participants who were not completely satisfied with the resource person commented on aspects such as time and amount of on-site lecturing, approachability of the resource person, and absence of resource person during stages two and four of the educational travel experience.

The resource person plays a key role in facilitating learning, as outlined in Chapter 2, particularly related to setting a group climate conducive to effective learning. If expertise was one criterion for selecting the resource person, it can be said that each person was an authority in his/her field. Related to educational qualifications, twelve of these twenty-three resource people possessed a Ph.D. in the subject matter of the educational travel tour. The others possessed the appropriate academic credentials related to the subject matter of the tour. Another vital requirement of the resource person, the ability to relate and communicate to adult students, could not be sufficiently analysed based on the information in the files. It was, however, discussed by the providers as a very important aspect when selecting the appropriate resource person for the educational travel tour.

Of the tours offered by the Faculty the frequency and degree of planned learning activities was greatest in stage three. In this stage visitations were made to the remains of early civilizations in order to gain an understanding of their developments and accomplishments. Marine life was observed in its natural habitat then later examined in detail in a well-equipped laboratory. And, the sights and sounds of beloved classic operas and significant contemporary works played by the world's greatest musicians were seen and heard at first hand.

A third essential requirement in facilitating learning involved the development of mutual trust and respect between the supplier and the resource person. This was of particular importance when the resource person was not accompanied by an on-site administrator and was given the dual responsibility of being the 'escort' and 'resource person'.

It was discovered in the early courses offered by one unit that the on-site administrator or 'escort' played an important role in satisfying tour clients. The escort's duties were many and varied – psychologist, diplomat, troop leader, flight attendant, entertainer, news reporter, restaurant critic, efficiency expert, and overall trouble-shooter. With an escort present during stage three the resource person was free from such responsibilities and able to focus on enhancing the learning experience.

The degree and frequency of planned learning activities was moderate during stage one. The Faculty along with the chosen resource people offered various types or combinations of learning activities during the first stage. These included the following: an information evening, a single pre-tour lecture session, a lecture series consisting of 3 to 8 lectures, or an orientation session. In stages two (travel there), four (travel back) and five (recollection and evaluation) the degree and frequency of planned learning was either low or non-existent. A planned learning activity during the travel there and travel back stages was found in only one of the possible 29 educational travel tours. There was no planned learning activity during stage five for any of the offered tours, although, for one tour the provider organized a post-tour social gathering. Given these findings, it can be concluded that overall the Faculty of Extension has not been providing an optimal educational experience. The Faculty has concentrated on providing planned learning in stages three and one, and there is a lack of provision for learning in stages two, four and five of the educational travel experience.

Implications

The purpose of the case study was to help us better understand educational travel by looking at one example in-depth. Supplying educational travel is not an easy task. There are certain 'essentials' to providing educational travel regardless of supplier, destination, duration or clientele. In brief, these essentials include organizational skills, appropriate staffing and provision of planned learning.

It seems that when it comes to planning and implementing an educational travel tour one can never be over-prepared. The Faculty of Extension staff associated providing a high quality educational travel product with being very well organized. They were consciously meticulous about the small, intangible points such as warmth, special attention and other tiny gestures. One could probably say that this type of service to their clientele had a great deal to do with the high percentage of repeat participants. Therefore, since the educational travel product is largely organizational in nature, important 'essentials' include an amalgam of personnel, a variety of expertise and an obsession for detail. Without the expertise and means to organize, the product would not exist.

Other important staff include the resource person and the tour escort. The quality of the resource person is perhaps the most important element that determines the success of an educational travel tour. He/she must possess both the knowledge of the subject matter and also have the skills necessary in being a facilitator of learning. He/she must be able to interact with adults, and be capable of handling the pressure of being 'teacher' for all of the five stages of the educational travel experience. If the number of people in the tour group is large (i.e. over 14) then it is essential to have an escort accompany the tour. This would free the resource person from the responsibilities of dealing with on-site administrative duties, consequently enhancing the learning experience.

A third essential item for providing an educational travel experience involves planned learning. The supplier should consider organizing learning activities throughout all of the five stages of the educational travel experience in order to facilitate 'praxis' (see Chapter 2). At the Faculty of Extension the most neglected stage was the final one. A post-tour debriefing is a very important component of the learning experience, as it allows the traveller an opportunity to reflect, assimilate and integrate the impressions of the trip while they are still fresh in his/her mind. Other neglected stages included two and four, travel between home and the destination. Ideally the facilitators should also be promoting learning activities during these stages, even if it is as simple as encouraging discussion among group members about the subject matter of the tour.

Educational travel should not be an expensive luxury holiday. Some of the tours offered by the Faculty over-emphasized the use of Western-like accommodation in exotic countries. Such luxury oriented tours are paradoxically sending mixed messages to participants. If these tours are truly 'educational' in the cultural sense, then there must be a greater emphasis on the educational component of interaction between host and guest. Is it appropriate to be learning about the culture of a nation which experiences shortages of water and power from the comforts of a Western-type hotel? Perhaps the learning objectives should be modified to suit the actual experience if local infrastructures are not used.

Richter (1989, p.184) writes that family-owned small hotels, pensions, church dormitories, campgrounds, and bed and breakfasts are defined as 'alternative' tourism. This form of tourism is based on the assumption that people want to experience the destination rather than the conventional type of tourism where the focus of the experience is on the inside of their hotel. If the local infrastructures were used, then the experience could be more geared toward getting to know the local people of the destination and of going beyond the 'luxury holiday' and into a real learning experience.

The educational travel program at the Faculty of Extension is at an embryonic stage. However, there is significant room for its expansion. According to Kulich (1987), upcoming university continuing education segments include:

1. the mature non-employed adults seeking enrichment through study;
2. wage earners who are seeking to enhance their knowledge and skills in liberal arts; and,
3. professionals who are seeking to maintain and update their skills and knowledge.

If the future adult education segments are as Kulich predicts, then there should be provision of:

1. general interest/personal development educational travel tours for both non-employed and wage earners; and,
2. job-related tours for professionals seeking to update their knowledge and skills.

An example of the former would be to offer subsidized study tours to non-employed individuals; and, an example of the latter would be to offer an architectural design study tour in England to professional architects.

Conclusion

This case study of the Faculty of Extension at the University of Alberta provides a valuable illustration of the role of Universities and similar institutions in providing educational travel experiences. As part of an academic environment the Faculty of Extension is perceived positively through its association with the University of Alberta. The Faculty should be able to take advantage of this reputation by being an innovator in the educational travel field, for there is considerable room for expansion including targeting other markets and providing products or tours related to a variety of subjects.

If tourism is to be the experience that it could be, then tourists need to relearn the value of travel. University faculty, through educational travel programs such as that at the University of Alberta, could be playing a proactive role in educating people on the importance of respecting the dignity of the culture being visited and to gain an understanding of the host society.

Throughout its history, the university has changed in order to serve the needs brought about by the evolution of society. It will be necessary in the near future for universities to adapt to the most recent challenges of providing lifelong learning opportunities in a learning society. At present, the University of Alberta does not appear to have made sufficient provisions. It must try to evolve with the upcoming population where adult education will play an important role. The time has arrived for the Faculty of Extension and other similar extension bodies to prepare for the anticipated growth in demand for educational travel opportunities for the challenging years ahead.

References

Kalinowski, K.M., 1989, Educational travel: a case study, University of Alberta Faculty of Extension, 1984–1988, Unpublished master's thesis, University of Alberta, Edmonton

Kulich , J., 1987, The university and adult education: the newest role and responsibility of the university, 170–190 in Leirman, W. Kulich, J., eds, *Adult Education and the Challenges of the 1990s*, Croom Helm, New York

Richter, L., 1989, *The politics of tourism in Asia*, University of Hawaii Press, Honolulu

Weiler, B., Kalinowski, K.M., 1991, Participants of educational travel: a Canadian case study, *Journal of Tourism Studies*, 1 (2): 43–50

4 CASE STUDY

Australians Studying Abroad: A Private Sector Success Story in Educational Tourism

Christopher Wood

Origins and History

Australians Studying Abroad (ASA) is Australia's oldest study tour company which now runs programmes throughout the world for Australians, Americans, Canadians, and New Zealanders. ASA was founded in 1977 by an art historian, Christopher Wood, who envisaged a semester abroad system modeled upon those of universities from the United States of America. The structure of Australian universities, their lack of familiarity with the concept of giving credits for overseas travel, and their belief that in a free university system, expensive education abroad would disadvantage less wealthy students mitigated against such a scheme. Wood therefore decided, on the advice of a number of professors, to set up a private company which would run tours each with an academic programme of at least ninety hours of lectures and site visits which would thereby equal the number of formal teaching hours in one humanities subject in a university year.

ASA's first tours established a pattern by which an Australian academic led a tour with modular courses taught in European cities by American and British scholars. The first tours, which were for art history students, toured Greece for two weeks and then ran one-week lecture and site visit programmes in Rome, Florence, Venice and Paris. By 1980 the content of tours was transformed to general cultural history. Organizers and lecturers agreed that their virtue was not in augmenting a single discipline but in giving general perspectives of the history of European culture in ways which were impossible in a classroom in the New World. These general tours are now used by twelve Australian Universities and colleges, some of whom give students degree credits for research projects developed on them. The institutions provide group leaders and ASA provides tour handbooks, lecture programmes in Europe, and travel services. As a type of travelling school ASA has also run some thirty such tours for members of the general public.

During the 1980s ASA often reverted to tours concentrating upon single subjects with particular faculties, professional associations and special interest groups. Tours have been developed for the Royal Australian Institute of Architects, Victorian State Correctional Services, the National Trust of Australia,

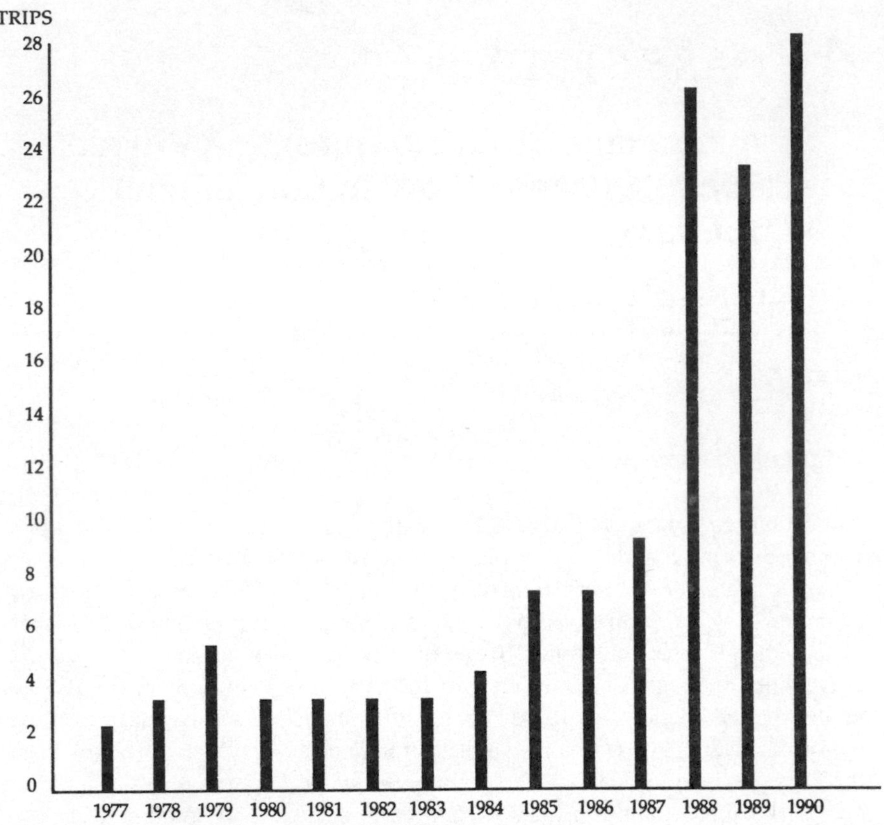

Figure 4.1 Number of ASA Tours per year, 1977–1990

Victoria, the National Gallery Society of Victoria and a number of Alumni organizations. University and college faculties also developed specialized programmes such as a performing arts tour of the United States of America (1980/81), Contemporary Politics and Society in China (1980/81), Graphics in Japan (1985/6), Social Planning in Europe (1986/7; 1988/9; 1990/91), Architectural Technology in Italy (1989/1990), Architecture in the U.S.A. (1990) and Horticulture and Landscape Planning in Europe (1991).

In the early 1980s, Academic Travel Abroad, Washington, D.C., commissioned ASA to develop tours in Australia for the Smithsonian Institution and the Denver Museum of National History and in 1986 Wood became academic co-ordinator for Elderhostel programmes in Melbourne, Australia. Australians Studying Abroad has also organized programmes in Europe for North Americans. In 1985 Wood ran North Italian programmes for the Rhode Island School of Design. In 1988, Information Age Travel, ASA's new parent company, ran thirty short programmes in Italy for the Lyon Travel Agency, Vermont, as add-ons to Italian Elderhostel programmes and in 1990 the organization ran add-on tours for two hundred

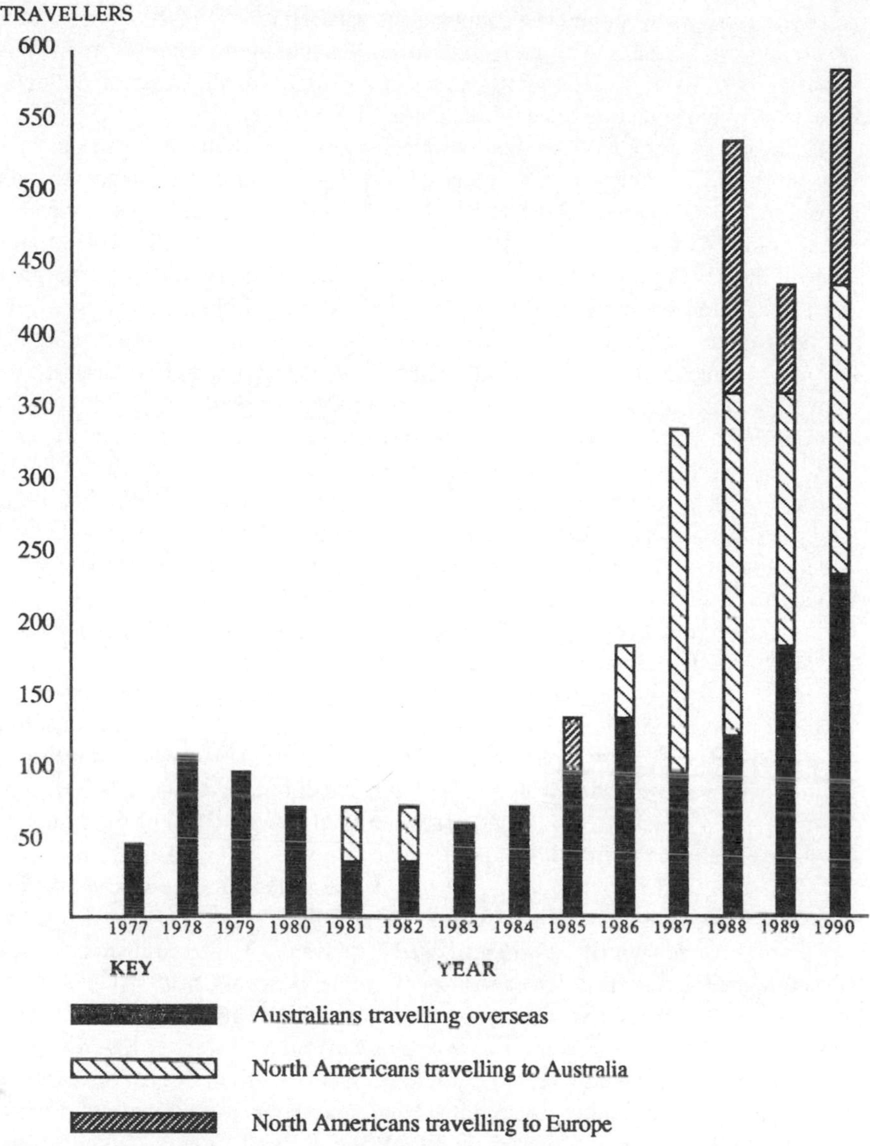

Figure 4.2 ASA Travellers, 1977–1990

participants in the Experiment in International Living's European and Australian homestay programmes. In 1990, ASA also organized a tour of Italy for the Friends of the Walter's Art Gallery, Baltimore. These programmes have given the company a certain international status as a specialist working with institutions throughout the world, a reputation which is a prime consideration in the company's future planning.

To date, ASA has run some fifty tours of its own to Europe, Asia and America. Another sixty tours have been organized for, or in partnership with, twelve

Australian tertiary academic institutions, four Australian secondary schools, three Australian professional institutions and three Australian associations, trusts and societies, two Australian alumni associations and eight North American colleges, associations and societies and adult education organizations.

Figure 4.1 is a graph of the total number of tours run by the company in each year since 1977. Until recently, most of these tours have been organized for November, December and January to fit the months when Australian education institutions took their annual vacations. Until 1987, this bound ASA to an annual cycle of the developing and marketing of tours from February to October before a short, very intensive touring programme. This condemned the company to a very uneven annual cash flow pattern. Tours are now spread more evenly throughout the year because of the development of adult education tours and because institutions have come to accept study tours as part of their curricula.

Figure 4.2 graphs the number of Australians travelling overseas with ASA versus the number of North Americans travelling to Australia, and the number of North Americans travelling to Europe with the company since 1987. The trend toward even numbers of Australians travelling outbound with the company, North Americans travelling inbound and North Americans travelling to Europe, is one which ASA aims to perpetuate. This not only gives the company a valuable international reputation but protects it against the dangers of currency fluctuation. In March, 1991, Arthur Frommer interviewed Chris Wood for America's cable television station, *The Travel Channel*. Frommer concentrated in this interview upon the opportunities North Americans have for joining ASA tours in Australia, Asia and Europe. ASA is at present appointing an agent in New York and Chris is giving seminars for Academic Travel Abroad, Washington, in June, 1991. ASA's ultimate aim is therefore to become an international company basing its reputation upon the excellence of its tours rather than any one market or destination.

ASA does tend to avoid such programmes as scientific expeditions or bird watching tours as these are the province of specialist companies. A new scheme, however, partnered with the Vermont-based Experiment in International Living, is pioneering environmental education tours for adolescents from Australia and North America. ASA has also entered a consortium called 'The Educational Travel Group' with the University of Western Australia, University Extension, the University of Queensland's TraveLearn, the Council of Adult Education and three other specialist companies, Australian Academic Tours, Australis and Alumni Travel. The last of these follows its director Robert Lovell's interest in the politics of Asia while the other organizations are specialists in natural science programmes. This has allowed ASA to involve itself in new fields which its own academic expertise could not cover. The make-up of this consortium reflects a tendency in Australia for universities to specialize in scientific tours leaving private companies to work in the humanities and social sciences.

This diversity of activity reflects the great range of educational tourism which in the English-speaking world is fast becoming an industry paralleling, but having little to do with, general tourism. ASA is typical of some 2,000 educational tourism companies in the United States, Great Britain, Canada, New Zealand, and Australia in many respects. These companies have seldom been developed by the tourism industry but rather by academics, educators and enthusiasts who wish to share their love of a subject or experience with others. They are seldom documented in major national and international tourism studies but their importance is coming to be recognized more and more in surveys of traveller interests. Their growth in Australia has been dramatic in recent years. When ASA was founded in 1977 it was alone in this field in Australia. In the early 1980s it gained three or four counterparts. In 1990 there were at least fifty companies offering educational tours out of Australia and within the country.

With only overseas models to guide it, ASA developed by trial and error. Until 1987, for example, it concentrated upon developing the academic programmes for tours and used travel agents to book the travel and deal with clients. This inhibited its growth. From 1977 to 1980 a number of travel agents, themselves inexperienced in tour design and organization, were used. Then, in 1980, ASA commenced an eight-year partnership with Wandana Travel, a company which had pioneered special interest travel in the 1970s. Wandana's tours had been expensive and had concentrated upon exotic destinations such as the Middle East and South America. Its staff had to adjust to running inexpensive programmes for students to Europe and were forced to deal with a new group of clients who were often better educated but less wealthy than Wandana's traditional clientele.

Wandana Travel brought much valuable experience to the partnership. ASA for the first time was forced to embrace the professionalism of a large, highly respected travel agent, a balancing-act developed between the informality, intellectualism and liberalism of academia and the conservatism of the tourism industry. One negative outcome was the slowing of ASA's growth by inhibiting the development of its status as an independent force in the travel industry (ASA was seen as Wandana's rather eccentric academic arm). However, on the positive side, Wandana never attempted to control the academic development of ASA. Previous travel agents had pressured Wood to popularize tours by down-playing their educational qualities and selling more conventional images of fun and adventure. Wandana's directors realized that the competitive strength of the small company was its ability to create a niche for itself in the tourism industry in which tourism companies could not compete.

Marketing

Unlike North Americans, who had been able to take educational tours and semesters abroad since the 1920s, Australians have tended in the past to travel independently, valuing freedom more highly than access to information. Before the development of the Boeing 747, they tended to travel in Europe for longer periods than Americans. Long sea voyages to Great Britain had formed this tradition which discouraged shorter, educational programmes abroad.

The educational tourism market, moreover, is dominated throughout the world by well-educated females and Australia in the 1970s did not have the vast number of older women with university degrees to be found in North America. The boom in mature-age tertiary education in the 1970s and 1980s has changed this situation, producing in the late 1980s and 90s a large market for educational tourism.

Australian students could not gain credits for tours and were also unfamiliar with the North American idea of attending a university or college in a different part of the country; even today, they invariably attend their local university. Only very successful honours students were helped by the universities with scholarships and advice concerning where to apply for a post-graduate degree overseas.

These and other factors governed ASA's slowed growth. In North America, companies such as The Lyon Travel Agency, Vermont, service large, well-established institutions such as The Experiment in International Living and Elderhostel rather than initiate academic tour programmes. Others, like Academic Travel Abroad, have very serious academic aims but also partner tours with large organizations such as The Smithsonian Institution and The National Trust for Historic Preservation. In Australia, such institutions and associations are smaller and have only recently become aware that they may derive revenue from running tours with a study tour company. Although ASA did partner programmes with special interest and educational bodies before the mid-80s it had no large feeder organization and depended for marketing upon its own academic reputation. Although this limited the company's market it did force it to develop expertise in the development of curricula for tours rather than become a large travel agent which merely serviced educational and special interest organizations. To survive, ASA has needed to keep abreast of academic developments in the disciplines its tours embraced. It is because of this expertise that ASA has been able recently to attract an increasing number of organizations as clients and partners both in North America and Australia.

Australia's tardiness in embracing the concept of educational tourism had consequences for ASA's development which set it apart in other ways from North American companies. It has meant that growth has been ideas driven rather than market driven. An early market survey commissioned by Wandana travel concluded that growth would be slow, that it would be useless to attempt to wholesale through conventional travel agents and that until the Australian populace became familiar with the philosophy of educational travel it would be wasteful to advertise in the media. This has meant that until the development of the Educational Travel Group in 1991, ASA has marketed using networks and mailing lists and has run all its tours as in-house programmes.

Early experience showed that it was necessary to convert Australians to the idea of educational travel before one could sell tours to them. Chris Wood's status as an historian and educational theorist became crucial to the development of the company and also its greatest problem. Like many small companies founded by specialists and enthusiasts ASA could not expand beyond the limits of Wood's energies and capabilities for many years. The paucity of Australian academics with any understanding of, or empathy with, the aims of educational tourism, forced ASA to depend to a large extent upon North American and British group leaders, and on-site lecturers in Europe. It has been difficult to find Australian academics and educators who believe in educational travel and are not motivated solely by the desire for free trips to exotic places. In 1985, one media commentator remarked wryly that there seemed to be more prospective tour leaders angling for free trips than people willing to pay to go on their tours. Unfortunately, although such companies as ASA now dominate the official educational tourism community in Australia, it is still possible that pseudo-study tours run by inexperienced teachers and academics using inexperienced travel agencies outnumber proper educational programmes. The motivation of such group leaders is often to go to new places with which they are not yet acquainted and so such tours are destination rather than curriculum driven. A thorough understanding of a place should, of course, be the first qualification for group leading and so such tours invariably fail in their purported educational aims.

Those who argue for educational tourism against mass or 'commodity' tourism usually claim that the niche marketing of the former is more cost effective than the mass advertising of the latter. Experience has shown, however, both in the United States and Australia, that the educational market itself is sub-divided into a myriad of smaller niches and that educational tours must be marketed with pin-point accuracy to succeed. Other factors also segment the educational tour market. Loyalties to particular companies and tour leaders (ASA is typical in that its tours have high return traveller rates), educational and professional status of clients, tour prices and levels of accommodation, all play their part.

In an industry which profits from lowering overheads, networking has become the key to success. Educational travel companies seldom print glossy brochures because their clients also know that these add to the prices of tours. Word-of-mouth recommendation drives the networks. Public lectures on educational tourism in general and on particular products are invaluable for marketing. ASA has found that a very powerful marketing tool is discussing, wherever possible, the nature of travel. For example, most educational travel clients listen almost exclusively to government radio stations. These stations will not push particular products but are happy to interview educational travel companies about more general issues such as the worth of education-on-the-move or tourism and the environment.

Networking also influences the educational, professional and socio-economic status of an educational tour company's clients. A typical ASA group in Spain (November, 1989) for example, included eight doctors, seven academics, two lawyers, one artist, one film maker, two architects, and five teachers. ASA's market has split into three clearly defined groups which reflect its product. The first is students who are often travelling with their own lecturers for the first time to Europe. Second, there are the architects and other professionals who join specific professional development programmes. The third group is a highly educated public which has travelled regularly for many years, does not like group travel, but joins study tours for the general education they give.

The profile of participants joining ASA tours is changing, with a marked tendency for the adult market to be older. This reflects harder economic times and the tyranny of the overdraft as well as the fact that the first generation of Australians to be highly educated is now entering its maturity. In ten years' time it is projected that ASA's market will be more like that of Elderhostel as this educated group ages.

One other element has dictated the marketing strategies of ASA in the late 1980s and early 1990s. American and Australian educational tour companies have

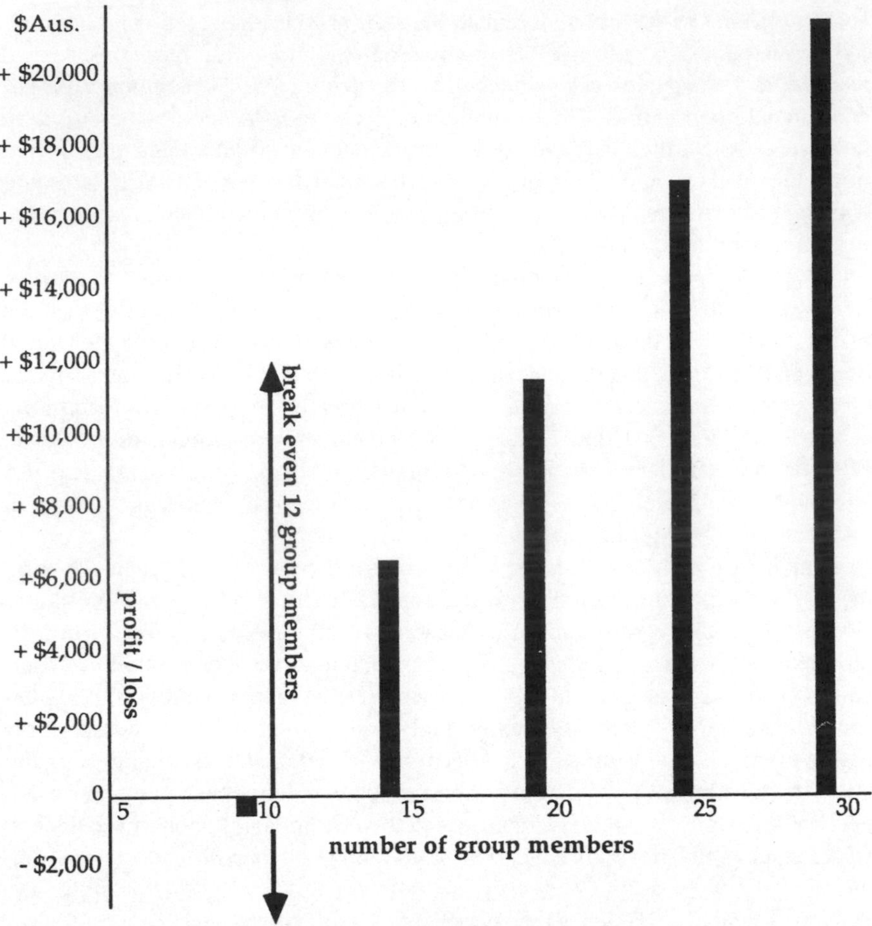

Figure 4.3 Costing chart for a tour costing $4,450 showing profit and loss for between 10 and 30 group members (normal group size = 20 people)

come to agree that the single most important element in determining the survival of a company is the size of its groups rather than the number of tours it runs. While most companies agree for educational reasons that the absolute maximum group size must be thirty, Figure 4.3, which reflects the costing of a typical ASA tour, shows that on a tour costed with break-evens of twelve members, profits rise dramatically when a group has more than twenty members. The single major reason for the development of The Educational Travel Group is the need to fill each other's groups. This signals the onset of wholesaling within the educational travel community itself. ASA tours are now offered by ten institutions and tour companies and it is possible, with the dramatic rise of educational tourism throughout the world, that educational tours will come to be marketed through non-educational travel agencies.

Developing a Philosophy of Educational Tourism

Perhaps the most profound influence upon the development of ASA is that it has been driven by ideas rather than responding to market forces. If the company is to give anything enduring to tourism in general it is in the philosophy it has evolved about travel and education.

The professors who advised the formation of ASA counselled that the company should concentrate on that which could not be done in a classroom. In its most primitive phase this meant showing art history students original works of art.

The experience of running the first group of tours in 1977 and 1978 led, in 1979, to the notion that traditional disciplinary boundaries in the humanities were inappropriate to educational travel. ASA's approach became synthesist rather than interdisciplinary, for the latter still recognizes the territoriality of specializations. It became obvious that the structures which have been evolved to give internal logic to the study of human activity in other cultures, while necessary in the classroom, are really only intellectual constructs which fast lose their meaning for the traveller. The logic which gives this synthesist approach its coherence derives from the relationship between perception, space and the object. Although ASA does not accept a disciplinary approach it nonetheless uses individual perspectives culled from religious, social, intellectual, political and economic history, from art history, historical geography, the physical and social sciences, anthropology, architecture, semiology, ecology, psychological geography and museology, bringing them to bear upon places, spaces and objects.

In an ideal situation, these individual perspectives ensure conceptual rigour but are not allowed to determine ASA's overall approach which is discursive. Group leaders and lecturers attempt to build holistic intellectual models of societies which make diverse realms of human activity sit together in a comprehensible way without recourse to Hegelian, Marxist, Culturalist, Semiotic or Structuralist logic.

This approach in part grew from Chris Wood's experience of the failure of many interdisciplinary courses in Australia. In Classical Studies, for example, it is not unusual for linguists, and political and art historians to teach three discrete components of a course without reference to each other, creating in the minds of students a confused model of a society in which interpretations of art, politics and drama have no relation to each other and sometimes even seem to contradict each other.

On tour, the education programme moves from specific objects to general concepts or a general sense of place to specific activities. Individual disciplinary perspectives in different places can therefore be moulded together into a general overview by creating a set of themes for the tour. Although ASA runs specialist tour programmes, the company believes that a 'special interest tour' is a tour which concentrates on one interest or subject to the exclusion of all others and attempts to avoid this approach because it denies the potential of the synthesism. For example, as much as possible, garden tours relate gardening to architecture and painting in order to set the history of horticulture within a wider context of attitudes to the environment.

One important limitation of classroom history is that it tends to teach in chapters. This way of organizing and rationalizing the past into periods has, of course, a heritage which goes back to thinkers like Hegel, Winckelman and Giorgio Vasari. Study tours, if they are carefully thought out, can portray history as a process, avoiding the tyranny of periods and styles. History can be understood as a temporal continuum through the visual analysis of change in customs and artefacts. One may decode the intricate web of perseverance and influence in the history of a culture in a way which is extremely difficult in a classroom. As time travellers, tour participants can move through a present which is a function of the past. A tour in Rome, for example, can treat the city as the object of urbanistic cultural memory. The rhythm of passage and congregational space, that is, of street and piazza, which all travellers perceive but few understand, can be seen as the conjunction of two different attitudes to planning separated by a millenium.

The Power of Ideas

ASA's future lies in that which has governed its past growth – its ability to excite travellers about ideas and not just about destinations. Its philosophy and its appeal hinge upon the notion that travel is a dialogue between imagination and place. It is ideas such as these, and their application on tours, which have unlocked the North American market to a small Australian company. This was consumated in 1991 when Arthur Frommer interviewed Chris Wood about ASA, stressing that it gave North Americans a unique opportunity to join an Australian study tour in Europe. As one of Australia's oldest educational tourism organizations, ASA will continue to be at the forefront of this emerging tourism niche. Given the downturn in mass tourism since Australia's Expo year, educational tourism and other forms of special interest tourism will become increasingly significant, perhaps finally gaining the attention of tourism policy-makers that they have long deserved.

5 REVIEW

Arts and Heritage Tourism

Heather Zeppel and C. Michael Hall

Introduction

Culture, heritage and the arts have long contributed to the appeal of tourist destinations. However, in recent years 'culture' has been rediscovered as an important marketing tool to attract those travellers with special interests in heritage and the arts. Throughout the world, museums, art galleries, heritage sites, historic buildings, archaeological monuments and sites, and arts festivals have become major tourism attractions. Rather than just being peripheral or added attractions, arts and heritage are increasingly becoming major catalysts for the whole travel experience. This chapter will examine the diversity of arts and heritage attractions, their popular appeal, and the motives and profiles of those tourists attracted by arts and heritage. The chapter does not analyse the impacts of arts and heritage tourism on the host population. However, a substantial amount of literature is available to readers wishing to examine some of the political and social dimensions of the impacts of arts and heritage tourism on host communities and indigenous populations (see Haulot, 1986; Altman, 1988; Cleere, 1989; Fowler, 1989; Hewison, 1989; Smith, 1989; Butts, 1990; Hall and Zeppel, 1990a; O'Regan, 1990; Zeppel and Hall, 1991).

Arts and Heritage Tourism

Arts and heritage tourism can be regarded as a subset of cultural tourism, which includes 'movements of persons for essentially cultural motivations such as study tours, performing arts and cultural tours, travel to festivals and other cultural events, visits to sites and monuments, travel to study nature, folklore or art, and pilgrimages' (World Tourism Organization, 1985, p.6). Heritage tourism is based on nostalgia for the past and the desire to experience diverse cultural landscapes and forms. In a broad sense, the term heritage can be used 'simply to describe those things – cultural traditions as well as artefacts – that are inherited from the past' (Hardy, 1988, p.333). Tangible remains of the past in the form of historic buildings, archaeological sites, monuments, and cultural artefacts on display in museums constitute the principal resources for heritage tourism (Konrad, 1982; Carlsson, 1986; McNulty, 1986). In addition to the cultural and built environments of an area, natural heritage can also include gardens, wilderness areas of scenic beauty, and valued cultural landscapes (Tassell and Tassell, 1990).

Many World Heritage sites are major tourist destinations, including the palace and park of Versailles (France), the old city of Dubrovnik (Yugoslavia), Kakadu National Park (Australia) and the pyramids of Egypt (Cheah, 1983). Heritage attractions are often a main reason for travel, indeed, 'individual heritage sites such as Notre Dame Cathedral and the Eiffel Tower in Paris, or the Tower of London and Shakespeare's birthplace at Stratford-upon-Avon in England, provide the motivation for people to visit a country in the first place' (Millar, 1989, p.14). Historical tourism is one main form of heritage tourism, being 'the Museum-Cathedral circuit that stresses the glories of the Past – i.e., Rome, Egypt, and the Inca' (Smith, 1989, p.5). Heritage tourism based on history tends to be education-oriented and includes guided tours of buildings, monuments and ruins, dramatic sound and light performances and the re-enactment of historically significant occasions.

Heritage tourism also includes local cultural traditions. 'Added to architecture, archaeology and natural sites, are family patterns, religious practices and the subtleties of refined traditions that combine in various ways to make up what we describe as the heritage of a country' (Collins, 1983, p.58). This community heritage embraces folkloric traditions, arts and crafts, ethnohistory ('ways of life'), social customs and cultural celebrations. In France, regional aspects of this 'minor heritage' include a focus on family life, conviviality, and the 'spirit of place' (Hoyau, 1988). Heritage tourism is thus a broad field of specialty travel including many special interest aspects of tourism ranging from examination of the physical remains of the past and natural landscapes to the experience of local cultural traditions.

Arts tourism, however, is directed at the visitor experience of paintings, sculpture, theatre and all other creative forms of human expression and endeavour. Visiting art galleries and attending arts festivals are principal visitor activities. Famous artists, 'exotic' art from other culture groups, well known schools of art, and particular forms or periods of art all attract visitors to the presentation and display of art objects in galleries and museums. Leonardo da Vinci's *Mona Lisa*, for example, constitutes a star attraction at the Louvre in Paris. With the performing arts, well known companies or individual performers often become a significant visitor drawcard in their own right. Arts festivals are a regular feature on the tourist calendar of many cities. The aesthetic, visual and theatrical appeal of the arts are increasingly being packaged and promoted as a special tourist experience.

'[Arts] tourism is experiential tourism based on being involved in and stimulated by the performing arts, visual arts and festivals. Heritage tourism ... is also experiential tourism in the sense of seeking an encounter with nature or feeling part of the history of a place' (Hall and Zeppel, 1990a, p.87). Through participation in arts, culture and heritage individuals can seek to escape the routines of everyday life and improve their social status and self

Table 5.1 Ranking of activities in the *Specialty Travel Index* by number of advertisers per activity

Spring/Summer 1988 Issue		Fall/Winter 1988 Issue	
Rank	Activity	Rank	Activity
1	Yacht/Charter Sailing (354)	1	Yacht/Charter Sailing (388)
2	Cultural Expeditions (302)	2	Cultural Expeditions (362)
3	Bicycle Touring (286)	3	Scuba Snorkelling (282)
4	River Rafting (282)	4	Trekking (274)
5	Scuba Snorkelling (272)	5	Nature Trips (271)
6	Hiking (265)	6	River Rafting (262)
7	Nature Trips (258)	7	Hiking (241)
8	Trekking (244)	8	Bicycle Touring (239)
9	Photography (184)	9	Photography (216)
10	Fishing (180)	10	Safari/Gameviewing (202)

Source: *Specialty Travel Index*, Spring /Summer, Fall/Winter 1988 issues. Figure in parentheses refers to number of advertisers (from Hall, 1989).

image. As Hughes (1987, p.212) commented, special cultural and artistic experiences 'are sources of arousal to compensate for the deficiencies of ordinary life'.

Arts and Heritage Travel Motivations

Cultural motivations for travel have been a significant factor in tourism since the sixteenth and seventeenth centuries (Thorburn, 1986). The Grand Tour was a journey made to the principal cities and classical sites of interest in Western Europe by the wealthy social élite of England for culture, education and pleasure. The Grand Tour followed a distinct travel circuit, with Italy and France providing most of the ancient ruins, classical antiquities and Renaissance sites which the classical Grand Tour traveller wished to experience. During the later romantic Grand Tour, in the nineteenth century, scenic tourism became a more dominant motive for travelling in Western Europe. 'The sites of classical antiquities and Renaissance treasures still dominated the pattern, but tourists were more concerned with the picturesque aspects of ruins and the emotional effects of scenes on their own feelings' (Towner, 1985, p.314). The once fashionable and genteel Grand Tour evolved into a mass tourism experience through the onset of cheaper forms of transport, social and economic change and the commercialization of travel (Feifer, 1985).

In the twentieth century, ever increasing numbers of people are participating in arts and heritage based forms of cultural tourism. 'Both culture and tourism have become democratized and are no longer confined to elites' (World Tourism Organization, 1985, p.23). Cultural expeditions, in fact, were the second most popular form of travel activity advertised in the *Specialty Travel Index* in 1988 (Table 5.1).

The growth in arts and heritage tourism, in particular, can be attributed to an increasing awareness of heritage, greater affluence, more leisure time, greater mobility, increased access to the arts and higher levels of education (Eastaugh and Weiss, 1989; Heinich, 1988). Widespread publications and television documentaries have also increased public awareness of art and heritage, with tourism now providing the opportunities to acquire cultural knowledge and cultural experiences. 'Travel is no longer to *see* for the first time. It is to *experience*' (Collins, 1983, p.59). In arts and heritage tourism, consumer consumption has become increasingly oriented towards the purchase of cultural experiences (theatre, music, festivals) and the consumption of 'cultural' goods through visits to art galleries, museums, and heritage sites (Heinich, 1988). As MacCannell (1976, p.10) commented, 'All tourists desire this deeper involvement with society and culture to some degree; it is a basic component of their motivation to travel'. Along with these important factors influencing travel trends, there has been worldwide recognition of arts activities, heritage sites and cultural facilities as tourist attractions (see Grossman, 1980; Wall and Sinnott, 1980; Weiner, 1980; Johnson, 1983; Tighe, 1985; Bell, 1986; Bwana, 1986; Dunstan, 1986; Korrés, 1986; Kuban, 1986; Lim, 1986; Mturi, 1986; Noblet, 1986; Thorburn, 1986; Tighe, 1986, 1990; Hall and Zeppel, 1990b; Moulin, 1990; Zeppel and Hall, 1991). As van Putten (1986, p.9) noted: 'With the growth in tourism, local authorities in many parts of the world are now asking themselves whether the historic monuments within their boundaries cannot be exploited as a source of income and development'. Therefore, cultural heritage and the arts are uniquely placed to meet the growing demand by tourists for richer travel experiences.

British Heritage Tourism

Heritage is the main strength of British tourism (Berrol, 1981; Capstick, 1985; Stevens, 1986; Thorburn, 1986; Fowler, 1987; Trippier, 1987; British Tourist Authority, 1988; Westwood, 1989; Lavery and Stevens, 1990; Urry, 1990). Indeed, 'the number of sites and monuments in Britain make it a leader in the international heritage tourism "craze"' (Moulin, 1990, p.6). English castles, country houses, cathedrals, archaeological sites and scenic landscapes have an enduring market appeal for both domestic and international tourists. Some 65 million visits were made to English historic houses during 1987 (British Tourist Authority, 1988). From 1976 to 1988 there has been a 22 per cent overall increase in visitation at historic buildings around England (Lavery and Stevens, 1990). English historic churches are visited annually by an estimated 10 million people, 18 per cent being overseas tourists (Marris, 1985). This level of heritage tourism generates a considerable economic impact. 'Throughout Britain it is estimated that £110 million was spent by visitors to historic buildings and gardens. About a third of these were foreign tourists, sixty-seven per cent of whom in 1984/85 visited historic sites, houses or cathedrals' (Hewison, 1987, p.27).

Table 5.2 The top 20 visitor attractions in England, 1987

Admission charged	('000 visits)	Admission free	('000 visits)
Madame Tussaud's	2,439	Blackpool Pleasure Beach	6,450
Alton Tower, Staffs	2,300	British Museum	3,700
Tower of London	2,289	National Gallery	3,567
Blackpool Tower	1,523	Westminster Abbey	3,500
Kew Gardens	1,336	Science Museum	3,166
London Zoo	1,304	Albert Dock, Liverpool	3,100
Natural History Museum	1,291	St. Paul's Cathedral	2,500
Thorpe Park, Surrey	1,060	York Minster	2,100
Benbom Brothers Theme Park, Margate	1,000	Canterbury Cathedral	2,000
Drayton Manor Park, Staffs	972	Tate Gallery	1,725

Source: British Tourist Authority/English Tourist Board 1988, *Sightseeing in 1987*, British Tourist Authority/English Tourist Board Research Services, London.

British Museum Tourism Museums and art galleries in England attract over 68 million visitors a year with overseas visitors representing 24 per cent of that total (Borley, 1988). Most overseas tourists (75 per cent) include a visit to a museum or gallery during their holiday in England (British Tourist Authority, 1984). In London '44 per cent of museum attendances is made up of tourists, compared with 21 per cent outside London' (Urry, 1990, p.118). A major cultural attraction such as the British Museum attracts a high proportion of foreign tourists. During the month of June, 47 per cent of visitors at the British Museum are from North America. By late August, non-English speaking tourists become more prominent while the North American proportion falls to 29 per cent of total Museum visitors (Capstick, 1985).

Major museums and art galleries, along with heritage sites, consistently rank among the most popular tourist attractions in England (Table 5.2). The British Museum and National Gallery each attract over 3.5 million visitors a year and are the most popular free cultural attractions in England. The Science Museum, Natural History Museum and Tate Gallery are also major visitor attractions in London. Other leading heritage drawcards are the Tower of London, Westminster Abbey and Canterbury Cathedral. Similarly, in Scotland, the most popular tourist attraction is the Burrell Collection of medieval, oriental and classical art in Glasgow, followed by Edinburgh Castle (Capstick, 1985). Since 1983, the Burrell Collection has been visited by over 4.5 million people (Watt, 1990).

A major growth area in British heritage tourism has been the development of on-site history museums, at areas of archaeological or industrial significance (Capstick, 1985; Hudson, 1987; Harris, 1989; Urry, 1990). These include the Beamish North of England Outdoor Museum, the Jorvik Viking Centre at York and Ironbridge Gorge with its focus on the Industrial Revolution. These popular heritage attractions provide a more experiential presentation of history for visitors, and reflect the growing trend towards experience based leisure, centred on educational elements (Lavery and

Stevens, 1990). At Jorvik, for example, 'high quality electronic, graphic and modelling techniques have been used to provide the ambience for the Viking village complete with all the sights, sounds and smells of that time' (Shepstone, 1987, p.132). The innovative Jorvik Viking Centre was visited by 866,855 people in 1987 (British Tourist Authority, 1988). Popular heritage museums, such as Jorvik, provide a catalyst for the provision of other related tourist services and facilities.

Museums and other heritage attractions also form key components of historical urban areas being revitalised for tourism (Wood, 1979; Hollis, 1983). In Liverpool, restored former warehouses at the Albert Dock complex now include the Merseyside Maritime Museum and the Tate Gallery North along with shops and other commercial developments. In 1987, an estimated 3.1 million people visited Albert Dock (British Tourist Authority, 1988). The presence of the Maritime Museum as a tourist attraction became a main selling point in attracting business to the dock complex (Capstick, 1985). Similarly, former warehouses have been converted into contemporary art display spaces for the National Gallery and a maritime museum in Wellington, New Zealand. Such developments indicate that museums are of growing importance to the regional tourist industry and may have significant economic impacts.

Economic Benefits of Heritage Tourism and Regional Development Heritage attractions represent a valuable tourism resource for northern England. Developing the tourism industry provides an economic alternative to the decline of traditional manufacturing industries in this region (Urry, 1990). Tourism evaluation studies conducted in Leeds (Harewood House, the Leeds City Art Gallery and Henry Moore Centre), Calderdale (Piece Hall, Shibden Hall, the Eureka! project [the first children's museum in Britain]), Manchester (Heaton Park, Castlefield Urban Heritage Park, Greater Manchester Museum of Science and Industry) and Scunthorpe (Normanby Hall) have emphasized the economic importance of heritage tourism (Greene, 1987; Buckley and Witt, 1989). Estimates of the overall economic impact of tourism in the early 1980s were £45.5 million in Manchester, £39.4 million in Leeds and about £13 million in Calderdale. An estimated 1,500 jobs in Calderdale alone are directly attributable to tourism. Other past and present industrial areas in England are also turning to the development of heritage tourism projects (restored industrial sites, museums, visitor centres, heritage trails) in order to assist economic regeneration and regional prosperity (Green, 1982; Thorburn, 1986; Oglethorpe, 1987; Martin and Mason, 1988; Harris, 1989; Liddle, 1989).

Glasgow – 'Cultural Capital of Europe' Culture is increasingly being utilized and promoted as a tourist drawcard for many city regions. The European Commission officially designated Glasgow, an industrial city in Scotland, as 'Cultural Capital of Europe' for 1990. Athens, Amsterdam, Berlin, Florence and Paris, with their well known cultural history, have previously received this title. The nomination as 'Cultural Capital of Europe' marked Glasgow's transformation, over a 10 year period, from a declining industrial region 'to one of the United Kingdom's first postindustrial cities, basing its economy around the service industries and most notably around the arts' (*EC News*, 1990). Glasgow's investment in the arts, museums, festivals and other visitor attractions has greatly expanded the local tourist industry. 'In 1984, 700,000 tourists came to Glasgow; by 1987, this figure had jumped to four million' (Hawkins, 1990, p.22). 'Two-thirds of visitors now consider that there is a wide variety of interesting museums and art galleries to visit in the city. And at least one-third think that there are so many cultural activities available that they wish they were able to stay longer' (Urry, 1990, p.156).

For its year of culture, the city of Glasgow developed a diverse program of 2,000 events, including visual arts, classical music, jazz, opera, performing arts, folk music, historical exhibitions, museum displays, drama and Scottish cultural traditions. Major art shows featured works by Edgar Degas, Camille Pissaro and Vincent van Gogh. An estimated 9 million visitors were expected to participate in the various cultural events, including 1.5 million local people (Rothwell, 1990). The special emphasis on arts and culture during 1990 undoubtedly attracted large numbers of tourists who would otherwise not be likely to have visited Glasgow. Using the arts as a tourist drawcard therefore generated significant economic and social benefits for Glasgow. The social benefits included renovated historical buildings, new cultural facilities and a renewed civic pride in local people. The cultural focus of 1990 also allowed the city of Glasgow to build and reaffirm its new image as a rewarding destination for arts and heritage tourism.

American Historic Sites

Visiting historic buildings and heritage sites has become a popular tourist activity in America. In the state of Virginia, the top tourist attraction is Colonial Williamsburg (63 per cent), followed by the Skyline Drive in the Blue Ridge Mountains (49 per cent). Colonial Williamsburg comprises some 138 original eighteenth century or early nineteenth century town buildings, together with costumed historical interpreters who re-enact and explain this period of colonial history. In 1984, over 1 million people visited Colonial Williamsburg, bringing the total visitation, since 1932, to over 27 million people (Colonial Williamsburg, 1985). The state of Virginia considers its main visitor strengths to be its historic atmosphere and historic sites along with scenery, mountains and friendly people (Makens, 1987). Visitor surveys in Virginia have also revealed that 'historian' travellers, on the average, tend to be older people with higher incomes, more likely to stay in a hotel/motel when travelling and they also stay longer in an area. 'Historian' travellers were also found to be more family-oriented and education-oriented in their vacation activities. 'Fun is secondary to learning for this group. Historians travel to increase their knowledge of people, places and things. Beyond this, they travel to a great extent for their children's benefit' (Solomon and George, 1977, p.17).

'It is very probable that U.S. historic sites host more than 100 million visitors per year and thus rank as tourist attractions of major importance' (Makens, 1987, p.11). One of the most popular historic sites in America is The Alamo in Texas, a battlefield site which attracted over 2.5 million visitors in both 1982 and 1983. Overall in Texas, from 1979 to 1982, there was a 45 per cent increase in recreational visitors to national historic areas. In New Mexico, attendance at State historic monuments increased by 79 per cent from 1972 to 1982 (Makens, 1987). Attendance at historic houses owned by the U.S. National Trust for Historic Preservation had a growth rate of 25 to 30 per cent during 1982–84 (Mawson, 1984). These visitation figures indicate a strong interest by American tourists in experiencing their own history and national heritage. American historic sites mainly relate to Revolutionary war and Civil war battlefields, the westward movement and frontier days, colonial settlement, early business and industrial enterprises, and venues associated with various US presidents (Winks, 1976). Indian cultural sites are also a significant tourist attraction in the south west region of America (Weighe, 1989) (see also chapter 7 by Harron and Weiler). Heritage tourism is a growing travel phenomenon in America.'As the United States population ages, there will be increased interest in "understanding one's roots", leading to increased interest in historic sites as visitor attractions' (Makens, 1987, p.120). Indeed, surveys of senior travellers over 55 in America, a fast growing segment of the travel market, have found that 51.4 per cent of this group consider visiting museums and historic sites an important reason for travel. These mature travellers are also seeking intellectual and spiritual enrichment from their vacation activities. Both 'Active Resters' (under 64) and the 'Older Set' (over 64) regard visiting historic sites as an important vacation activity (Shoemaker, 1989). Furthermore, visitor surveys conducted by the U.S. National Trust For Historic Preservation and Colonial Williamsburg have shown that people visiting historic sites were primarily attracted by the 'atmosphere' and ambience associated with these sites (Colonial Williamsburg, 1985; Mawson, 1984). This would seem to indicate that 'historian' tourists are motivated more by a search for heritage *experiences* than by a detailed interest in factual history.

Australian Heritage Tourism

The natural environment and cultural attractions of Australia are key components of both the domestic and international tourist market. Overseas travellers are particularly seeking to experience uniquely Australian scenery and wildlife, with a growing interest also in Australian culture, arts and heritage (Hall, 1991). The 1988 International Visitor Survey identified the percentage of various international tourists, by nationality, which visited the major cultural and heritage attractions in Australia (Table 5.3).

The survey results in Table 5.3 illustrate that visitors from Japan place a high priority on visiting heritage attractions such as Ayers Rock, the Sydney Opera House, the Australian War Memorial and also historic venues. Visitors from Malaysia, Singapore, Hong Kong and various European

Table 5.3 Principal international visitor groups, by nationality, visiting cultural and heritage sites in Australia

State	Attraction	Nationalities
NSW	Sydney Opera House	Japan (93%), Scandinavia (86%)
NSW	Museum/Art Gallery of NSW	Scandinavia (34%), Germany (28%)
Vic.	Museum of Victoria	Malaysia (30%), UK/Ireland (27%)
Vic.	National Gallery of Victoria	Scandinavia (29%), Netherlands (28%)
Vic.	Captain Cook's Cottage, Fitzroy Gardens	Japan (70%), Singapore (41%)
Vic.	Sovereign Hill at Ballarat	UK/Ireland (26%), Malaysia (23%)
SA	State Museum/Constitution Museum/ Art Gallery	UK/Ireland (46%), Hong Kong (42%)
WA	Pioneer World/ Elizabethan Village	Singapore (24%), Hong Kong (22%)
Tas.	Port Arthur	Scandinavia (79%), France (76%)
Tas.	Richmond Historic Township	Japan (95%), Malaysia (56%)
ACT	National Gallery	Scandinavia (48%), Singapore (47%). Note: Other Countries (56%)
ACT	War Memorial	Japan (86%), Hong Kong (82%)
NT	Ayers Rock	Japan (97%), Switzerland (88%)
NT	Kakadu National Park	Italy (53%), Switzerland & Germany (46%)

Source: *International Visitor Survey 1988*, Bureau of Tourism Research, Canberra.

NOTE: % factor refers to proportion of each nationality group, who are visitors to that State, visiting cultural and heritage tourist attractions.

countries also exhibit this preference for visiting historical attractions as well as major Australian museums and art galleries. Heritage tourism represents an expanding market sector of the Australian tourist industry. 'In Australia, slowly at first but with increasing rapidity, the entrepreneurial potential of heritage tourism is being recognized. National Parks, the Great Barrier Reef, rainforests and ... heritage buildings are valuable, not only intrinsically, but as tourism resources. These are areas that tourists, both Australian and overseas will visit; places where they will stay, play and pay' (Black, 1990, p.15).

This heritage based travel trend is also of growing importance within the local tourism market. 'Visits to sites of cultural and historical significance are a particular feature of domestic tourism' (Department of the Arts, Sport, the Environment, Tourism and the Territories, 1988, p.80). A popular Australian heritage tourist attraction is Sovereign Hill, an historical theme park at Ballarat in Victoria. Sovereign Hill is a recreated 1850s' gold mining township, where role playing characters in historical costumes bring to life the early goldmining days. In 1988, 498,000 visitors came to Sovereign Hill, while overall, this historical theme park has been visited by over 8 million people. International visitors from the United Kingdom and Europe comprise the majority of the 1 in 5 visitors to Sovereign Hill who are from overseas (Akers, 1989).

Arts and cultural attractions are of growing importance to the Australian tourism industry (Dunstan, 1986; Noblet; 1986; Roeper, 1986; Spring, 1988; Australia Council, 1990a; Cameron, 1990). The 1986 International Visitor survey revealed that '29 per cent of overseas tourists visited museums and art galleries, 19 per cent visited outdoor folk museums or historic parks and 16 per cent attended live theatre and music performances' (Industries Assistance Commission, 1989).

> Australia's cultural buildings, museums and galleries are a drawcard for international tourism. Sydney Opera House is the most popular place in Australia for tourists, attracting almost half of all international visitors. In 1988 25 per cent of international visitors from the UK, Europe, the USA and Canada went to the theatre or concerts. Around 41 per cent of them visited an art gallery or museum (Australia Council, 1989a, p.18).

Art Gallery attendance is also increasing around Australia. Over the two year period from 1986 to 1988 there were nearly a million extra visitors to the many public art galleries (state, national, metropolitan and regional) in Australia (Australia Council, 1989b). A survey of international visitors found that the most frequent reason given for visiting galleries and museums was a general or special interest in art, culture or history (44 per cent) followed by a desire to see examples of Australian art and culture (36 per cent), with many people visiting a gallery specifically to see Aboriginal art (Australia Council, 1990a).

The Australian National Gallery represents a major tourist attraction for Canberra and draws the majority of its audience from outside the national capital region. Four special art exhibitions at the National Gallery have attracted over 500,000 visitors with more than 75 per cent of these people coming from interstate. Many visitors came to Canberra specifically to see these four special art exhibitions, generating an additional A$45 million in visitor expenditure during the periods of the exhibitions (Holding, 1989). The special exhibition 'Civilization: Ancient Treasures of the British Museum' (24 March–11 June) attracted 190,162 visitors to the National Gallery while related souvenir sales totalled nearly A$1 million in the first two months alone (*Muse News*, 1990). One hotel in Canberra also linked their newspaper advertising with the 'Civilization' exhibition, offering special benefits to the cultural tourist along with hotel accommodation. In Australia, the economic benefits of arts tourism are increasingly being recognized by cultural institutions and tourist service industries.

Tourism and Aboriginal Culture The Australian tourism industry is further recognizing that 'Aboriginal art and culture are also important features to some tourists' (Industries Assistance Commission, 1989). A 1989 survey has revealed high interest by international visitors (49 per cent) in experiencing Aboriginal culture, with one in five overseas visitors specifically going to an Australian museum or art gallery to see Aboriginal art. A further 30 per cent of international visitors purchased Aboriginal arts and crafts, worth an estimated A$30 million in arts tourism revenue for Australia. 'Visitors from the USA/Canada and Continental Europe are the most interested in Aboriginal arts and culture and were the most frequent buyers of Aboriginal art and souvenirs' (Australia Council, 1990b, p.1). Aboriginal cultural centres, with a tourism focus, include the Tandanya Aboriginal Cultural Institute in Adelaide, South Australia (opened 1 Oct., 1989) and the Dreamtime Cultural Centre in Rockhampton, Queensland (opened 9 April, 1988). These centres are primarily being operated as commercial tourist ventures, by presenting displays of traditional Aboriginal culture and hosting Aboriginal art exhibitions while also selling Aboriginal craft souvenirs. Over 50,000 people have visited the Dreamtime Cultural Centre at Rockhampton, with a third of these visitors coming from overseas. During the first nine months of opening, Tandanya in Adelaide was visited by some 30,000 people, many from overseas (28 per cent) and interstate (10 per cent). Tandanya is being marketed principally as an international tourist attraction, with Aboriginal art exhibitions at the 1990 Edinburgh Fringe Festival being used to promote Tandanya to the overseas travel market (James, 1990). By promoting Aboriginal culture as a tourist drawcard, such ventures indicate that 'cultural activities are ... adding to the diversity of attractions that Australia offers' (Industries Assistance Commission, 1989).

Heritage Tourism in China

In China, heritage attractions are regarded as a major asset in the development of international tourism (Tisdell and Wen, 1991). The richness of numerous archaeological sites, historic oriental buildings and multiethnic culture groups with diverse customs, food and craft traditions all attract international tourists to visit China (Oudiette, 1990). Well known historic sites include the Great Wall of China, the Summer Palace in Beijing and the Terra Cotta Warriors, a major tourist attraction for the city of Xian. Discovered in 1974, the Terra Cotta Warriors include 7,500 life-size clay figures of warriors and horses buried around 200BC to guard the tomb of the first Qin Emperor (Coutts, 1986). About 300,000 overseas tourists visited Xian during 1987, stayed an average of 2.4 days and spent an amount equivalent to US$32 million. Tourists come to Xian principally to visit various historical sites, with the Terra Cotta Warrior and Horse Museum being the most popular attraction; visited by 90 per cent of all visitors to Xian, including 250,000 international tourists and one million Chinese people in 1987 (Mings and Liu, 1989). The typical tourist travel pattern consists of touring Xian and its vicinity in buses, proceeding from one historical site to another. One day is usually spent visiting the Qin tomb, the Terra Cotta Warrior and Horse Museum, the ancient village museum of Banpo (an archaeological site dating from 5000 to 4000BC) and the imperial country estate of Huaqing Hot Springs, all to the north-east of Xian. A second day is often spent visiting historical attractions within the city of Xian such as the Wild Goose Pagoda, a drum or bell tower, the great mosque and other sites, along with souvenir shopping. Based on the tourist appeal of its heritage sites, the city of Xian has entered into a period of major hotel construction which will eventually increase the number of hotel rooms by 150 per cent. This rapid growth has followed on from 'new central Chinese government policies of the early 1980's (which) acknowledged the potential economic and social benefits to be derived from the development of international tourism' (Mings and Liu, 1989, p.333). With government impetus and continuing international interest in experiencing Chinese cultural history, heritage based tourism will continue to be a major part of the Chinese travel industry .

Art Galleries in Paris

The world's major public art galleries are well patronized by cultural tourists. The paintings and sculptures on display at the Louvre in Paris, for example, now attract 5 million visitors a year (Brooks, 1990). A controversial new glass pyramid entrance and further exhibition space at the Louvre are meeting the needs of a growing arts tourism market. 'By 1993, the Grand Louvre will exhibit 2,000 more paintings and already galleries for temporary exhibitions are bringing more art loving visitors' (Sriber, 1990a, p.16). Paris also has a wealth of other art museums for tourists with a special interest in different art styles and forms to visit and enjoy, their quality and diversity reinforcing the 'international prestige of French museums' (Gordon, 1991). These include the D'Orsay Museum, housed in an ornate former railway station, the Rodin Museum, the Museum of Decorative Arts, the Picasso Museum and the Orangerie Museum, featuring large oval galleries exhibiting Monet's famous impressionist paintings of waterlily ponds. The Picasso Museum, housed in a baroque mansion, has about 4,000 visitors a day. The museum displays 203 paintings and 158 sculptures along with 2,000 other artefacts and sketches covering Picasso's entire artistic life (Eckardt, 1987). These diverse art museums support the tourist image of Paris as a city especially associated with art.

The Georges Pompidou National Centre of Art and Culture is another popular tourist attraction in Paris. An estimated 7.3 million visits are made annually to the Pompidou Centre, with the visitors being from the Paris region (58 per cent), the provinces (13 per cent) or foreigners – who comprise a third or more of the visiting public. The Pompidou Centre is 'undeniably popular, both in specifically tourist terms (the building is an attraction on account of its architecture and the view of Paris it affords) and for more cultural ends' (Heinich, 1988, p.200). In addition, the area surrounding the Pompidou Centre building is 'currently the high spot of Parisian popular culture with its buskers, pavement artists and fire-eaters' (Heinich, 1988, p.203). The Pompidou Centre offers cultural diversity and thus extends the tourist experience of Paris.

A further indication of the importance of cultural tourism to France was the designation of 1991 as the 'Year of the Art of Living' by the French Tourist Bureau. Various aspects of French culture will be further promoted as tourist attractions, including Museums and art galleries along with opera, dance, concerts, churches, gardens, military history and historic routes. In Paris, the purchase of a Museum Card already gives visitors direct admission to some 60 museums and monuments in the Paris region (Sriber, 1990b). Arts and heritage attractions thus continue to be central to the tourist experience of Paris and other regions of France.

Special Art Exhibitions

Special art exhibitions are a major visitor drawcard at public art galleries and may generate substantial economic benefits for the host city (Wall and Knapper, 1981). For instance, the 855,000 visitors who came to view 'The Vatican Collections: The Papacy and Art' exhibition held at the New York Metropolitan Museum of Art in 1983 generated more than US$2 million in admission fees, while the 426,000 out-of-town visitors (out of the 855,000 people who viewed the Vatican exhibition at the Met) spent some US$101 million while in New York' (Danilov, 1988, p.205). Similarly, the 'Pompei A.D. 79' exhibition was shown in just four American cities yet attracted 2.5 million people. The Dallas Museum of Fine Arts hosted 'Pompei A.D. 79' from January 2 to March 18, 1979. Surveys indicated that 37.1 per cent of the respondents (137,000 people) were visitors from outside the Dallas-Fort Worth Metropolitan area generating an estimated direct impact of US$5.4 million. 'Of the out-of-town visitors, almost 70 per cent (96,000) indicated that the *primary* purpose of their visit was to visit "Pompei"' (Vandell, et al., 1979, p.203), while over 80 per cent had come from over 100 miles or more away. These visitors also experienced additional cultural attractions while in Dallas; nearby museums had a substantial increase in visitation while 'Pompei A.D. 79' was on display.

In 1985, 'The Entombed Warriors' exhibition at the City Art Centre in Edinburgh, Scotland, attracted 221,128 visitors. This Chinese exhibition included 11 life-size figures of warriors and horses excavated from the tomb of the first Qin emperor. Extensive media coverage throughout the exhibition generated overwhelming public interest, indeed, 'queues outside the Art Centre were ... a daily feature for the duration of the exhibition' (Coutts, 1986, p.25). A survey revealed that 26 per cent of visitors were Edinburgh residents and 60 per cent were day visitors while 14 per cent were longer stay visitors. The special content of the exhibition also attracted many first time visitors. 'Most of the respondents (82 per cent) had not visited the City Art Centre and as many as 15 per cent said they did not normally visit galleries and museums' (Coutts, 1986, p.26). The success of this exhibition also had social significance for Edinburgh, in particular, 'a civic and national pride that such a unique exhibition had been mounted in Scotland rather than in London' (Coutts, 1986, p.26). Therefore, apart from visitor popularity and economic benefits, special art exhibitions can also represent a socially important event for the host city or region.

Vincent van Gogh – a Tourist Attraction

Famous artists have become the focus for special art exhibitions and also for tourist promotion. The artistic achievements of Vincent van Gogh were celebrated by Holland during 1990 in a highly publicized manner. Indeed, the marketing campaigns were intended to make 1990, the centenary of van Gogh's death, a major arts tourism event for the Netherlands (Moulin, 1990). Dutch tourism policies have particularly emphasized the promotion of cultural heritage and art as a visitor drawcard (Cornelissen, 1986). Some 800,000 visitors were expected to attend the main retrospective exhibition of 135 paintings at the van Gogh Museum in Amsterdam. Another 600,000 people were expected to view an exhibition of 250 van Gogh drawings at the Kroller-Muller Museum in Otterlo (Turner, 1990). Further exhibitions associated with van Gogh were held at other museums and galleries around Holland and also in West Germany, Glasgow and Paris. Other special events in the Netherlands included a van Gogh meal in the town of Sleen based on *The Potato Eaters* and, in Amsterdam, the premiere of an opera based on Vincent van Gogh. 'Thus, the Van Gogh centenary functions as a cultural shorthand which leads to an eclectic assimilation of a variety of Dutch cultural objects' (Moulin, 1990, p.5). The tourism marketing campaigns focused on van Gogh attracted more than a million visitors to the Netherlands in 1990 (Loudon, 1990). The Dutch travel industry clearly benefited from packaging and promoting the international artistic reputation of Vincent van Gogh primarily as a tourist attraction for Holland.

Sculpture as a Tourist Attraction

Major sculptural works are another attraction for the arts tourist. Michelangelo's original statue of *David* in Florence represents a special tourist drawcard for this historically and culturally important region of Italy. The artistic appeal of Florence, a city with 500,000 residents, attracts 1.7 million visitors annually (Urry, 1990). Similarly, the unusual sculptural display at Frogner Park in Norway is a main tourist attraction in the city of Oslo. Created by the sculptor, Gustav Vigeland, the main feature of the sculpture park is a 15 metre high monolith carved into 121 human figures entwined together. Tourists on the site can also walk amongst 36 large granite statues of human figures, a sculptured fountain and 20 bronze trees depicting various stages of human life unfolding among the branches (*Landscape Australia*, 1990). New sculptural art forms can also be a tourist attraction. The Shona stone sculptures of Zimbabwe are renowned as a major contemporary African art form. Shona sculptures are based on spiritual themes and depict animal and human figures. These sculptural works constitute a significant added tourist attraction for Zimbabwe, a country where the main priority of most visitors is to experience the grandeur of Victoria Falls. Shona sculptures are displayed at the National Gallery in Harare and in outdoor sculptural parks at Chapungu village, near Harare, and Tengenenge, a workshop centre for Shona sculptural production. Major exhibitions in Paris, London, New York and Sydney are also exposing Shona sculptures to a western arts audience. This target group may constitute possible future tourists to Zimbabwe based on their special interest in Shona sculpture (Strachan, 1989).

Art and Cultural Festivals

Art Festivals serve as major tourist attractions for city regions. High quality performing arts events are packaged and promoted as a tourism product specifically aimed at the art tourism market sector. Visitor surveys consistently indicate that tourists at arts festivals tend to be 'up-scale', they 'represent a large, well educated and high-income market segment – one which should be highly attractive to the travel and tourism industry' (Tighe, 1986, p.2). A special interest in the visual arts, performing arts (opera, music, ballet, theatre) and other art forms is a major motivating factor for visitor attendance and participation in festivals. The Wagner Ring Festival in Seattle draws close to 75 per cent of its audience from outside the state of Washington. The economic impact of the Festival is an estimated US$6 million. The main tourist source markets for the Wagner Ring Festival are New York, Chicago and Houston. Airline tour packages for this Festival proved to be the most successful travel packages offered by one airline company for the Pacific Northwest region (Lorentzen, 1981). Art Festivals clearly have strong tourist drawing power. In 1985, the Spoleto Festival in Charleston, South Carolina, was attended by 85,000 people. A 1984 survey revealed that 37 per cent of visitors were from outside of South Carolina and Georgia and that 86.9 per cent of the visitors came specifically to attend the festival. The direct economic impact of the 1984 Spoleto Festival was estimated to be US$12 million with tourist expenditure on travel and accommodation being major cost items. Some 80 per cent of visitors to the festival stayed for 4 or more days (nearly 30 per cent stayed 7 or more days) compared to the average non-festival visitor who stayed less than 4 days (Spoleto Festival, nd). Art festivals can both attract and retain additional tourists while also raising the tourist profile and cultural image of a destination.

Arts and heritage tourism are an important aspect of the Canadian tourist economy. Visiting historic and cultural attractions accounted for 29 per cent of Canadian tourism spending in the early 1970s (Galt, 1974). In a visitor survey conducted in Canada in the late 1970s, '42 per cent of respondents had participated in pastimes such as visiting museums, galleries and historical places, while 32 per cent had attended theatre, opera, ballet and concerts' (*Performing Arts*, 1980). Canadian cultural festivals also serve to attract those tourists with a special interest in music, folk traditions, the visual arts or performing arts. The value of arts tourism in Canada is further supported by a study of the economic impact of three theatrical festivals in southern Ontario: the Shakespearean Festival at Stratford, the Blyth Festival at Blyth and the Shaw Festival at Niagara-on-the-Lake (Wall and Mitchell, 1989). The Shakespearean Festival at Stratford, a town of 27,000 people, attracted 487,100 visitors in 1985. Expenditures by the festival organizations and visitors to the festival both make an important contribution to the local economy of the host region. Furthermore, tourist demand for accommodation, food and souvenirs during the festivals has led to growth in the retail and service sectors in each host town. At Niagara-on-the-Lake, 49 per cent of businesses earn more than half their revenue from tourists attending the Shaw Festival. Apart from economic benefits, the festivals also have positive social and cultural impacts. As Wall and Mitchell (1989, p.140) observed: 'The festivals both benefit from and contribute to the ambience of their host communities'. Because of their economic and social benefits, art festivals are increasingly being promoted as a special event tourist drawcard.

The Adelaide Festival

In South Australia, economic studies have been conducted on the impact of the Adelaide Festival of Arts (Brokensha and Tonks, 1985; McDonald, 1989; McDonald, 1990). In March 1990, a total of 10,380 visitors and 47,088 Adelaide residents paid to attend performances at the Adelaide Festival generating an estimated A$10 million for the South Australian economy (Lloyd, 1990; McDonald, 1990). The interstate visitors came principally from Victoria (36 per cent) and New South Wales (26 per cent) while a further 16 per cent of Festival visitors came from overseas. The Adelaide Festival represents a significant tourist attraction, 'for half the estimated number of visitors, the Festival was the *main* reason for coming to Adelaide' (McDonald, 1990, p.7). Festival visitors also spend more and stay longer than other typical tourists in Adelaide. Moreover, the Festival generated 'an increase in hotel demand of over 10,000 room nights let above trend' (McDonald, 1990, p.18), representing the highest level of room nights recorded for the city of Adelaide (Lloyd, 1990). Festival visitors also spent an average A$107 per day (excluding ticket sales) compared to the A$62 per day spent by a typical visitor to Adelaide. In addition, an estimated 4,850 Adelaide residents chose to remain home and attend the Festival. This increased the local economic impact of the 1990 Festival by retaining an estimated A$4.1 million in visitor expenditure in Adelaide that these 'holidaying at home' residents would have spent elsewhere.

Conclusions

Arts and heritage tourism represent a growing market segment for both domestic and international tourism. Already an important component in the special interest tourism market, arts and heritage tourism are rapidly becoming integrated into the mainstream tourism industry in certain destinations. Heritage and history are vital components of the British tourism industry, the visual arts are a major drawcard for Paris, the Netherlands promoted Vincent van Gogh as a prime tourist attraction during 1990, and China is developing its international tourism industry based around archaeological sites and historic buildings. Special art exhibitions and regular arts festivals have also become an established arts tourism product in Canada, America, Australia, Britain and many other countries. As a special tourism resource, arts and heritage attractions often generate large-scale attendance figures and widespread economic benefits. Arts and heritage tourism are being developed to offset the effects of economic restructuring, provide a rationale for urban redevelopment, to establish new tourism markets, and also to boost the cultural image and raise the tourist profile of cities and regions. Furthermore, heritage sites and arts activities are uniquely placed to respond to the growing tourist demand for personally enriching travel experiences. With their enduring visitor appeal and marketability, arts and heritage attractions are therefore being increasingly promoted as essential parts of the tourism experience in many countries, cities and regions.

References

Akers, M., ed., 1989, *Sovereign Hill annual report 1988–1989*, Ballarat Historical Park Association, Ballarat

Altman, J., 1988, *Aborigines, tourism and development: the Northern Territory experience*, North Australia Research Unit, Casuarina

Australia Council, 1989a, *Annual report 1988–89*, Australia Council, Sydney

Australia Council, 1989b, *The arts: some Australian data*, 3rd ed., Australia Council, Sydney

Australia Council, 1990a, *Arts participation by international visitors to Australia*, Arts Facts Research Paper No. 2, Policy & Research Division, Australia Council, Sydney

Australia Council, 1990b, *International visitors and Aboriginal arts*, Arts Facts Research Paper No. 4, Policy & Research, Strategic Development Unit, Australia Council, Sydney

Bell, E., 1986, Conservation and tourism: the ancient capital of Antigua Guatemala in the 20th century, 97–100 in *Conservation and tourism, Second international congress on architectural conservation and town planning, Basle, 1–4 April 1985*, Heritage Trust, London

Berrol, E., 1981, Culture and the arts as motives for American travel, 199–200 in *Innovation and creativity in travel research and marketing – keys to survival and opportunity*, Travel and Tourism Research Association Twelfth Annual Conference Proceedings, June 7–10, 1981, Bureau of Economic and Business Research, Graduate School of Business, University of Utah, Salt Lake City

Black, N.L., 1990, A model and methodology to assess changes to heritage buildings, *The Journal of Tourism Studies*, 1 (1): 15–23

Borley, L., 1988, Museums and tourism, 11–17 in T. Ambrose, ed., *Working with museums*, Scottish Museums Council, Edinburgh

British Tourist Authority, 1984, *Overseas visitor survey, 1 October 1982–30 September 1983,* British Tourist Authority, London

British Tourist Authority/English Tourist Board 1988, *Sightseeing in 1987*, British Tourist Authority/English Tourist Board Research Services, London

Brokensha, P., Tonks, A., 1985, *An interim report on the economic impact of the 1984 Adelaide Festival of Arts*, South Australian Institute of Technology, Adelaide

Brooks, G., 1990, The European experience, *Historic Environment*, 7 (3/4): 99–101

Buckley, P.J., Witt, S.F., 1989, Tourism in difficult areas II: Case studies of Calderdale, Leeds, Manchester and Scunthorpe, *Tourism Management*, 10 (2): 138–152

Bureau of Tourism Research, 1989, *International visitor survey 1988*, Bureau of Tourism Research, Canberra

Butts, D.J., 1990, Nga Tukemata: Nga Taonga o Ngati Kahungunu (The awakening: the treasures of Ngati Kahungunu), 107–117 in P. Gathercole and D. Lowenthal, eds, *The politics of the past*, Unwin Hyman, London

Bwana, O., 1986, Conservation and tourism: the case of Lamu, 81–85 in *Conservation and tourism, Second international congress on architectural conservation and town planning, Basle, 1–4 April 1985*, Heritage Trust, London

Cameron, F., 1990, Here comes the seriously green tourist machine, *The Weekend Australian, Property*, 10–11 November: 7

Capstick, B., 1985, Museums and tourism, *The International Journal of Museum Management and Curatorship*, 4: 365–372

Carlsson, O., 1986, Denkmalpflege und tourismus: miteinander, füreinander, 23–33 in *Conservation and tourism, Second international congress on architectural conservation and town planning, Basle, 1–4 April 1985*, Heritage Trust, London

Cheah, P., 1983, World heritage sites and tourism potential, *Heritage Australia*, 2 (2): 60–63

Cleere, H.F., ed., 1989, *Archaeological heritage management in the modern world*, Unwin Hyman, London

Collins, R.E., 1983, Tourism and heritage conservation – the Pacific experience, *Heritage Australia*, 2 (2): 58–59

Colonial Williamsburg, 1985, *Annual report*, Colonial Williamsburg Foundation, Williamsburg, Virginia

Cornelissen, J.A.T., 1986, Dutch tourism; a big industry in a small country, *Tourism Management*, 7 (4): 294–297

Coutts, H., 1986, Profile of a blockbuster, *Museums Journal*, 86 (1): 23–26

Danilov, V.J., 1988, Corporate sponsorship of museum exhibits, *Curator*, 31 (3): 203–230

Department of the Arts, Sport, the Environment, Tourism and the Territories, 1988, *Directions for tourism: a discussion paper*, AGPS, Canberra

Dunstan, D., 1986, Packaging the developing arts for an increase in tourist trade, 18–23 in *Tourism and the arts*, Policy & Planning Division, Australia Council, Sydney

Eastaugh,A., Weiss, N., 1989, Broadening the market, 58–67 in D.L. Uzzell, ed., *Heritage interpretation volume 2 The visitor experience*, Belhaven Press, London

Eckardt, W. von, 1987, Picasso in Paris, *Travel & Leisure* (Australia edition), 2 (3): 60–65, 78–80

E C News , 1990, Glasgow: European capital of culture, *E C News*, 8(2)

Feifer, M., 1985, *Tourism in history: from imperial Rome to the present*, Stein and Day, New York

Fowler, N., 1987, *Making the most of heritage*, HMSO, London

Fowler, P., 1989, Heritage: a post-modernist perspective, 57–63 in D.L. Uzzell, ed., *Heritage interpretation, vol. 1, The natural and built environment*, Belhaven Press, London

Galt, G., 1974, *Investing in the past: A report on the profitability of heritage conservation*, Heritage Canada, Ottawa

Gordon, H., 1991, At large in Paris? Just pray for rain, *The Weekend Australian, Review*, 5–6 January: 10, 13

Green, D., 1982, Tourist rites for Wales, *Tourism Management*, 3 (3): 199–200

Greene, J.P., 1987, Museums and urban regeneration: The Greater Manchester Museum of Science and Industry, 37–43 in P.M. Summerfield, ed., *Proceedings of the council of Australian museums associations conference Perth W.A. 1986*, History Department, Western Australian Museum, Perth

Grossman, L., 1980, The time is ripe to tap tourists' cultural awakening, *Performing Arts*, Winter: 24–25

Hall, C.M., 1989, Special interest travel: A prime force in the expansion of tourism?, 81–89 in R. Welch, ed., *Geography in action*, University of Otago, Dunedin

Hall, C.M., 1991, *Introduction to tourism in Australia: impacts, planning, and development*, Longman Cheshire, South Melbourne

Hall, C.M., Zeppel, H., 1990a, Cultural and heritage tourism: the new grand tour?, *Historic Environment*, 7 (3/4): 86–98

Hall, C.M., Zeppel, H., 1990b, History, architecture, environment: cultural heritage and tourism, *Journal of Travel Research*, 24 (2): 54–55

Hardy, D., 1988, Historical geography and heritage studies, *Area*, 20: 333–38

Harris, F., 1989, From the industrial revolution to the heritage industry, *Geographical Magazine*, 61 (5): 38–42

Haulot, A., 1986, Politique du tourisme et protection du patrimoine, 14–22 in *Conservation and tourism, Second international congress on architectural conservation and town planning, Basle, 1–4 April 1985*, Heritage Trust, London

Hawkins, G., 1990, Touting for tourists, *Culture and Policy*, 2 (1): 21–27

Heinich, N., 1988, The Pompidou Centre and its public: the limits of a utopian site, 199–212 in R. Lumley, ed, *The museum time machine: putting cultures on display*, Routledge, London and New York

Hewison, R., 1987, *The heritage industry: Britain in a climate of decline*, Methuen, London

Hewison, R., 1989, Heritage: an interpretation, 15–23 in D. Uzzell, ed., *Heritage interpretation, vol. 1, The natural and built environment*, Belhaven Press, London

Holding, C. (Minister for the Arts, Tourism and Territories), 1989, *Address to the annual general meeting of the Australian Federation of Friends of Galleries and Museums*, The Australian National Library, Canberra, 14 September

Hollis, S.M., 1983, The arts and center-city revitalization: a case study of Winston-Salem, *The Journal of Arts Management and Law*, 13 (2): 29–48

Hoyau, P., 1988, Heritage and 'the conserver society': the French case, 27–35 in R. Lumley, ed., *The museum time machine: putting cultures on display*, Routledge, London and New York

Hudson, K., 1987, *Museums of influence*, Cambridge University Press, Cambridge

Hughes, H.L., 1987, Culture as a tourist resource – a theoretical consideration, *Tourism Management*, 8 (3): 205–216

Industries Assistance Commission, 1989, *Travel and tourism*, Report No. 423, Australian Government Publishing Service, Canberra

James, C., 1990, Tandanya – a troubled dreaming, *The Advertiser*, 21 August: 17

Johnson, W., 1983, If its Tuesday this must be ballet, *American Arts*, July: 12–14

Konrad, V.A., 1982, Historical artifacts as recreational resources, 392–416 in G. Wall and J.S. Marsh, eds, *Recreational land use: perspectives on its evolution in Canada*, Carleton University Press, Ottawa

Korrés, M., 1986, Die Akropolis: restaurierung und die besucher, 122–130 in *Conservation and tourism, Second international congress on architectural conservation and town planning, Basle, 1–4 April 1985*, Heritage Trust, London

Kuban, D., 1986, Direct and indirect uses of restoration for tourism: the Caravanserail, Erdine; the harbour site, Antalaya; the Ibrahim Pasa Museum, Istanbul, and other examples, 49–55 in *Conservation and tourism, Second international congress on architectural conservation and town planning, Basle, 1–4 April 1985*, Heritage Trust, London

Landscape Australia, 1990, Landscape Australia looks abroad: sculpture in Scandinavia, *Landscape Australia*, 12 (1): 103–105

Lavery, P., Stevens, T., 1990, Attendance trends and future developments at Europe's leisure attractions, *Travel and Tourism Analyst*, 2: 52–75

Liddle, B., 1989, The case for modern industrial tourism, *Area*, 21: 405–406

Lim, W., 1986, Bu Ye Tian conservation project, Singapore, 63–68 in *Conservation and tourism, Second international congress on architectural conservation and town planning, Basle, 1–4 April 1985*, Heritage Trust, London

Lloyd, T., 1990, Festival a magnet for visitors, *The Advertiser*, 31 March: 3

Lorentzen, S.A., 1981, Building a cultural tourism industry in America: The launching of a Wagner festival, 207–213 in *Innovation and creativity in travel research and marketing – keys to survival and opportunity*, Travel and Tourism Research Association Twelfth Annual Conference Proceedings, June 7–10, 1981, Bureau of Economic and Business Research, Graduate School of Business, University of Utah, Salt Lake City

Loudon, B., 1990, The best kept secret in Europe, *The Weekend Australian, Review*, 20–21 October: 12

MacCannell, D., 1976, *The tourist: a new theory of the leisure class*, Schoken Books, New York

Makens, J. C., 1987, The importance of U.S. historic sites as visitor attractions, *Journal of Travel Research*, 25 (3): 8–12

Marris, T.G., 1985, English churches and tourism, *Tourism recreation research*, 10 (1): 60

Martin, B., Mason, S., 1988, The role of tourism in urban regeneration, *Leisure Studies*, 7 (1): 75–80

Mawson, R., 1984, *Summary report: who visits historic houses and why,* National Trust for Historic Preservation, Washington D.C.

McDonald, S. 1989, *The 1988 Adelaide Festival: an economic impact study*, Centre for South Australian Economic Studies, University of Adelaide, Adelaide

McDonald, S. 1990, *The 1990 Adelaide Festival: The economic impact, Volume 1 summary*, Centre for South Australian Economic Studies, University of Adelaide

McNulty, R., 1991, Cultural tourism: new opportunities of wedding conservation to economic development, 34–41 in *Conservation and tourism, Second international congress on architectural conservation and town planning, Basle, 1–4 April 1985*, Heritage Trust, London

Millar, S., 1989, Heritage management for heritage tourism, *Tourism Management*, 10 (3): 9–14

Mings, R., Liu, W., 1989, Emerging tourism in China – the case of Xian, *Tourism Management*, 10 (4): 333–336

Moulin, C., 1990, Cultural heritage and tourism evolution, *Historic Environment*, 7 (3/4): 3–9

Mturi, A.A., 1986, Problems and prospects for urban conservation in Tanzania: Zanzibar Stone Town, Bagamoyo, Dar es Salaam and Kilwa Kivinje, 86–96 in *Conservation and tourism, Second international congress on architectural conservation and town planning, Basle, 1–4 April 1985*, Heritage Trust, London

Muse News, 1990, From the people who brought you the British Empire..., *Muse News*, 1/2: 19

Noblet, A., 1986, Consolidating this profitable partnership, 24–28 in *Tourism and the arts*, Policy & Planning Division, Australia Council, Sydney

Oglethorpe, M.K., 1987, Tourism and industrial Scotland, *Tourism Management*, 8 (3): 268–271

O'Regan, S., 1990, Maori control of the Maori heritage, 95–105 in P. Gathercole and D. Lowenthal, eds, *The politics of the past*, Unwin Hyman, London

Oudiette, V., 1990, International tourism in China, *Annals of Tourism Research*, 17 (1): 123–132

Performing Arts , 1980, The tourism and culture connection across the land, *Performing Arts*, Winter: 26–27

Roeper, J. de., 1986, The Adelaide festival as a tourist attraction, 13–17 in *Tourism and the arts*, Policy & Planning Division, Australia Council, Sydney

Rothwell, N., 1990, Culture with a capital C, *The Weekend Australian, Weekend*, 5–6 May: 9

Shepstone, T., 1987, Future tourism projects, *Tourism Management*, 8 (2): 131–133

Shoemaker, S., 1989, Segmentation of the senior pleasure travel market, *Journal of Travel Research*, 27 (3): 14–21

Smith, V., (ed.), 1989, *Hosts and guests: the anthropology of tourism.*, 2nd ed., University of Pennsylvania Press, Philadelphia

Solomon, P.J., George, W.R., 1977, The bicentennial traveler: a life-style analysis of the historian segment, *Journal of Travel Research*, 15: 14–17

Spoleto Festival , nd, *Spoleto Festival 1984 survey*, Spoleto Festival, Charleston, South Carolina

Spring, J., 1988, Arts and entertainment in tourism, 349–354 in B. Faulkner, and M. Fagence, eds, *Frontiers of Australian tourism. The search for new perspectives in policy development and research*, Bureau of Tourism Research, Canberra

Sriber, C., 1990a, Take a look at Louvre after facelift, *The Weekend Australian, Weekend*, 12–13 May: 16

Sriber, C., 1990b, France is a feast for culture vultures, *The Weekend Australian, Review*, 17–18 November: 13

Stevens, T., 1986, Heritage & leisure: The essential partnership, *Leisure Management*, 6 (3): 25–26

Strachan, N., 1989, The other face of Zimbabwe, *Holiday and Travel News*, Oct./Nov.: 18–20

Tassell, C., Tassell, M., 1990, The Tasmanian rural landscape, *Heritage Australia*, 9 (4): 12–15

Thorburn, A., 1986, Marketing cultural heritage: does it work within Europe?, *Travel & Tourism Analyst*, December: 39–48

Tighe, A.J., 1985, Cultural tourism in the U.S.A., *Tourism Management,* 6 (4): 234–251

Tighe, A.J., 1986, The arts/tourism partnership, *Journal of Travel Research,* 24 (3): 2–5

Tighe, A.J., 1990, 1991 outlook for cultural travel, 123–125 in *1991 Outlook for travel and tourism, Proceedings of the sixteenth annual travel outlook forum,* U.S. Travel Data Center, Washington D.C.

Tisdell, C., Wen, J., 1991, Foreign tourism as an element in PR China's economic development strategy, *Tourism Management,* 12 (1): 55–67

Towner, J., 1985, The grand tour: A key phase in the history of tourism, *Annals of Tourism Research,* 12: 297–333

Trippier, D., 1987, Tourism in the 1990's – UK government view, *Tourism Management,* 8 (2): 79–82

Turner, J., 1990, The merchants of Vincent, *ARTnews,* 89 (3): 155

Urry, J., 1990, *The tourist gaze: leisure and travel in contemporary societies,* Sage, London

Vandell, K.D., Barry, T.E., Starling, J.D., Seib, P., 1979, The arts and the local economy: the impact of 'Pompei AD 79', *Curator,* 22 (3): 199–215

van Putten, H., 1986, Welcoming speech, 9 in *Conservation and tourism, Second international congress on architectural conservation and town planning, Basle, 1–4 April 1985,* Heritage Trust, London

Wall, G., Knapper, C., 1981, *Tutankhamun in Toronto,* Department of Geography Publication Series No. 17, University of Waterloo, Waterloo

Wall, G., Mitchell, C., 1989, Cultural festivals as economic stimuli and catalysts of functional change, 132–141 in G.J. Syme, B.J. Shaw, D.M. Fenton, and W.S. Mueller, eds, *The planning and evaluation of hallmark events,* Avebury, Aldershot

Wall, G., Sinnott, J., 1980, Urban recreational and cultural facilities as tourist attractions, *Canadian Geographer,* 24 (1): 50–59

Watt, R.A., 1990, The Burrell Collection: foreword, *Arts of Asia,* 20 (3): 94–95

Weighe, M., 1989, From desert to Disney World: the Sante Fe Railway and the Fred Harvey Company display the southwest, *Journal of Anthropological Research,* 45 (1): 115–137

Weiner, L., 1980, Cultural resources: an old asset – a new market for tourism, 187–192 in D.E. Hawkins, E.L. Shafer, and J.M. Rovelstad, eds, *Tourism marketing and management issues,* George Washington University, Washington D.C.

Westwood, M., 1989, Warwick Castle: preparing for the future by building on the past, *Tourism Management,* 10 (3): 235–239

Winks, R., 1976, Conservation in America: national character as revealed by preservation, 140–149 in J. Fawcett, ed., *The future of the past: attitudes to conservation 1174 – 1974,* Thames and Hudson, London

Wood, A.C., 1979, Tourism: an asset... or a liability?, *Historic Preservation,* 31: 39–43

World Tourism Organisation, 1985, *The state's role in protecting and promoting culture as a factor of tourism development and the proper use and exploitation of the national cultural heritage of sites and monuments for tourism,* World Tourism Organization, Madrid

Zeppel, H., Hall, C.M., 1991, Selling art and history: cultural heritage and tourism, *Journal of Tourism Studies,* 2 (1): 29–45

6 CASE STUDY

The Festival of Pacific Arts: An Emerging Special Interest Tourism Event

Heather Zeppel

Festivals as a Form of Special Interest Tourism

Festivals, carnivals and community fairs add vitality and enhance the tourist appeal of a destination. Festivals are held to celebrate dance, drama, comedy, film and music, the arts, crafts, ethnic and indigenous cultural heritage, religious traditions, historically significant occasions, sporting events, food and wine, seasonal rites and agricultural products. Visitors primarily participate in festivals because of a special interest in the product, event, heritage or tradition being celebrated. The special appeal of festivals derives from their atmosphere of fun and celebration 'and their "ambience", which elevates them above ordinary life' (Getz, 1989, p.125).

Festivals are generally organized for a variety of reasons, 'including enhancing or preserving local culture and history, providing local recreation and leisure opportunities, and enhancing the local tourism industry' (Long and Perdue, 1990, p.10). Festivals can be essentially community-based, focused on 'local themes and values', largely aimed at attracting outside visitors or, increasingly, rely for their continued success on appealing to both outsiders and local visitors (Heenan, 1978). Visitor motivations for festival attendance include the five main elements of spectacle, ritual, games, sharing experiences and authenticity, which in the context of festivals means 'an event which is community-based, so that visitors believe they are sharing in an authentic local celebration' (Getz, 1988, p.25). Festivals also seem to attract particular types of tourists, including 'high-contact travellers' who seek cross-cultural experiences, 'explorers' who mix with the host society and 'allocentrics' with their cultural/educational motives and a search for the exotic (Pearce, 1982).

Festivals can be categorized as either special events (Getz, 1989) or as hallmark events (Ritchie, 1984; Hall, 1989a). The Canadian National Task Force on Tourism Data defined special events as 'A celebration or display of some theme to which the public is invited for a limited time only, annually or less frequently'. This definition was influenced by an orientation to local community-based festivals (Getz, 1989). In contrast, hallmark events are generally regarded as major, large-scale tourist events with an international status (Hall, 1989b; Wall and Mitchell, 1989). 'Hallmark tourist events... are major fairs, festivals, expositions, cultural and sporting events which are held on either a regular or a one-off basis'

(Hall, 1989a, p.263). Hallmark events, including special interest festivals, have significant economic, physical, socio-cultural, psychological and political impacts on the destination area and host group which has generated the event (Ritchie, 1984; Schaffer, 1986; Pelletier, 1988; Wang and Gitelson, 1988; Hall, 1989c; Hall, 1989d; Wall and Mitchell, 1989; Long and Perdue, 1990).

Festivals are an important segment of events tourism, 'which can be defined as the systematic development and marketing of special events as tourist attractions and as image-builders for destinations' (Getz, 1988, p.252). The positive tourism impacts of major festivals include promotional opportunities offered to the host region through media coverage and favourable responses generated in visitors attending the festival. A Canadian study of festivals held in the Ottawa region, for example, revealed that all of the festivals promoted a positive image of Ottawa, with their artistic, cultural and entertainment aspects being a major drawcard for participants (Coopers and Lybrand Consulting Group, 1989). As such, festivals are an important type of special interest tourism.

Festivals are increasingly being promoted as a special tourist attraction (South Australian Tourism Development Board, 1987; Getz, 1988; Frisby and Getz, 1989; Ralston and Stewart, 1990; Getz, 1991). 'Festivals generally are viewed by their organizers and host communities as being social or cultural celebrations. More and more, they are also being viewed as tourist attractions which have a considerable economic impact on the surrounding region' (Frisby and Getz, 1989, p.7). Festivals thus represent an important tourist asset in the special interest tourism market. The following case study examines the Festival of Pacific Arts as a specific form of special interest tourism. In particular, the Festival of Pacific Arts illustrates the transformation of a community-based cultural celebration into a special interest tourism event attracting an international audience.

The Festival of Pacific Arts

The Festival of Pacific Arts is a major international cultural festival. Twenty six Pacific nations are represented in the Festival, which brings together cultural participants from throughout the entire Pacific Ocean region. The Festival primarily celebrates the cultural heritage of indigenous peoples in the Pacific, including Melanesian, Polynesian and Micronesian culture groups as well as the Aboriginal and Torres Strait Island cultures of Australia. The Festival of Pacific Arts has been held in Fiji (1972), New Zealand (1976), Papua New Guinea (1980), Tahiti – French Polynesia (1985) and Australia (1988). In 1992 the Festival will be held on Rarotonga in the Cook Islands. The first Festival, called the South Pacific Festival of Arts, was held in Suva, Fiji in an attempt to combat the erosion of traditional artistic and cultural practices in the face of increasing western influences. 'South' was dropped from the Festival's name in 1985 in recognition of the participation by Hawaii and the Micronesian nations from the north Pacific (Simons, 1989).

Table 6.1 Cultural delegations at the 5th Festival of Pacific Arts, Townsville, 14–27 August 1988

Country	Number of Delegates
Australia	300
American Samoa	42
Cook Islands	47
Easter Island (Chile)	7
Federated States of Micronesia	65
Fiji	110
French Polynesia	140
Guam	56
Hawaii	82
Marshall Islands	56
Nauru	44
New Caledonia	88
New Zealand	73
Niue	31
Norfolk Island	4
Northern Marianas	82
Papua New Guinea	250
Solomon Islands	58
Tokelau	21
Tonga	42
Tuvalu	32
Vanuatu	43
Wallis/Futuna	41
Western Samoa	46
Pitcairn Island	Exhibition only

Source: Duke, A., 1989, *Report on planning & staging the 5th Festival of Pacific Arts held in Townsville, Australia, 14–27 August 1988*, Festival of Pacific Arts Ltd., Appendix 11: 'Participating Countries', p.17.

The 5th Festival of Pacific Arts

The 5th Festival of Pacific Arts was held in the city of Townsville in north Queensland, Australia, from 14–27 August, 1988. Cultural delegations from 24 Pacific nations attended the Festival (Table 6.1). There were 1,760 participants at the 5th Festival of Pacific Arts, making it the largest indigenous cultural event ever held in Australia (Isaacs, 1988). An estimated 20,000 visitors attended this Festival (Creagh, 1988). As a special interest tourism event, the Festival in Townsville was considered to be 'a significant addition to the attractions bringing visitors to the North' (*Townsville Bulletin*, 1988a, p.4).

The Australian Commonwealth government allocated A$4.8 million in funding for the 5th Festival of Pacific Arts with an additional A$237,000 provided for the training of indigenous liaison officers. Sponsorship of A$60,000 was received from the Overseas Telecommunications Commission (OTC) for the Festival media centre, while the Australian Film Commission provided A$30,000 sponsorship for the Festival film program. Admission to all Festival events was free of charge (Duke, 1989).

There was extensive international interest in the 5th Festival of Pacific Arts. There were 432 accredited media representatives from 29 countries in Townsville to report on the Festival. This media coverage included 110 film/video makers, 98 print journalists, 78 radio presenters, 62 television staff, 44 photographers, 7 technicians and 33 other journalists (Duke, 1989). As stated earlier, such media coverage provides a valuable tourism promotion opportunity for destinations, in this case Townsville, and the 5th Festival of Pacific Arts featured in 'the many articles, photo series, television items and documentaries produced for overseas consumption' (*Townsville Bulletin*, 1988c, p.3).

The visitors' book at 'The Past in the Present', the main exhibition at the 5th Festival of Pacific Arts, provides a record of international and Australian visitors at the Festival in Townsville.

> Apart from participating countries, visitors came from West Germany, Spain, England, Sweden, America, Holland, Japan, Brazil, Israel, Scotland, Austria, France, Denmark, Luxembourg, Canada, Panama, Italy, Africa, Philippines and Bermuda. Overseas visitors accounted for approximately 50 percent of the 1,010 signatures in the visitor's book. Of the remainder approximately half represented visitors from all Australian states and half North-Queensland residents (Duke, 1989, p.14).

The Festival Programme

The 5th Festival of Pacific Arts included traditional dancing performances, contemporary plays, indigenous rock groups, exhibitions of artefacts, a craft village, a film program, storytelling and a cultural forum. Special events at the Festival included an American Samoan feast and kava ceremony, a Tahitian wedding celebration and a sacred Tahitian fire-walking ceremony. Traditional song and dance performances were a major feature of the Festival. These performances were generally held outdoors in Townsville, at the craft village and Queen's Park, at Alma Bay on Magnetic Island (a 20 minute ferry ride from Townsville), in the Flinders Mall and on a specially constructed stage built out over the sea at the rock pool. The open-air venues used for the Festival encouraged a casual and relaxed atmosphere, while the close proximity of performers often resulted in members of the audience joining in with the dancing (Duke, 1989). Throughout the Festival visitors were drawn into a first-hand experience of Pacific cultural traditions. Rather than just being spectators and observers, many visitors took the opportunity to become active participants in the variety of special cultural learning experiences offered by the Festival.

Culture as a Tourist Attraction

'Exotic' Pacific cultures have long held a special fascination and appeal for western audiences. Major attractions include the vibrant song, dance and music traditions of the Pacific region along with the visually striking body adornment and decoration of the performers. This special interest by international visitors in experiencing 'authentic' Pacific culture has contributed to the Festival of Pacific

Plate 6.1 Tahitian dancer performing at the 5th Festival of Pacific Arts. (Courtesy of the *Townsville Bulletin*)

Arts becoming a major tourist event. With the Festival held in Townsville, the varied performances by Aboriginal and Torres Strait Islander groups were a significant added attraction for overseas tourists. The 5th Festival of Pacific Arts also provided an unparalleled opportunity for many Australian visitors to experience the full range of Pacific cultural traditions at one occasion.

The participating cultural groups at the Festival varied in the amount of western influence, the degree of authenticity in costumes and dance styles, and the extent to which performances were oriented towards a tourist audience. While dance styles were largely based on traditional forms, the attire worn by performers ranged from traditional costumes to modified traditional items (commercial face paints, artificial leis) and also contemporary clothing (sarongs, thongs, watches). The overall colour, drama and spectacle of the Festival, however, more than fulfilled most visitor expectations of experiencing 'traditional' Pacific culture.

Pacific Culture/Tourist Culture

The Polynesian dance performances included choreographed dance routines from Tahiti, the Cook Islands and American Samoa. In the best Hollywood tradition, the Tahitian and Cook Islands dancers presented vigorous hip-shaking *tamure* dancing. Both groups selected members of the audience to perform their own versions of *tamure* dancing and were popular performing groups at the Festival. 'The song and dance troupes were exuberant and of a high standard, with both the Cook Islands dancers and the French Polynesian groups excelling, their drum orchestras marvels of pulsating percussion' (Roces, 1989, p.52). More traditional Polynesian dance performances from Western Samoa, Tonga, Wallis/Futuna, Tuvalu, Tokelau and Niue featured action songs (emphasizing graceful hand, arm and head movements), paddle dances and war dances. Teenage pupils from the Kamehameha High School in Hawaii performed *hula* dances and *mele* or song chants accompanied by traditional bamboo and gourd percussion instruments. Tourist acts included a Cook Islands woman husking a coconut with her teeth, Western Samoan machete juggling and a Samoan dance performed with blazing firebrands. All the Polynesian dance performances were popular spectator events throughout the Festival.

Traditional Melanesian Culture

Melanesian dance performances were among the most authentic and traditional cultural events presented at the 5th Festival of Pacific Arts (Kaeppler, 1989; Simons, 1989). Cultural performances from Papua New Guinea included the yam harvest dances of the Trobriand Islands, a west New Britain war dance, a Gogodala ceremonial dance performed with tall totemic masks and the colourfully plumed and painted Mt. Hagen group in their Western Highlands 'sing sing'. The spectacular body decoration of performers from Papua New Guinea attracted a large tourist audience at Festival performance venues.

Visitors with a special interest in other traditional aspects of Melanesian culture were also well rewarded at the Festival. The Solomon Islands presented a bamboo band and panpipe music along with traditional dances from the island of Malaita, and Polynesian dances from Bellona Island. The male performers from Ambrym Island in Vanuatu wore their traditional costume of a pig tusk on the chest, a bark belt and the *nambas*, a finely woven penis covering. Fiji's multicultural performance, however, included Indian sitar music, a Chinese fan dance and ribbon dance, Rotuman (Polynesian) singing and Banaban (Micronesian) dances along with a Fijian men's spear dance and action songs by the Fijian women.

Contemporary Pacific Culture

Contemporary cultural presentations at the Festival included plays, theatre, ballet, indigenous rock groups and a film program.The Marli Biyol Company presented the plays *Barungin* and *The Dreamers*, by Aboriginal playwright Jack Davis. Raun Raun Theatre from Papua New Guinea staged a play called *Sido* in *tok pidjin*, featuring traditional costumes, dance, drama, mime, comedy, oratory and singing to the beat of *kundu* drums. The Festival film programme, 'Adventures in Paradise', included films on the craft practices, history and contemporary issues affecting indigenous people in the Pacific. Feature films included *Cannibal Tours*, *Half Life*, *Short Changed*, *Tukana* and the Australian premiere of the New Zealand film *Ngati* (Duke, 1989). Contemporary cultural events at the Festival had a younger audience that also included more indigenous people, particularly at the rock group performances.

Festival Craft Village

The craft village provided a major focus for cultural activities during the 5th Festival of Pacific Arts. The Pacific island style village consisted of a complex of open-sided pole frame huts with palm frond thatched roofs. In a lively and bustling atmosphere, visitors walked around the craft village watching and questioning various Pacific craftspeople at their work, with the more adventurous participating in craft making. Visitors also had the opportunity to purchase craft products, watch dance performances, take photographs and mingle with performers wearing traditional costumes. 'It was the festival at the people level; the Pacific way at its casual best' (Roces, 1989, p.52). Craft activities demonstrated at the village included the carving of dugout canoes, the making of *tam tam* slit gong drums by Vanuatu craftsmen, Hawaiians creating flower leis, women from Papua New Guinea weaving *billum* bags, and Aboriginal women burning patterns onto wooden *coolamon* bowls with a hot wire. Ground ovens were also prepared at the craft village, enabling visitors to participate in Polynesian feasting. With its diversity of cultural activities and Pacific ambience, many people regarded the craft village as the most successful part of the 5th Festival of Pacific Arts (Kaeppler, 1989; Roces, 1989; Simons, 1989; Thompson, 1989a).

Fire Walking: Drama and Spectacle

A special highlight of the Festival in Townsville was the sacred Tahitian fire walking ceremony, *umu-ti*, held at Alma Bay on Magnetic Island. It was the first time this ritual event had been performed outside of French Polynesia. Watched by a crowd of about 3,000 people, the fire walking ceremony included sacred incantations, ritual dances and strict protocol. The Tahitian high priest, Raymond Graffe, stood on basalt rocks heated to 230 degrees celsius as 71 Tahitians and more than 200 onlookers, including the Mayor of Townsville, walked barefoot across the hot rock oven. The fire walking ceremony was traditionally performed to obtain favours from the gods at a time when food was scarce (*Townsville Bulletin*, 1988b; Roces, 1989). The ceremony performed at the Festival, however, constituted a unique tourist spectacle and was given national media coverage.

Tourism and the 5th Festival of Pacific Arts

The Festival of Pacific Arts ranks among one of the largest indigenous cultural gatherings in the world but the Festival held in Townsville was not a mass tourism event. Bicentennial celebrations were held throughout Australia in 1988 with special events being staged in each State and Territory to commemorate 200 years of European settlement. The major Australian tourism event of the Bicentennial year was World Expo 88 held in Brisbane, the capital city of Queensland, from 30 April to 30 October, 1988. Advertised as 'A once-in-a-lifetime experience', World Expo 88 represents the largest international event ever staged in the Southern Hemisphere. Originally forecast to attract 7.8 million people, World Expo 88 instead finished with a total attendance of 15,560,447 visitors (Department of the Arts, Sport, the Environment, Tourism and Territories, 1989).

Even though the 5th Festival of Pacific Arts was held in 1988, it was not a Bicentennial event (*Images*, 1987). Rather, it represented a special Townsville celebration of Pacific culture shared with domestic and overseas visitors with special interest in indigenous arts and crafts. The Festival was not targeted at the mass tourist market, and as a result attracted far fewer visitors. However, 'the Pacific festival in Townsville was of a richer cultural significance than the travel posters and slick slide shows, or pocket presentations of many of the participating nations at Expo' (Roces, 1989, p.55).

Economic Impact

The selection of Townsville to host the 5th Festival of Pacific Arts was considered 'a major coup for North Queensland – and a boost to the city's evolving tourism industry' (Horton, 1988, p.2). Funds were spent locally by the Festival organizers on accommodation, catering, transport and security arrangements, on the preparation of Festival venues and by the employment of temporary Festival staff (Duke, 1989). Expenditures by international and Australian visitors attending the Festival, the media contingent and also by the Pacific cultural delegations (on film, food, souvenirs, and tours) added to the overall economic impact of the event. With some 2,000 performers and perhaps 20,000 visitors, the Festival in Townsville meant 'a welcome addition to the area's tourism and visitor revenue' (Creagh, 1988, p.17). As a special interest tourism event, the 5th Festival of Pacific Arts significantly boosted tourism related trade in Townsville.

Politics, Tourism and Promotion

In addition to being a major tourist attraction, the 5th Festival of Pacific Arts also served to meet the cultural and political aspirations of indigenous people participating in the event. The 5th Festival of Pacific Arts was advertised by the indigenous Festival organizers as 'Not a Bicentennial Event'. The Bicentennial year of 1988 saw many Aboriginal rallies and protests about the 200 years of European occupation of Australia (Hall, 1989d). In this climate, the Festival in Townsville became a means for expressing the political opinions of Aboriginal and Torres Strait Island people. Red, yellow and black Aboriginal land rights flags were highly prominent at both the opening and closing ceremonies for the Festival. The high profile of any hallmark event, including the 5th Festival of Pacific Arts, provides a platform for political protest (Hall, 1989d). Political lobbying from the Aboriginal community also saw the inclusion of a forum on the Festival program to discuss common problems shared by indigenous people in the Pacific. The forum was only approved two weeks before the Festival began and it was designated a 'cultural' rather than a political forum (Hellmers, 1988). A common theme expressed at the Festival's cultural forum was the oppression of indigenous people by colonizing countries and the significance of indigenous artistic revival as a means of building a sense of cultural pride and identity (Thompson, 1989a; Thompson, 1989b).

Not all delegates agreed with Aboriginal attempts to politicize the Festival, a participant from Guam observed that 'the politics of the Bicentennial have got into the wheels of the Festival' (Hellmers, 1988, p.21). Another participant from American Samoa felt that the Festival in Townsville 'was a blatant exercise in political propaganda hiding behind the facade of an artistic festival' (Powell, 1988, p.45). The multicultural Fijian presentation at the Festival, called 'Unity in Diversity', was also regarded by one reviewer as an exercise in propaganda following the Fijian initiated military coups in that Pacific nation (Roces, 1989). Some local residents and visitors, including the director of the first Festival in Fiji, were perturbed by the politicization of a cultural festival (Carell, 1988). However, it is difficult to avoid or ignore political issues affecting indigenous people in the Pacific region. The 4th Festival of Pacific Arts, for example, was to have been held in New Caledonia in December 1984 but outspoken indigenous Kanak groups strongly lobbied that their political struggle for independence from France be integrated into the Festival activities (Fraser, 1984). Due to this internal political situation the Festival was cancelled and rescheduled to Tahiti in 1985 (Carell, 1988; Portus, 1988). The 5th Festival of Pacific Arts, however, made a definite statement about the quest of indigenous people for political and cultural self determination. Without this input, 'many believe the Festival runs the risk of becoming a cute tourist attraction, thereby perpetuating a showcase of culture removed from any real base' (Hellmers, 1988, p.23). Such recognition of a 'living Pacific culture' perhaps contributed to the success of the Festival as an authentic cultural event and as a high quality form of special interest tourism. In any case, despite some controversy over the raising of indigenous political issues, most people who attended the 5th Festival of Pacific Arts appeared to enjoy participating in a unique cultural celebration (Kaeppler, 1989; Roces, 1989; Simons, 1989).

Selling Pacific Culture

As a tourist event, the Festival of Pacific Arts also sought to provide a 'marketplace for the traditional living arts of Oceania' (Pita, 1979, p.27). In other words, some commoditization of culture took place (Crocombe, 1983; Graburn, 1984; Smith, 1989). This was demonstrated at the Townsville Festival craft village where most craftspeople were producing replicas of traditional artefacts and also contemporary art forms for sale as tourist souvenirs. In addition, Polynesian dance performances were often tailored to meet tourist expectations for the 'Hollywood' created images of Pacific culture. The Cook Islands' performance at the 5th Festival of Pacific Arts, while very entertaining, consisted mainly of choreographed dance routines. The 'slick, touristic show' was perceived to be the 'right' type of performance for the Cook Islands to present to a largely western audience (Simons, 1989). The Cook Islands proudly claim that dance is one of their main exports, with commercial dance groups performing in Japan, Europe, America and Australia. The costumes and adornment of performers have also been affected by tourist images of the Pacific. Grass skirts, for example, were not traditional in Polynesia (Crocombe, 1983). Similarly selected aspects of Polynesian material culture and the performing arts are presented to tourists at the Polynesian Cultural Centre in Hawaii, which attracts over one million visitors annually (Stanton, 1989).

Pacific cultural traditions have a significant market value as tourism assets (Pita, 1979; Stanton, 1989). Cultural delegations from Fiji and Tahiti at the Festival in Townsville were well aware that their cultural performances constituted a tourist attraction and a major drawcard for visitors (Roces, 1989). It is no coincidence that tourism has become a major part of the economy in both Fiji (F$185 million in 1986) and French Polynesia (Armstrong, 1988). 'Tourism is a key industry for Tahiti. It accounts for $150 [million] in revenue, employs 4,000 people and the foreign exchange it brings in equates to one quarter of Tahiti's import bill' (Economist Intelligence Unit, 1989, p. 90). Tourist brochures were distributed at the Townsville Festival craft village by Tahiti, the Northern Marianas, American Samoa and New Zealand (for the Maori Arts and Crafts Institute at Rotorua). The Festival of Pacific Arts not only represents a tourist attraction for the host community but also acts to promote tourism in the Pacific region by 'advertising' the special cultural attractions of participating countries.

An Emerging Special Interest Tourism Event

Since its inception in 1972, the Festival of Pacific Arts has been steadily growing in importance and international repute as a major special interest tourism event in the Pacific region. 'The Festival has grown as a dynamic institution, becoming itself part of contemporary Pacific culture' (Simons, 1989, p.299). While the main aim of the Festival has been to revitalize Pacific cultural traditions, host countries have also regarded the event as a significant tourist attraction. Indeed, after the first Festival held in Suva, Fiji, a Solomon Islands administrator remarked: 'The main benefit of the Arts Festival will be to the tourist trade' (Francis Bugotu quoted in Crocombe, 1983, p.89). In March 1976, some 30,000 visitors attended the second South Pacific Festival of Arts in Rotorua, New Zealand. The Festival was a popular tourist event, with visitors queueing to gain admission to the performance venues. Indeed, Rotorua's 'first aim was to provide a tourist attraction' (*Pacific Islands Monthly*, 1976, p.20). Continuing its growth as a special interest tourism event, the third South Pacific Festival of Arts in Port Moresby was considered 'the biggest event of 1980 in the South Pacific' (*Paradise*, 1980, p.13). The growing tourist interest in experiencing Pacific cultural traditions at this Festival also raised the question of whether the event was maintaining cultural heritage or becoming a tourist spectacle. 'Is it to attract tourists looking for a quick visual and aural "fix" or is it for ordinary people and visiting artists?' (De'ath, 1979, p.60). The analysis in this case study suggests that the Festival of Pacific Arts has become something between these two extremes: a special interest tourism event.

The 5th Festival of Pacific Arts proved to be a major special interest tourism event for the city of Townsville. Held at the peak of the tourist season, the exhibition and performance venues were thronged with international and local visitors for the duration of the Festival. Special interest groups represented in the audience for this Festival included groups of indigenous people, those with an interest in arts and crafts, anthropologists, ethnomusicologists, people who had attended previous festivals, photo-journalists and documentary film makers as well as the majority of visitors with a general interest in experiencing Pacific cultural traditions. Publicity for the 5th Festival of Pacific Arts was mainly aimed at informing Aboriginal and Torres Strait Island communities around Australia of the forthcoming Festival. Advertising for this target audience included 5,000 mailed Festival invitations, articles placed in publications directed at indigenous people, plus radio and television interviews about the Festival broadcast on indigenous media programs. In addition, four Festival newsletters were produced and these were more widely distributed to the arts network, tourism authorities and media organizations (Duke, 1989). A comprehensive illustrated article, publicizing the Festival, also appeared in the August 1988 issue of *Panorama*, the in-flight magazine of Ansett, a major Australian domestic airline (Portus, 1988). Potential overseas visitors with a special interest in Pacific culture may have also noticed the preliminary article about the Festival of Pacific Arts which appeared in the April 1988 issue of *Pacific Islands Monthly* (Creagh, 1988).

For the people of Townsville, the 5th Festival of Pacific Arts was a highly successful special interest tourism event. In particular, the Festival represented an exotic tourist attraction '...to the squadrons of home video makers; to the whites reclining in their deckchair *South Pacific* dreams...' (Hellmers, 1988, p.20). The authentic presentation of Pacific cultural traditions, the colourful costumes and vibrant dance performances brought a special excitement and ambience to the otherwise conservative European character of Townsville. The Mayor of Townsville particularly noted that 'Townsville had benefitted greatly from the festival not only culturally and socially but economically and promotionally' (*Townsville Bulletin*, 1988c, p.3). By attracting special interest tourists and 'selling' Pacific culture, Townsville used the 5th Festival of Pacific Arts to boost the local tourism industry and also enhance its own image as a rewarding tourist destination.

Conclusions

Festivals are an increasingly important segment of the special interest tourism market. The 5th Festival of Pacific Arts proved to be a major tourist event for the city of Townsville. International and local visitors, performers and spectators came to Townsville to experience 'authentic' Pacific culture and to be involved in the ambience generated by the large cultural gathering at the Festival. Economically, the Festival also boosted tourism related trade in Townsville. The transformation of the Festival of Pacific Arts from a community-based cultural celebration to a special interest tourism event has been largely determined by its growing reputation as a spectacular cultural event and an international tourist drawcard.

The Festival of Pacific Arts, as a major cultural exposition, is also acting to both maintain and change the way in which unique Pacific cultural traditions are being presented to a world audience. As a special cultural event, both for indigenous participants and visiting tourists, the Festival of Pacific Arts provides an apt example that 'to survive and prosper in the decades ahead, tourism must develop some capability to serve multiple constituencies' (Heenan, 1978, p.32). Community festivals are increasingly being developed into tourist events. Growing visitor interest in experiencing unique aspects of community culture and traditions will ensure the further development and promotion of festivals as significant tourist drawcards in the special interest tourism market.

References

Armstrong, D., 1988, Tourism '88: challenges and opportunities, *Pacific Islands Monthly*, 59 (2): 41–48

Carell, V., 1988, Tropicalities: festival, *Pacific Islands Monthly*, 59 (11): 46–47

Coopers and Lybrand Consulting Group, 1989, National capital region 1988 festivals study, *Recreation Canada*, 47 (4): 24–29

Creagh, C., 1988, Pacific artists gather, *Pacific Islands Monthly*, 59 (4): 17

Crocombe, R., 1983, Creative arts: the soul of a people, 82–90 in *The South Pacific: an introduction*, University of the South Pacific/Longman Paul, Auckland

De'ath, C., 1979, Whose festival?, *Post-Courier* (Papua New Guinea) [Special issue: Independence Anniversary Edition], September: 58, 60, 61

Department of the Arts, Sport, the Environment, Tourism and Territories, 1989, *Annual report 1988–89,* Australian Government Publishing Service, Canberra

Duke, A., 1989, *Report on planning & staging the 5th Festival of Pacific Arts in Townsville, Australia, 14–27 August 1988*, Festival of Pacific Arts Ltd., Canberra

Economist Intelligence Unit, 1989, The Pacific islands, *International Tourism Reports*, 4: 70–99

Fraser, H., 1984, The fourth South Pacific Festival of Arts, *Pacific Islands Monthly*, 55 (11): 20–23

Frisby, W., Getz, D., 1989, Festival management: a case study perspective, *Journal of Travel Research*, 28 (1): 7–11

Getz, D., 1988, Festivals and events: defining the product, 251–252 in *Tourism research: expanding boundaries*, Bureau of Economic and Business Research, Graduate School of Business, University of Utah, Salt Lake City

Getz, D., 1989, Special events: defining the product, *Tourism Management*, 10 (2): 125–137

Getz, D., 1991, *Festivals, special events and tourism*, Van Nostrand Reinhold, New York

Graburn, N.H.H., 1984, The evolution of tourist arts, *Annals of Tourism Research*, 11: 393–419

Hall, C.M., 1989a, The definition and analysis of hallmark tourist events, *GeoJournal*, 19 (3): 263–268

Hall, C.M., 1989b, Hallmark tourist events: analysis, definition, methodology and review, 3–19 in G.J. Syme, B.J. Shaw, D.M. Fenton, and W.S. Mueller, eds, *The planning and evaluation of hallmark events*, Avebury, Aldershot

Hall, C.M., 1989c, Hallmark events and the planning process, 20–39 in G.J. Syme, B.J. Shaw, D.M. Fenton, and W.S. Mueller, eds, *The planning and evaluation of hallmark events*, Avebury, Aldershot

Hall, C.M., 1989d, The politics of hallmark events, 219–241 in G.J. Syme, B.J. Shaw, D.M. Fenton, and W.S. Mueller, eds, *The planning and evaluation of hallmark events*, Avebury, Aldershot

Heenan, D.A., 1978, Tourism and the community: a drama in three acts, *Journal of Travel Research*, 16 (4): 30–32

Hellmers, L., 1988, Arts… or politics, *Pacific Islands Monthly*, 59 (10): 20–23

Horton, A., 1988, Townsville's festival of cultural harmony, *The Weekender* (*Townsville Bulletin* magazine), 13 August: 1–3

Images, 1987, Pacific arts festival planning gathers momentum, *Images: a quarterly report on cultural & heritage matters from the ministry of the environment and the arts*, 4 (1): 2

Isaacs, J., ed., 1988, *Arts of the Pacific*, Festival of Pacific Arts Ltd., Townsville

Kaeppler, A., 1989, A report on the fifth festival of Pacific arts, *Pacific Arts Newsletter*, 28: 1–3

Long, P.T., Perdue, R.R., 1990, The economic impacts of rural festivals and special events: assessing the spatial distribution of expenditures, *Journal of Travel Research*, 28 (4): 10–14

Pacific Islands Monthly, 1976, Rotorua!, *Pacific Islands Monthly*, 47 (5): 19–20

Paradise, 1980, When islanders get together…, *Paradise*, 26: 13–17

Pearce, P., 1982, *The social psychology of tourist behaviour*, Pergamon, Oxford

Pelletier, J., 1988, The social, ethnic and economic impacts of festivals and events, 253–256 in *Tourism research: expanding boundaries*, Bureau of Economic and Business Research, Graduate School of Business, University of Utah, Salt Lake City

Pita, Aiono Dr. F.T.L., 1979, The role of the South Pacific arts festival in the preservation and promotion of traditional living arts in Oceania, 27–32 in *SPC – UNESCO symposium on the preservation of traditional living arts in Oceania (Port Moresby, Papua New Guinea, 2–4 July 1979)*, South Pacific Commission, Noumea

Portus, M., 1988, Pacific pageant, *Panorama, Ansett inflight magazine*, August: 49–52

Powell, S., 1988, 'Divise' festival, *Pacific Islands Monthly*, 59 (10): 45

Ralston, L.S., Stewart, W.P., 1990, Methodological perspectives of festival research studies, *Annals of Tourism Research*, 17: 289–291

Ritchie, J.B.R., 1984, Assessing the impact of hallmark events: conceptual and research issues, *Journal of Travel Research*, 23 (1): 2–11

Roces, A., 1989, Captain Cook's past comes to Townsville: Geo goes to the fifth Festival of Pacific Arts in Townsville, *GEO, Australasia's Geographical Magazine*, 11 (2): 47–55

Schaffer, W.A., 1986, The financial impact of the Atlanta Arts Festival, 147–155 in *Technology and tourism: a growing partnership*, Bureau of Economic and Business Research, Graduate School of Business, University of Utah, Salt Lake City

Simons, S.C., 1989, The fifth festival of Pacific arts, *Oceania*, 59 (4): 299–310

Smith, V.L., ed., 1989, *Hosts and guests: the anthropology of tourism*, University of Pennsylvania Press, Philadelphia

South Australian Tourism Development Board, 1987, *Tourism in South Australia, the strategic plan: the South Australian tourism plan 1987–89*, National Library of Australia, Canberra

Stanton, M.E., 1989, The Polynesian Cultural Centre: a multi-ethnic model of seven Pacific cultures, 247–262 in V.L. Smith, ed., *Hosts and guests: the anthropology of tourism*, University of Pennsylvania Press, Philadelphia

Thompson, L., 1989a, South Pacific festival: self-determination in the South Pacific, *Simply Living Magazine*, 3 (10): 39–45

Thompson, L., 1989b, South Pacific arts festival, *Paradise*, 72: 13–17

Townsville Bulletin, 1988a, Pacific arts festival promises spectacle, *Townsville Bulletin*, 15 August: 4

Townsville Bulletin, 1988b, Taking a walk on the warm side, *Townsville Bulletin*, 22 August: 1

Townsville Bulletin, 1988c, Festival 'lacked media support', *Townsville Bulletin*, 27 August: 3

Wall, G., Mitchell, C., 1989, Cultural festivals as economic stimuli and catalysts of functional change, 132–141 in G.J. Syme, B.J. Shaw, D.M. Fenton, and W.S. Mueller, eds, *The planning and evaluation of hallmark events*, Avebury, Aldershot

Wang, P., Gitelson, R., 1988, Limitations with the economic benefits of short-term events, 257–261 in *Tourism research: expanding boundaries*, Bureau of Economic and Business Research, Graduate School of Business, University of Utah, Salt Lake City

7 REVIEW

Ethnic Tourism

Sylvia Harron and Betty Weiler

The key objective [of ethnic tourism] is to experience events, lifestyles, attitudes, cultures, political outlooks, and theological views utterly different from what you ordinarily encounter at home. Unless that happens, why travel? (Frommer, 1989, p.xv).

Introduction

This chapter provides an overview of the phenomenon of ethnic tourism. It begins by drawing on well-known ethnic tourism researchers and scholars to define ethnic tourism in the context of special interest tourism. The chapter then goes on to review the major case studies of ethnic tourism that have been published since the inaugural cases presented in Smith's (1977) first edition of *Hosts and Guests: The Anthropology of Tourism*. Research findings are presented under three themes: the tourist's perspective, the ethnic tourism product and the impacts of ethnic tourism. The final section in this chapter presents issues and principles for future development of ethnic tourism, based on the results of case studies as well as the work of major international organizations and leading tourism scholars.

The Context and Meaning of Ethnic Tourism

Terms such as ethnic, cultural and heritage tourism are common in the tourism literature, yet there is very little consistency in the way in which they are used. Often but not always there is a reference to exposure to 'exotic' or 'quaint' cultures (Hitchcock and Brandenburg, 1990, p.21; Smith, 1989, p.4). Many would agree that ethnic tourism 'capitalizes on and therefore fosters the tourists' desire to meet native people, promoting the idea that museums or cultural centers are no substitutes for actual human contact' (Sweet, 1990, pp.6–7), yet this quote was used to describe what Sweet calls 'adventure tourism'.

This chapter is concerned with ethnic tourism as a type of special interest tourism. In some cases, ethnic tourism implies a 'better' form of tourism, but in most cases it suggests simply a 'different' type of travel. What makes special interest tourism different, as stated in the introductory chapter of this book, is the primary motive of the tourist. This chapter focuses on travel

Table 7.1 Role of culture and ethnicity in different forms of tourism

Ethnic Tourism	Cultural Tourism
Primary Importance	
Cultural practices as defining a unique ethnicity of interest to tourists – e.g. among the Balinese, Toraja, Thai hill tribes, Borneo long-house communities, etc.	Role of physical artefacts of cultures and general bustle of everyday life in providing Asian flavour to experience of tourists – e.g. the array of dress and physical appearance, the sight and smell of food stalls, etc., which make a destination seem exotic to tourists
Secondary Importance	
Designated villages or special performances supplementing other forms of tourism (recreational, historical, environmental) – e.g. excursion to Cherating village, daytime performances of Javanese puppet theatre, etc.	Role of local culture in providing a physical setting for other forms of tourism which imprints them with a sense of uniqueness – e.g. the setting provided by fishing villages and rice paddies for resorts on the East coast of Malaysia

Source: Wood, 1984, p.361.

motivated primarily by the search for first hand, authentic and sometimes intimate contact with people whose ethnic and/or cultural background is different from the tourist's.

Although there are a number of forms of tourism that include culture and ethnicity in their itinerary, these are not necessarily ethnic tourism. Ethnic tourism, for our purposes, does not include mass tourism such as resort tourism, tour group travel by air or cruise ship and other forms of mainstream travel where ethnic experiences are incidental and not the main focus of the trip. Ethnic tourism always involves some form of direct experience with the host culture and environment, usually by visits to native homes and villages to observe and/or participate in native customs, ceremonies, rituals, dances and other traditional activities. Other tourist activities may include photography and studying or purchasing local artefacts, art and crafts. Face to face contact with indigenous people, while often sought, does not always occur, but regardless, the human element is important.

Ethnic tourism is distinguished from cultural tourism by a number of authors (Wood, 1984; Smith, 1989: Graburn, 1989). Wood's framework (see Table 7.1) is perhaps the best illustration of the differences between the two. According to Wood, ethnic tourism involves first hand experience with the practices of another culture, while cultural tourism involves exposure to culture in an indirect way, more as a backdrop than as the specific focus of travel. In addition, ethnic tourism may be perceived by the visitor as more 'intimate' (Klieger, 1990, p.38) and more 'authentic' (Greenwood, 1982). Wood also distinguishes between primary and secondary ethnic tourism; this chapter is restricted to those activities which fall into Wood's category of 'primary ethnic tourism' (Wood, 1984, p.361).

In addition to cultural tourism, other close relatives of ethnic travel include:

- environmental or nature-based tourism (for examples, see Chapter 9 by Valentine)
- arts and heritage/historical tourism (see Chapter 5 by Zeppel and Hall)
- adventure tourism (depending on whose definition, ethnic tourism may be a form of adventure tourism or vice versa, as illustrated in the earlier quote by Sweet)

In addition, there are less familiar but growing forms of special interest tourism such as anthro-tourism (Gordon, 1990, p.6) and archaeological tourism (Daltabuit and Pi-Sunyer, 1990). This chapter includes these as subsets of ethnic tourism. The relationship of ethnic tourism to 'alternative travel' or 'sustainable tourism' is addressed in a later section of this chapter.

The Tourist's Perspective

As with many forms of special interest tourism, there is very little published data on the tourists themselves. Most research has focused on the product or the impacts of ethnic tourism. One of the few studies providing profile data of ethnic tourists is Dearden and Harron's study of trekkers in the hills of Northern Thailand (see Chapter 8). These ethnic tourists were relatively young, the majority were tertiary-educated and a third were in professional occupations. The profile of participants in a residential study program of Australian Aboriginal culture revealed that participants were mainly between 21 and 50 years old, with tertiary qualifications, and more than a third were teachers (Dwyer, 1988). In addition, a limited amount of research on the market for Aboriginal tourism in Australia found that the key target markets are as follows. For general interest in Australian Aboriginal culture/heritage, the market is made up of young singles and, to a lesser extent, family groups with children. For visiting national park sites with Aboriginal artefacts, the market is mainly white collar. In both cases, the target market has an above-average income of Aus$30,000 and over (AGB: McNair, 1988).

Although the demand for ethnic travel has been explored in a few studies, it is still poorly understood. Research has focussed mainly on culture as a travel motive and a destination attribute of mainstream tourism (Burchett, 1988; Ritchie and Zins, 1978). As recently as a decade ago, it was assumed that ethnic travel catered for 'only a limited number of visitors motivated by curiosity and elite peer approval' (Smith, 1977, p.4). This demand appears to have been stimulated in recent years by such movies as *The Gods Must be Crazy* (Gordon, 1990) and television documentaries of exotic cultures and environments. The impacts of media coverage and travel guidebooks have not been systematically investigated but may be signficant in the growth of ethnic travel.

As for what tourists actually want to experience, the results of studies range from a desire for 'more information' (Burchett, 1988, p.6; AGB: McNair, 1988) to seeking the truly exotic and unusual (Graburn, 1989, p.31). Surveys of visitors to Australian Aboriginal sites found that interest in lifestyle, religion, food, and hunting were high, while interest in art, craft, dances and performances were relatively low (Moscardo and Pearce, 1989).

Ethnic tourism is often marketed with a focus on the destination's unique cultural attributes or identity (Wood, 1984, p.361; Swain, 1989, p.85). However, it would appear that a not-too-close-encounter for not-too-long-a-time with another culture is preferred (deKadt, 1979, p.50: Smith, 1989, p.57; see also Chapter 8, Dearden and Harron case study) and in some cases tourists prefer to reaffirm their preconceived images of primitive or unusual cultures rather than confront real issues and change (Klieger, 1990, p.39).

The Ethnic Tourism Product

Insight into what is actually being offered to ethnic tourists is probably better revealed by perusing travel brochures and recent special interest travel indexes and magazines such as the *Specialty Travel Index* (a U.S. publication), *Special Interest Holidays Magazine* (a U.K. magazine) *Adventure Travel* (U.S.) and *RealTravel* (now part of a Canadian magazine called *Explore*) than by reading published research. For example, *Adventure Travel '89* advertises such tours as the Japan Cultural Odyssey, a seventeen day trip by rail through Japan including accommodation in traditional minshuku and ryokan and led by a Japanese-speaking American guide; the New Guinea Tribes and Islands, nineteen days trekking to highland villages, exploring by dugout canoe, sleeping in traditional shelters, and 'learning about the culture of this island group'; and the Ladakh Cultural Treks, visiting high passes, remote monasteries and isolated villages with an 'emphasis on Ladakhi culture'. The *Specialty Travel Index* includes such companies as Adventures of the Mind, which specializes in anthropological field seminars of one to four weeks duration to study the indigenous peoples of virtually every continent; and Cross Cultural Adventures, which takes small groups to the festivals of South India or on the Road to Timbuktu.

Many of the tour companies offer trips to more than one destination, and stress personal contact with exotic people and participation in local events. In the case of Aboriginal tourism in Australia, the brochure *Come Share Our Culture: A Guide to Northern Territory Aboriginal Tours, Arts and Crafts* is updated annually and provides a comprehensive guide to what is offered in the Territory, where most Aboriginal tourism occurs. Included are half and full day trips which include visits to environmental and cultural points of interest such as Aboriginal communities and missions, bush camps, handicraft centres, rock arts sites, archaeological sites and burial sites. Longer tours, up to thirteen days in length, include more outdoor recreation and natural attractions such as guided fishing, overnight camping and participation in corroborees. Most of these tours emphasize interaction with Aboriginals and learning about culture, history and lifestyle (Altman, 1989, p.464).

Research into indigenous tourism in developed countries has focused on Aboriginals in Australia (Altman, 1989; Burchett, 1988), Eskimos (Inuit) (Smith, 1989) and native Indians (Sweet, 1990) in the United States. Burchett observed that because of visitors placing pressure on tour operators for information about Australian Aboriginality, they are 'being fed a line of half truths which perpetuates the idea... that Aboriginality [is] an exotic, inanimate curio, rather than... a living, complex culture' (Burchett, 1988, p.6). According to Smith (1989, p.60), ethnic tourism in Alaska provides opportunities to attend Eskimo dance performances and dog team demonstrations, pan for gold and sample native foods, but typically with a white guide in mid-summer and with little or no face-to-face contact with Eskimo people. In contrast, visits to the Pueblo Indians of the American Southwest offer personal interaction with 'real Indians' as well as a glimpse at traditional native life (Sweet, 1990, p.6).

Ethnic tourism in developing countries, based on the results of published studies, also appears to be quite variable in content and quality. Some involve local forms of transportation such as mule, dugout canoe and horse carts (Daltabuit and Pi-Sunyer, 1990, p.12; Swain, 1990, p.26). Many but not all offer opportunities to 'sample' the local culture and religion by viewing or participating in rituals, meals and performances (Crystal, 1989, p.141; Swain, 1989, p.83; Goering 1990, p.20; Adams, 1990; Swain, 1990, p.26). Virtually all offer opportunities to photograph traditional dress, architecture and living conditions as well as purchase local products (Hitchcock and Brandenburgh, 1990; Klieger, 1990; Mirante, 1990, p.35; Swain, 1990, p.26; Gordon, 1990, p.6), but of course there is considerable variation in what can and cannot be photographed and purchased.

In many cases, the tour guide (or tour operator) acts as a 'cultural broker' (Cohen, 1985; Smith, 1989, p.66), buffering the visitor from the unfamiliar and fostering communication. This can be a very positive aspect of ethnic tourism, particularly when tour guides facilitate genuine interpersonal contact between host and guest. However, studies have found that individuals filling these roles tend to be 'marginal' members of the community at best (Smith, 1989, p.66) and outsiders at worst (Smith, 1989, p.60; Crystal, 1989, p.166), which can create difficulties:

> The middleman is the broker in ethnic exoticism who mediates and profits by the interaction of tourist and touree, and who, in the process, very frequently manipulates ethnicity for gain, stages 'authenticity', peddles cultural values, and thus becomes an active agent in modifying the situation in which and from which he lives (van den Berghe and Keyes, 1984, p.347).

The Impacts of Ethnic Tourism

A discussion of the impacts of ethnic tourism on host cultures and societies is virtually impossible except on a case-by-case basis. Much depends on the nature of the differences between host and guest and on the nature of the travel experience being offered. Moreover, 'in any interpretation of the impacts of tourism development, the issues emphasized are those chosen by the writer. Thus we find radically different assessments of the tourism experience for the same place by researchers using the same available data' (Johnston, 1990, p.36). However, while the assessment of the problems are filtered through the cultural lens of the researcher, there are common sets of benefits and problems.

Positive benefits are most often economic, including higher incomes, greater levels of employment, and reduced cost and/or higher standard of living (Altman, 1988; Johnston, 1990; Smith, 1989). Many researchers, however, emphasize the tendency for economic benefits to accrue mainly to outside entrepreneurs (Crystal, 1989; Goering, 1990).

Clearly, ethnic tourism has the *potential* to be a positive force for ethnic revitalization. In the case of Aborigines in Australia, ethnic tourism has served as a mechanism for re-educating and re-establishing pride in and knowledge of traditional skills and values (Burchett, 1988, p.10). The revival of religious ceremonies, art forms and craft production are common consequences of ethnic tourism (Smith, 1989, p.78; Crystal, 1989, p.148, 162; Hitchcock and Brandenburgh, 1990, p.23). Research has also documented the contribution of tourism in strengthening ethnic and political identity (Swain, 1990, p.29; Johnston, 1990, p.31; Klieger, 1990, p.38).

Unfortunately, the negative impacts of ethnic tourism, although perhaps not as severe as mainstream tourism, can be significant. The commoditization of culture and the denigration of sacred sites are commonly identified as outcomes of ethnic tourism (Crystal, 1989, p.150,163; Hitchcock and Brandenburgh, 1990, p.22; Klieger, 1990, p.38). Social impacts such as increased social tension, sociocultural breakdown and a loss of sense of identity and place do occur (Daltabuit and Pi-Sunyer, 1990, p.9; Goering, 1990, p.21; Johnston, 1990, p.35).

While there is some reinforcement of inequities as a result of cross-cultural contact between the 'haves' (the tourists) and the 'have-nots' (the host population), the demonstration effect of such contact may not be significant, given the fleeting contact typical of most ethnic tourism experiences. Furthermore, other forms of tourism and other forces of change (such as extractive industries) probably cause greater damage both culturally and environmentally (Smith, 1977; Altman, 1988; Burchett, 1988). What is important to recognize, of course, is the cumulative effects of even brief encounters and the potential negative impacts of increasing numbers of ethnic tourists.

In reality, the social, cultural and economic effects of tourism are difficult to isolate from the broader effects of modernization and development. Research confirming a causal link between tourism and negative impacts has been scant (deKadt, 1979). However, there is a tendency to attribute all negative impacts to tourism, particularly when large numbers of foreigners visit remote or isolated communities.

While there seem to be some commonly recognized problems that occur at least in part because of tourism, there seem to be few 'generic' solutions or strategies to solve such problems; 'for if anything has been learned about tourism it is that even common problems may require culture-specific responses'. (Richter 1989, p.206). Having acknowledged this limitation, the final section of this chapter outlines some new approaches to tourism that may be appropriate, if not to all forms of tourism, then at least to ethnic tourism.

Issues and Principles for Consideration in Ethnic Tourism

A number of organizations such as women's, environmental and labour groups have become aware of the social, economic, environmental, and political problems associated with tourism. Working independently of both industry and government, those concerned non-governmental organizations (NGOs) simultaneously attempt to monitor their performance and encourage diversification of the tourism industry.

Table 7.2 The Ecumenical Coalition on Third World Tourism code of ethics for tourists

A Code of Ethics for Tourists
1. Travel in the spirit of humility and with a genuine desire to learn more about the people of your host country. Be sensitively aware of the feelings of other people, thus preventing what might be offensive behavior on your part. This applies very much to photography.
2. Cultivate the habit of listening and observing, rather than merely hearing and seeing.
3. Realize that often the people in the country you visit have time concepts and thought patterns different from your own. This does not make them inferior, only different.
4. Instead of looking for that 'beach paradise', discover the enrichment of seeing a different way of life, through other eyes.
5. Acquaint yourself with local customs. What is courteous in one country may be quite the reverse in another – people will be happy to help you.
6. Instead of the Western practice of 'knowing all the answers', cultivate the habit of asking questions.
7. Remember that you are only one of thousands of tourists visiting this country and do not expect special privileges.
8. If you really want your experience to be a 'home away from home', it is foolish to waste money on travelling.
9. When you are shopping, remember that the 'bargain' you obtained was only because of the low wages paid to the maker.
10. Do not make promises to people in your host country unless you can carry them through.
11. Spend time reflecting on your daily experience in an attempt to deepen your understanding. It has been said that 'what enriches you may rob and violate others'.

Source: Ecumenical Coalition for Third World Tourism in Frommer, 1988, p.9.

One interest group which has worked extensively in producing tours, surveys, resources and other research information is the Ecumenical Coalition for Third World Tourism (ECTWT). A product of the World Council of Churches conferences, it seeks to support networks of communication between various groups concerned about tourism in developing countries. The ECTWT has published a book on tourism prostitution and a *Resource Book on Alternative Tourism*; it also sponsors workshops and research projects, and promotes alternative tourism programmes and models (Gonsalves, 1987).

As early as 1960, the World Council of Churches had been expressing concerns over tourism and its effects. At the 1975 conference in Penang, it tabled the 'Code of Ethics for Tourists' (see Table 7.2) which has since been reproduced in several places, including the brochures of commercial tour operators. At the Manila conference in 1980, it was decided that:

> . . . discovery and development of alternative ways of travel is needed. It is also a requirement that we find ways to return tourism to the people so that the experience of travel will enrich all. By exposure of travellers to living situations in the host country understanding is increased and solidarity established. Visitors who are able to handle the situation should be given the opportunity to know the real situation of the country they visit rather than the facade that tourism usually provides. By returning the travel industry to the people the economic benefits can be more fully shared, and the people can participate fully in decision making (O'Grady, 1980, as quoted by Gonsalves, 1987, p.9).

However, while basically sympathetic with the laudable goals of this 'concerned' alternative tourism, some critics are cautious in their appraisal. Butler (1989) claims alternative tourism is another buzzword for the 1980s; like sustainable development, 'it sounds good, implies thought and concern and a different approach and philosophy' (Butler, 1989, p.9). However, alternative tourism may 'penetrate further into the personal space of residents, involve them to a much greater degree, expose often fragile resources to greater visitation, [and] expose the genuine article to tourism to a greater degree' (Butler, 1989, p.13). It can mean anything to anyone, and such is the concern for the impacts, and the hope for authentic experiences, that tourists are ready to accept and support the concept of alternative tourism, even if they do not understand it. 'It appeases the guilt of the "thinking tourists" while simultaneously providing the holiday experience they want' (Wheeller, 1990, p.298).

> Concerned 'alternative tourism' is thus in a quandary: While unable to transform mass tourism, the small scale nature of its projects, and the selected character of its public, precludes it from becoming a realistic alternative to conventional mass tourism (Cohen, 1987. p.16).

While it may be an 'unrealistic alternative to conventional mass tourism', alternative tourism may be an appropriate model for specialized, culturally based regional tourism, provided control remains with the local population. However, there are examples where good intentions and local control of resources have still failed to carry off an alternative tourism plan (De Burlo, 1987; Chapin, 1990). Alternatively, the apparent increased interest in authentic, honest presentations of 'genuine cultural exchange' on the part of the tourists (Burchett, 1988; Dwyer, 1988; AGB: McNair, 1988; Moscardo and Pearce, 1989; Sweet, 1990), could be effectively tapped to provide a model of tourism development which emphasizes tourist education, and local control of the information and image projected.

One form of control is the education of tourists as to appropriate, culture-specific behaviour. Beyond the 'Code of Ethics' mentioned earlier, one model of tourist development which attempts to educate tourists about local cultural realities is the Ladakh Ecological Development Group (Ledeg). Ledeg seeks 'to promote sustainable development that harmonizes with and builds on traditional Ladakhi culture' (Goering, 1990, p.21). The input from tourists provides both financial and psychological support for the general goals of sustainable development. The education is reciprocal. Ledeg provides Western tourists with guidelines for responsible behaviour, attempting to educate them on the culture and history of Ladakh and how tourism fits into this broader context. It also helps dispel, for the Ladakhis, the inaccurate impressions of the West that accompany these visitors.

A few countries, such as Bhutan, have short circuited this *post-hoc* response by strictly controlling the development and direction of tourism from the beginning. However, Bhutan itself is dependent in part on India, which controls access to the kingdom. In contrast to its near neighbour, Nepal, which the Bhutanese feel has 'sold its soul for tourism', tourism in Bhutan is restricted to expensive group tours with 'about 200 tourists at a time and only three or four towns open to visitors' (Richter, 1989, p.177). The focus of this élitist approach is presumably the cultural attractions of the tiny Himalayan kingdom, there being little encouragement for trekking, nor any casinos, nightclubs or amusement parks. This small scale tourism is also easier to control and remains the monopoly of the King's relatives. Bhutan's tourism program is probably the youngest and smallest in Asia and may, as it develops, provide valuable insights into the relationship between tourism development, political control, and cultural integrity.

However, many countries cannot afford the luxury of such extremes. Unless a country restricts entry visas and controls the itineraries and activities of its tourists, tourism is likely to happen regardless of what any politician, local resident or tourism official desires. Faced with a choice, if the local people do not get involved in tourism, it is possible it will be imposed upon them from the outside. Aboriginal tourism in Australia (Boveington, 1988), Eskimo tourism in Alaska (Smith, 1989), and the Tana Toraja of Indonesia (Crystal, 1989) have been faced with such a dilemma.

Tana Toraja Regency was a relatively isolated but culturally significant area on the island of Sulawesi in Indonesia. It did not play a major role in national development until the government took an active interest in promoting international tourism based on the Toraja's elaborate funeral rituals. If the local Torajas opened their villages and ceremonies to tourism for the sake of economic gain, they stood to compromise their cultural integrity and their 'ancestral prerogative of ritual self-determination' (Crystal, 1989, p.151). If they personally excluded tourism, enterprising neighbours and outside entrepreneurs stood to profit from the 'death ceremonies' of the Toraja, not only as observers, but as looters and purchasers of their material culture. Now, a decade after Crystal's research into the Toraja's tourism dilemma, international tourism is an integral part of the local economic, social and cultural life. However:

> [there has been] little effort to orient, communicate with, or educate visitors about traditional Toraja culture . . . . Despite the fact that all foreign tourists to Tana Toraja are cultural tourists, drawn to the area because of its impressive ceremonial system and vital traditional arts, to date no effective effort at communication concerning Toraja culture has been undertaken (Crystal, 1989, p.166).

The great paradox of Tana Toraja tourism, as Crystal sees it, is that although the area is visited by some 40,000 visitors a year, including tourists, social scientists, government officials and international art dealers, the cultural integrity of the area remains intact. At the same time, the benefits of tourism do not amass to the traditional leaders who are responsible for maintaining this cultural vitality.

It is also important to keep in mind that culture is not a static entity as all 'viable cultures are in the process of "making themselves up" all the time' (Greenwood, 1982, p.27). By the very fact that there is some interaction between residents and visitors, all ethnic or cultural tourism consists of some manipulation of culture. The question then is 'whether the culture will adapt and yet retain its fundamental character through a period of change or whether tourists will destroy the qualities that attracted them in the first place' (Goering, 1990, p.24).

Conclusion

The increasing ease with which we are able to travel internationally is both good and bad for ethnic tourism. Certainly, hard-to-visit people and places are now more accessible to those with a desire to experience foreign culture, and new destinations and experiences continue to emerge. On the other hand, continued demand for the exotic and the unusual has its price:

> The ethnic/adventure tourism industry can turn exotic cultures into commodities and individuals into amusing 'objects' for tourist 'consumption'. Over time, novel encounters become routine for both host and guest, and cultural 'presentations' become more and more removed from the reality of everyday life. The jaded tourism marketeers then move on to other groups as yet unaffected by tourism (Klieger, 1990, p. 38).

The pattern is unhealthy at best and in some cases spells disaster for destinations. Adopting some or all of the principles of alternative tourism would be a major step toward the sustainment of ethnic tourism on a local and global scale.

References

Adams, K.M., 1990, Cultural commoditization in Tana Toraja, Indonesia, *Cultural Survival Quarterly*, 14 (1): 31–34

AGB: McNair, 1988, *Aboriginal tourism survey*, Prepared for the Victorian Tourism Commission, Melbourne

Altman, J. C., 1988, *Aboriginals, tourism and development: the Northern Territory experience*, Australian National University, North Australia Research Unit, Darwin

Altman, J., 1989, Tourism dilemmas for Aboriginal Australians, *Annals of Tourism Research*, 16 (4): 456–476

Boveington, J.T., 1988, Distinct cultures: tourism and remote traditionally oriented Aboriginal communities of the Northern Territory, 211–221 in B. Faulkner and M. Fagence, eds, *Frontiers in Australian tourism: The search for new perspectives in policy development and research*, Bureau of Tourism Research, Canberra

Burchett, C., 1988, Aboriginal tourism in Australia's Northern Territory, in L. J. D'Amore and J. Jafari, eds, *First global conference: Tourism – a vital force for peace*, Montreal

Butler, R.W., 1989, Alternative tourism: pious hope or Trojan horse? *World Leisure and Recreation*, 31 (4): 9–17

Chapin, M., 1990, The silent jungle: ecotourism among the Kuna Indians of Panama, *Cultural Survival Quarterly*, 14 (1): 42–45

Cohen, E., 1985, The tourist guide: the origins, structure and dynamics of a role, *Annals of Tourism Research*, 12 (1): 5–29

Cohen, E., 1987, Alternative tourism – a critique, *Tourism Recreation Research*, 12 (2): 13–18

Crystal, E., 1989, Tourism in Toraja (Sulawesi, Indonesia), 139–168 in V. Smith, ed., *Hosts and guests: the anthropology of tourism*, 2nd ed., University of Pennsylvania Press, Philadelphia

Daltabuit, M., Pi-Sunyer, O., 1990, Tourism development in Quintana Roo, Mexico, *Cultural Survival Quarterly*, 14 (1): 9–13

De Burlo, C., 1987, Neglected social factors in tourism project design: the case of Vanuatu, *Tourism Recreation Research*, 12 (2): 25–30

deKadt, E., 1979, *Tourism: passport to development? Perspectives on the social and cultural effects of tourism in developing countries*, Oxford University Press, Oxford

Dwyer, A., 1988, The necessity for authenticity and integrity – a tour operator's viewpoint, *Aboriginal culture and tourism conference*, Halls Gap, Northern Territory

Frommer, A., 1988, *The new world of travel 1989*, Prentice Hall, New York

Goering, P.G., 1990, The response to tourism in Ladakh, *Cultural Survival Quarterly*, 14 (1): 20–25

Gonsalves, P.S. 1987, Alternative tourism – The evolution of a concept and establishment of a network, *Tourism Recreation Research*, 12 (2): 9–12

Gordon, R., 1990, The prospects for anthropological tourism in Bushmanland, *Cultural Survival Quarterly*, 14 (1): 6–8

Graburn, N.H.H., 1989, Tourism: the sacred journey, 21–36 in V. Smith, ed., *Hosts and guests: the anthropology of tourism*, 2nd ed., University of Pennsylvania Press, Philadelphia

Greenwood, D.J., 1982, Cultural authenticity, *Cultural Survival Quarterly*, 6 (3): 27–28

Hitchcock, R.K., Brandenburgh, R.L., 1990, Tourism, conservation, and culture in the Kalahari desert, Botswana, *Cultural Survival Quarterly*, 14 (2): 20–24

Johnston, B.R., 1990, "Save our beach dem and our land too!" the problems of tourism in "America's paradise", *Cultural Survival Quarterly*, 14 (2): 31–37.

Klieger, P. C., 1990, Close encounters: "intimate" tourism in Tibet, *Cultural Survival Quarterly*, 14 (2): 38–42

Mirante, E. T., 1990, Hostages to tourism, *Cultural Survival Quarterly*, 14 (1): 35–38

Moscardo, G., Pearce, P.L., 1989, Ethnic tourism: understanding the tourists' perspective, 387–394 in *Tourism research: globalization the Pacific Rim and beyond*, Travel and Tourism Research Association, Honolulu

O'Grady, R., ed., 1980, *Third world tourism*, Christian Conference of Asia, Singapore

Richter, L. K., 1989, *The politics of tourism in Asia*, University of Hawaii Press, Honolulu.

Ritchie, J. R. B., Zins, M., 1978, Culture as a determinant of the attractiveness of a tourist region, *Annals of Tourism Research*, 5: 252–267

Smith, V.L., ed., 1977, *Hosts and guests: the anthropology of tourism*, University of Pennsylvania Press, Philadelphia

Smith, V.L., 1989, Eskimo tourism: micro-models and marginal men, 55–82 in V. Smith, ed., *Hosts and guests: the anthropology of tourism*, 2nd ed., University of Pennsylvania Press, Philadelphia

Swain, M.B., 1989, Gender roles in indigenous tourism: Kuna Mola, Kuna Yala, and cultural survival, 83–104 in V. Smith, ed., *Hosts and guests: the anthropology of tourism*, 2nd ed., University of Pennsylvania Press, Philadelphia

Swain, M.B., 1990, Commoditizing ethnicity in southwest China, *Cultural Survival Quarterly*, 14 (1): 26–29

Sweet, J.D., 1990, The portals of tradition: tourism in the American Southwest, *Cultural Survival Quarterly*, 14 (2): 6–8

van den Berghe, P.L., Keyes, C.F., 1984, Introduction: tourism and re-created ethnicity, *Annals of Tourism Research*, 11 (3): 343–352

Wheeller, B., 1990, Is responsible tourism appropriate? in *Tourism research into the 1990s*, University College, Durham

Wood, R.E., 1984, Ethnic tourism, the state, and cultural change in Southeast Asia, *Annals of Tourism Research*, 11 (3): 353–374

8 CASE STUDY

Tourism and the Hilltribes of Thailand

Philip Dearden and Sylvia Harron

You've had your fill of history and culture; of monuments that have stood still for centuries; of mass produced vacations that are as predictable as picture postcards.
"You want more than a holiday".
You want an experience that stimulates the mind and challenges the spirit. An experience that promises to make your pulse beat just a little faster. An experience that lives and breathes adventure at every turn.
Take a deep breath and step this way... to "Trekking in North Thailand" (Brochure, Camp of Troppo Trekking, 1990).

Introduction

Trekking in northern Thailand started some 20 years ago. For most of that period it remained a fairly small and localized activity. The last five years have, however, witnessed spectacular growth. It is now estimated that over 100,000 people go trekking in the area annually. This is double the number that trek annually in Nepal. The attraction for this activity, unlike Nepal, is ostensibly a cultural one – to see the hilltribe people. The purpose of this paper is to provide a brief overview of this activity within the context of specialized tourism. It is based upon extensive fieldwork in the area since 1984 that has used a wide variety of research approaches including participant observation, interviews, content analysis and surveys. More extensive discussions are available in Dearden 1988, and Harron 1991.

The Context

Understanding of the geographical, historical and cultural context is critical to an understanding of the nature of the tourist activity. Northern Thailand is a rugged and largely inaccessible area (Figure 8.1). About 75 per cent of this area is classified as Highlands, ranging between 500 and 2,500m in height, where slopes are steep and soils often poor. It is these Highland areas that are largely occupied by the so-called hilltribes who have traditionally made a livelihood through slash and burn agriculture. There are some 23 different ethnic groupings that are generically referred to as hilltribes (Bhruksasri, 1989); six of these, Karen, Akha,

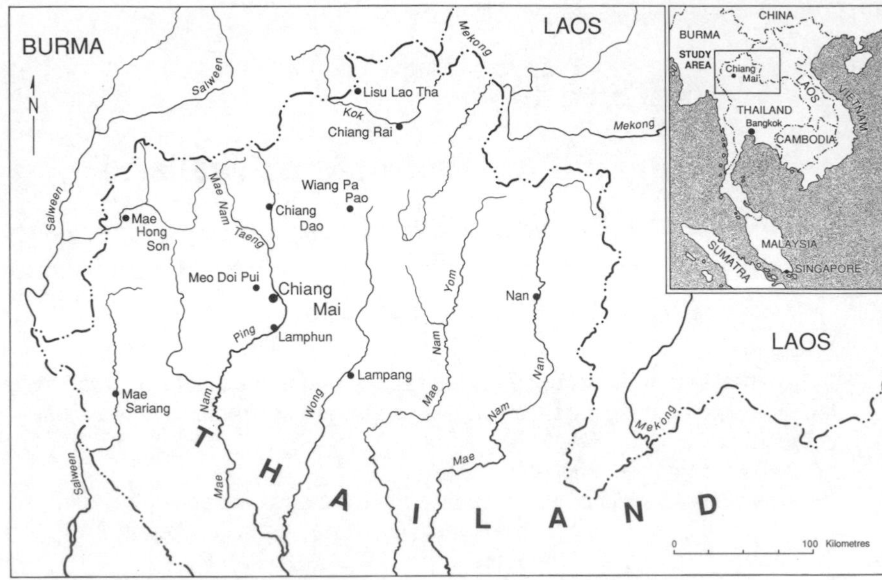

Figure 8.1 Map of northern Thailand

Lisu, Hmong, Lahu and Yao constitute the vast majority of the estimated half million population.

Most of the hilltribes are considered recent immigrants into the area and are perceived as a source of problems by the Thai Government. Due to their dominant mode of agricultural activity, swiddening, they are seen as a main cause behind deforestation in northern Thailand. A recent survey suggests that the hilltribe peoples destroy about 775,000 rai (124,000 ha) of forest annually (*Bangkok Post*, January 21, 1990). Reliable estimates of the rates of associated soil erosion are not available but can be safely assumed to be substantial. The hilltribe people also grow opium, with an estimated 28,000 rai (4,480 ha) cultivated in 1988, despite the extensive efforts of drug control agencies (*Bangkok Post*, January 21, 1990). Furthermore, in the past the hilltribes have been associated with insurgencies, and many are not, nor do they consider themselves to be, Thai citizens.

In contrast to the generally unfavourable light with which the hilltribes are seen by the Government, is their attraction for tourists. Still retaining their traditional and colourful dress in many instances, in their small villages often perched high on the mountain tops, the hilltribes exude an aura of romance in an increasingly unromantic world. Unfortunately, in actuality, there is little romance in an existence that is constantly bordering on the hungry, where populations are growing and per capita food supplies decreasing, and where a vicious cycle of debt gets larger every year as money needs to be borrowed to buy food.

It is within this context that hilltribe trekking must be considered. Attention will now be directed toward trekking as an activity before turning to an examination of the people who go trekking and a discussion of trekking as a form of specialized tourism.

Trekking

Trekking as an organized, commercial tourist activity is of fairly recent origin, although more robust, explorer types appear to have been taking to the hills for some time. The earliest descriptions originate from work undertaken by Cohen in the early 1970s (1979, 1982, 1983) and an early survey undertaken by the Tribal Research Institute in Chiang Mai (Maneeprasert et al., 1975). Chiang Mai, the largest city in northern Thailand, is the main centre for trekking tours. Cohen (1983) mentions 'about a dozen' trekking companies there in 1977, by 1985 there were some 54, and by 1990 in excess of 100. These companies advertise and organize treks to areas throughout northern Thailand. They assemble the participants, usually ranging between 6 and 14 trekkers, and provide a guide, food and transport for the trek. The assembled party are then transported to the area by 'silor', a modified pick-up truck, and the walking begins.

The trips vary considerably in terms of degree of exertion required and the nature of the villages visited. Few average over 6 hours walking per day. Many overnight in villages that have one or more trekking groups staying practically every night, while others are lucky enough to get further off the common trekking routes and visit villages that are less accustomed to tourists. Modal trip length is 3 nights. During this period the trekkers hike from village to village, over 90 per cent ride an elephant, and just under that number have a rafting experience. These figures are derived from interviews with 173 trekkers in Chiang Mai. They cannot be considered representative for trekking as a whole in northern Thailand, but personal experience in other trekking centres such as Mae Hong Sorn and Chiang Rai suggests that these are fairly typical.

The Trekkers

Cohen (1979) characterized the early trekkers as budget, world-traveller, explorer types, fringing on the hippy culture. Interviews undertaken with 208 respondents in Chiang Mai in 1989 and 1990 help provide some greater insight into this clientele. One hundred and thirty one people were interviewed following their trek; 42 were interviewed before their trek with 27 of these also completing post-trek interviews. A further 35 non trekkers were also interviewed to find out why they did not go trekking.

The socio-economic profile for the trekkers shows an equal split between male and female participants, with a mean age of 28 years. There was little confirmation of the 'aimless drifter' characterization often associated with the market. Fifty-eight per cent had university and college degrees, a further 24 per cent had attended college. About a third could be classified as professionals (e.g. doctors, lawyers, managers, and programmers), while 17 per cent were teachers and 14 per cent were still students. Europeans constituted 57 per cent of the participants, North Americans 22 per cent and Australia/New Zealand 17 per cent. Most were on an extended trip and were travelling independently.

The total trip length exhibited a large range from two weeks to five years, with a mean length of six months. The length of time spent in Thailand ranged from

Plate 8.1 Visitor interacting with Hilltribe children

eight days to eight months with a mean length of 40 days and a modal length of 28/30 days (25 per cent). On average, trekkers reported spending US$27.81 per day.

The trip characteristics of trekkers differ significantly from the profile of all visitors to Thailand as reported by the Tourism Authority of Thailand (TAT). The largest apparent difference is that while other Asian countries make up 60 per cent of the total visitors to Thailand, they do not as a rule go trekking. The Japanese and Malaysians (accounting for half of these visitors), do not as of yet make up a significant portion of the trekking clientele, although the numbers of these nationalities signing up for treks is increasing. The average length of stay in Thailand is 7 days. Approximately 33 per cent of all tourists to Thailand travel by group tour. Although some major tour companies include treks in their itineraries, all trekkers encountered in the sampling frame independently arranged a trek once they arrived in Thailand. The mean daily expenditure for all tourists to Thailand is US$100.22.

Comparison can also be made between trekkers and international budget travellers. Riley, in her 1988 paper on international long term budget travellers, characterized the average traveller as one who prefers 'to travel alone, is educated, European, middle class, single, obsessively concerned with budgeting his/her money, and at a juncture in life' (p.313). While her sample shares characteristics

Table 8.1 Why do you want to go on a trek?

	Responses in order stated						
	1st	2nd	3rd	4th	5th	Total	%
Hilltribes	31	29	13	13	5	91	52.9
Scenery	21	25	21	1	2	70	40.7
Get away from city	25	22	7	5	1	60	34.9
Seek new experience	30	13	2	1	2	48	27.9
Ride elephants	6	7	18	7	5	43	25.0
Raft	3	8	9	7	6	33	19.2
Hike	11	7	10	2	2	32	18.6
Adventure	10	7	3	6	2	28	16.3
See different side of Thailand	6	12	5	1	0	24	14.0
Physical challenge	6	8	3	2	2	21	12.2
Something to do	10	6	1	1	0	18	10.5
Smoke opium	1	0	5	5	1	12	7.0
Meet travellers	1	3	1	0	4	9	5.2
Fun	4	3	0	0	0	7	4.1
Need to go with guides	3	1	2	1	0	7	4.1
Other	4	5	1	1	1	12	7.0

n=172

with those interviewed in Chiang Mai, she is concerned with 'long term travellers', those on the road for one year or longer, rather than the participants in a specific activity. She found a 'surprising large number' were women (20–25 per cent). Meijer (1989) in a study of non-organized tourists in Bolivia reported 35 per cent were women. There appears to be a more even split between the sexes among trekkers. Americans were under represented in Riley's sample, as is noticeable in northern Thailand.

From this brief comparison it can be seen that while trekkers form a specialized segment of the overall tourist arrivals for Thailand, they are also marginally part of a global classification of 'long term budget travellers'. However, there are no specific criteria for inclusion in this category. These people may represent a further specialized segment of the non-institutionalized travel market. They are travelling on a small budget, not because they are poor, but because they want to take a longer trip. There is also the belief that budget travel will put them in touch with the 'local people' and they will have more authentic experiences than their counterparts in the four-star hotels. Status is achieved on the road by getting the best value. There is a similar obsession with not getting 'ripped off' in northern Thailand, but trekkers also realize, sometimes too late, that you get what you pay for.

Specialized tourism has been defined by the World Tourism Organization (1985) as 'involving group or individual tours by people who wish to develop

Table 8.2 What did you like best about your trek?

	1st response	2nd response	Total Frequency	Per cent
Raft	25	8	33	21.4
Whole experience	22	8	30	19.5
Seeing hilltribes	21	7	28	18.2
Trek group	19	6	25	16.2
Hiking	19	2	21	13.6
Elephant ride	10	10	20	12.9
Nights in village	11	5	16	10.4
Drugs	6	4	10	6.5
Scenery	3	7	10	6.5
Guide	3	6	9	5.8
Other *	15	4	19	12.3

n= 154

* Other: exercise, hot springs, waterfall, adventure, organization of trek, caves.

certain interests and visit sites and places connected with a specific subject'. Having described the nature of the clientele above, attention can now be directed toward the object of their interest. What are the motivations for trekking? What is their 'special interest'?

The obvious answer to this question is simply 'the hilltribes'. But is this true, and what is it about the hilltribes that the trekkers find so attractive? The results from the survey indicate that the hilltribes do indeed constitute the main motive behind most people wanting to go trekking. In relative order of priority, hilltribe related variables (visit the hilltribes, stay in hilltribe village and photograph the hilltribes) were ranked first. These were followed by 'scenery', 'get away from city', and 'seek new experience' respectively (Table 8.1). On the other hand when post trip satisfactions are examined it is the rafting experience that is ranked most highly (Table 8.2). Furthermore, when asked to name the tribes visited many respondents had great difficulty in recalling the names of any of the tribes, let alone the ones that were visited and in what order. Presumably tourists with a serious commitment to a specialized interest would not have experienced such difficulties.

This would argue that although the hilltribes provide the initial focus for the attraction, it is more the experience as a whole that is sought rather than a detailed and intimate encounter with the hilltribe culture. Indeed it could be argued that the very nature of the enterprise, taking over 100,000 trekkers per year through the hilltribe villages mitigates against the very thing that ostensibly the trekkers are looking for – contact with a supposedly remote and primitive people in an authentic setting. Anyone seeking the latter experience, therefore, would probably be trying to get as far away as possible from a trek, rather than join one.

This is not to argue that the trekkers are in any way dissatisfied with their experience – far from it. Trekkers were asked to rate their relative degree of

Table 8.3 How do you feel about your trekking experience?

Trekking...	Strongly Agree	Agree	Neutral	Disagree	Strongly Disagree	no response
is enjoyable	84(54%)	67(43%)	4(3%)	0	1(1%)	0
is worth $ spent	76(44%)	63(36%)	8(5%)	7(5%)	2(1%)	0
is touristy	20(13%)	63(40%)	37(24%)	31(20%)	4(3%)	1(1%)
is risky	2(1%)	29(19%)	20(13%)	76(49%)	27(17%)	0
is good experience	90(58%)	62(40%)	4(3%)	0	0	0
is exhausting	22(14%)	35(22%)	27(17%)	61(39%)	11(7%)	1(1%)
exploits hilltribes	7(4%)	61(39%)	39(25%)	40(26%)	5(3%)	1(1%)
gets away from touristy areas	11(7%)	84(54%)	26(17%)	25(16%)	8(5%)	2(1%)
is exciting	50(32%)	78(50%)	23(15%)	4(3%)	0	1(1%)
is a way to see remote areas of Thailand	51(33%)	83(53%)	12(8%)	7(4%)	1(1%)	1(1%)

n=156

agreement with statements relating to various aspects of their trip (Table 8.3). As can be seen, overall there was a strong endorsement for the experience with 'good experience', 'enjoyable' and 'worth the money spent' being the most strongly endorsed respectively. Furthermore, 99 per cent said that they would recommend trekking to their friends and only seventeen per cent said that they would not go again. From this it is apparent that although the hilltribes provide the primary focus for the 'specialized interest', this interest is a very broad one of which the hilltribes are but one part. On returning from the experience the trekkers do not indicate that the hilltribes were the highlight of the trip but do not appear to be dissatisfied in any way.

Discussion and Conclusion

Several points can be distilled from the foregoing within the context of specialized tourism and the situation in northern Thailand. The first is in relationship to the tourists themselves. Clearly the clientele described above do not fit the profile of the typical visitor to Thailand. Instead they can be described as being part of a more broadly-based 'international traveller' profile as described by authors such as Riley (1988), Meijer (1989), and as a maturing version of the earlier youth travellers as described by Cohen (1973, 1982). Thailand is but one stop on a more extended journey. Chiang Mai is one stop in Thailand. Nonetheless trekking can be considered part of specialized tourism as defined earlier. A significant proportion come to Chiang Mai specifically to trek (59 per cent) and the hilltribes are the primary motivation for that activity.

There are, however, many gradations of what may be considered 'specialized', rather than a simple dichotomy between 'specialized' and 'non-specialized'. These differences within the context of recreational activities have been explored by authors such as Bryan (1977, 1979). Duffus and Dearden (1990) have examined the nature of these differences with special reference to wildlife-oriented tourism. Initial clientele for such activities may be highly specialized and knowledgeable on the topic. As the activity becomes more popular a wider range of tourists are attracted and eventually the clientele becomes dominated by less-knowledgeable and specialized visitors. The nature of the attraction may change to accommodate not only higher numbers but also this less-knowledgeable clientele. The focus may change from a detailed examination of the object of specialization into a more general appreciation of the entire context at a more superficial level. Thus although the activity may still fall under the classification of specialized tourism, the clientele may tend toward the 'softer' end of that specialization continuum and be considered a generalized specialist. The same may be said of the 'international traveller' continuum. As the explorer types seek non-touristed areas they spearhead the touristic development of these areas, making it safe and accessible to their less intrepid cousins.

This seems to be the case in northern Thailand. Early travellers in the area were not faced with a plethora of ready-made trekking companies to accommodate their wishes but had to devise their own treks, find guides and be prepared for a fairly rigorous and unpredictable journey. It is only recently that activities such as elephant riding and rafting became a routine part of the offerings. Early trips focused more exclusively on the hilltribes and their way of life. These aspects now seem to have been eclipsed by the more general recreational activities available on the treks in terms of reported satisfactions (Table 8.2). This is consistent with the role of culture and ethnicity in different forms of tourism outlined in Table 7.1. In the former the ethnic group under consideration constitutes the prime focus for tourist interest; in the latter they become more a part of the local colour of the area rather than the focal attraction.

Such a change or evolution is not necessarily undesirable. It represents a broadening of the attraction base for the area, which not only helps relieve pressure on the original primary focus, but may also serve to attract a more broadly based clientele. Such diversity may assist in insulating the area in question from the vagaries of highly specialized markets. This may be especially true where the nature of the tourist activity itself may have an effect upon the nature of the attraction. Thus Dearden (1988) has described how trekking can influence the nature of the hilltribes in terms of such aspects as dress, consumer goods, and the nature and appearance of the villages. The overall thrust of such changes is to make the hilltribes and their villages appear less 'authentic' in the eyes of the trekkers. The very success of ethnic tourism may thus carry within it the seeds of its own destruction. As the tourism business increases so do the forces of change; more people come to the area, more money becomes available. In terms of the hilltribes this may mean that, superficially at least, the people begin to look and act more like their lowland Thai neighbours. They therefore lose some of their attraction to tourists who take their money elsewhere, where conditions are more 'authentic'.

This search for the authentic described above may be ameliorated by the transformation from primary to secondary tourism. If rafting is a significant proportion of trip satisfaction and one river provides the best rafting opportunity then, over time, the clientele may be prepared to sacrifice the necessity for their perception of 'authentic' hilltribes in exchange for the excellence of the rafting along that one river. From a tourism management point of view this also may have some advantages. Cultural change of traditional peoples is a difficult thing to understand let alone attempt to manage as a tourism focus. On the other hand activities such as rafting and elephant riding are much more amenable to external control.

In terms of this perspective, it does seem as if ethnic tourism is, perhaps more so than other forms of specialized tourism, an ephemeral phenomenon. Cohen (1989) argues that the authenticity seeking, countercultural reactionaries to conventional mass tourism, as exemplified by the trekkers of northern Thailand, become the unsuspecting victims of a more 'covert and insidious form of staged authenticity' (p.32). The prolific number of companies compete on the basis of a 'communicative staging' of the hilltribes and the experience offered to the trekkers. Communicative staging, as opposed to substantive staging, does not involve a transformation of the 'flow of tribal life', but convinces through rhetoric the authenticity of the villages. Hence, through judicious advertising, the hilltribes are offered up as 'primitive and remote' and the treks as a chance for 'adventure and excitement'.

This strategy can be successful for some time until the discrepancy between the advertising and reality becomes too great. At this point the staging manipulation must go beyond the merely communicative to the substantive. This calls for actual changes to be made to the substance of the attraction in an attempt to maintain authenticity. Authenticity itself is staged and a contrived 'tourist space' is created. The potential for such staged authenticity within ethnic tourism on any broad kind of scale is limited, without affecting the clientele attracted to such activities. Individual villages might be able to be substantially influenced along these lines if tourism is a major economic force, it is realized as such and a collective decision is made to substantively stage authenticity in order to maintain the activity. Alternatively 'authentic' villages can be specifically created as a contrived attraction. In either case it could be argued that the focus of the activity has become inauthentic (although see Cohen 1988 for a more thorough discussion of the concept of authenticity in tourism).

This is in contrast to many other forms of specialized tourism where the attraction base is more durable and insulated from the contaminating effects of the tourist activity. For example it has been argued that small-scale, nature-based tourism can be inherently sustainable if developed within certain guidelines reflecting carrying capacities (Brockelman and Dearden, 1990). Animals and nature can be manipulated in ways that human quarry cannot.

Finally attention must be drawn to the developmental context of the particular case study discussed here. There are many forces effecting change in the hills of northern Thailand – missionaries, government programmes, bilateral aid programmes, United Nations projects and the penetration of market forces to name but a few. The sum of these forces is to reduce the cultural heterogeneity of the hilltribe peoples and incorporate them more into the fabric of northern Thai society. Thus, even without the influence of tourism itself, this is a very rapidly changing scene and underscores the fragility of a heavy reliance upon a primary ethnic attraction as opposed to the secondary ethnic attraction that now appears to be emerging.

References

Bhruksasri, W., 1989, Government policy: highland ethnic minorities, 1–31 in J. McKinnon and B. Vienne, eds, *Hill tribes today: problems in change*, White Lotus, Bangkok

Brockelman, W., Dearden, P., 1990, The role of nature trekking in conservation: a case study in Thailand, *Environmental Conservation*, 17 (2): 141–148

Bryan, H., 1977, Leisure value systems and recreation specialization: the case of trout fishermen, *Journal of Leisure Research*, 9: 174–187

Bryan, H., 1979, Conflict in the great outdoors: towards understanding and managing for diverse sportsman preferences, *Sociological studies No.4*, Bureau of Public Administration, University of Alabama, University, Alabama

Cohen, E., 1973, Nomads from affluence: notes on the phenomenon of drifter-tourism, *International Journal of Comparative Sociology*, 14: 89–103

Cohen, E., 1979, The impact of tourism on the hill tribes of northern Thailand, *Internationales Asienforum*, 10 (1/2): 5–38

Cohen, E., 1982, Jungle guides in northern Thailand – the dynamics of a marginal occupational role, *The Sociological Review*, 30 (2): 234–266

Cohen, E., 1983, Hilltribe tourism, 307–325 in J. McKinnon and W. Bhruksasri, eds, *Highlanders of Thailand*, Oxford University Press, Kuala Lumpur

Cohen, E., 1988, Authenticity and commodization in Tourism, *Annals of Tourism Research*, 15: 371–386.

Cohen, E., 1989, Primitive and remote: hilltribe trekking in Thailand, *Annals of Tourism Research*, 16: 30–61

Dearden, P., 1988, Tourism in developing societies: some observations on trekking in the highlands of north Thailand, 207–216 in L.J. D'Amore and J. Jafari, eds, *Tourism – a vital force for peace*, First Global Conference, Montreal

Duffus, D., Dearden, P., 1990, Non-consumptive wildlife-oriented recreation: a conceptual framework, *Biological Conservation*, 53: 213–231

Harron, S., 1991, Characterizing an alternative tourism segment: trekking in northern Thailand, unpublished MA thesis, University of Victoria, Victoria, British Columbia.

Maneeprasert, M., Pokpong, K., Prangkio, C., 1975, *Reconnaissance survey of the impact of tourism in the highlands*, Tribal Research Centre, Social and Economic Change Committee, Chiang Mai

Meijer, W.G., 1989, Rucksacks and dollars: the economic impact of organized and non-organized tourism in Bolivia, in T.V. Singh, H.L. Theuns, F.M. Go, eds, *Towards appropriate tourism: The case of developing countries*, Peter Lang, Frankfurt

Riley, P.J., 1988, Road culture of international long-term budget travelers, *Annals of Tourism Research*, 15: 313–328

Tourism Authority of Thailand, 1989, *Annual statistical report 1988*, Tourism Authority of Thailand, Bangkok

World Tourism Organization, 1985, *The role of recreation management in the development of active holidays and special interest tourism and consequent enrichment of the holiday experience*, World Tourism Organization, Madrid

9 REVIEW

Nature-based Tourism[1]

Peter S. Valentine

> Ecotourism is big business. It can provide foreign exchange and economic reward for the preservation of natural systems and wildlife. But ecotourism also threatens to destroy the resources on which it depends. Tour boats dump garbage in the waters off Antarctica, shutterbugs harass wildlife in National Parks, hordes of us trample fragile areas. This frenzied activity threatens the viability of natural systems. At times we seem to be loving nature to death (Berle, 1990).

This quotation, from an editorial in the American nature conservation journal *Audubon*, at once expresses the hopes and fears many people hold for nature-based tourism. Is it the ideal, low impact, high value, dream tourism sought by host communities the world over? Is it ecologically sustainable development? Can it form the basis for community tourism in developing countries? Will it further destroy the ailing conservation programs by adding internal pressures to parks already under assault from external forces? Can we live with it? Can we live without it?

In this chapter the essential elements of nature-based tourism are explored and examples from around the world help illustrate its diversity of form. Existing literature is reviewed and an assessment made on the present state of knowledge about ecotourism and some of the most pressing issues awaiting research. An overall management perspective reflects the intimate link between nature-based tourism and nature conservation.

Nature and Tourism – The Context

The primary role of nature in attracting tourists to specific destinations is now well understood and in this broad sense most tourism may be described as nature-based. For example, in Africa the work of Ferrario has identified the dominance of natural resources: using features listed in 10 travel guides, a total of 2,100 items were classified into 21 'resource' classes. The three most important classes were all natural (Ferrario, 1982).

Plate 9.1 Group observing green turtle laying her eggs, Heron Island, Australia (courtesy of TraveLearn)

A survey of international tourists to Australia showed that 55.8 per cent of visitors viewed Australia's tourist assets as the 'natural environment' (Tisdell, 1984). During 1989 the Tourism Council of the South Pacific prepared four brochures in association with its South Pacific Islands Travel Manual (Dive, Fish, Adventure and Nature). All brochures are dominated by natural environment photographs and this emphasis in advertising is generally true throughout the travel industry. In the United States a survey of 'non-consumptive wildlife use' reported a total of 29 million US citizens participated in approximately 310 million nature trips away from their homes in 1980 (Boo, 1990, p.3). These figures include more than 1 million people making over 4 million international nature trips, very many of which are to Central and South America. Costa Rica, for example, has a very significant tourism industry based on its national park system – the best in Latin America. The remarkable array of flora and fauna, some 5 per cent of all the planet's biodiversity, seems well protected with 12 per cent of the land area in national parks and a further 15 per cent in other refuges and reserves. It is not surprising that tourism provides the third largest source of foreign exchange in the country, and that there are very many nature tour companies. Apart from the 16 national parks plus additional government reserves, there are at least 15 significant privately owned nature reserves which cater for nature tourism (Sheck, 1990, p.206).

The African wildlife connection is well known (Luard, 1985). The singular importance of encounters with wildlife has been documented (Valentine, 1984) including the role of crocodiles in tropical Australian tourism and bears in Canada and northern USA, whalewatching (Shaw, 1987) and 'gorilla tourism' (McNeely et al., 1990). In the latter case, the African country Rwanda gains over one third of its foreign exchange revenue from nature-based tourists visiting the Volcans National Park to see gorillas.

The importance of wildlife to people might be illustrated by the expenditure of some US$14 billion annually on wildlife viewing, photography, travel and feeding of wildlife (Vickerman 1988). This US Fish and Wildlife study included trips only if they were primarily for wildlife viewing. It did not include supporting equipment values. Other indications of the perceived attractive power of wildlife in tourism developments include the hotel in Kakadu National Park which is shaped like a crocodile and the numerous concrete and fibreglass models of animals used throughout the tourism industry. Walt Disney was perhaps one of the first to recognize this and certainly a person who made much from people's love of wildlife.

Apart from this well established link between most tourism and the environment, there has recently been an increasing focus on 'nature-based tourism' as a kind of special interest tourism, evidenced by a very high level of interest in and recent publications on the topic (e.g. Ingram and Durst, 1987, 1989; Laarman and Durst, 1987; Kutay, 1989; Boo, 1990; Goudberg, Cassells, and Valentine, 1991). The fact that this is a recent phenomenon is supported by the literature surveyed for this review – of the over 100 publications consulted, 60 per cent were published in the last three years. There had previously been numerous expressions of concern about the growing role of tourism in protected areas (for example Budowski, 1976; Coleman, 1980; Lucas, 1984; Marsh, 1987; Bateson, Nyman, and Sheppard, 1989; Neumann and Machlis, 1989) and responses include the development of guidelines to help park managers deal with tourism, especially in developing countries (McNeely and Thorsell, 1987; Thorsell and McNeely, 1988).

The focus of this chapter is to provide a framework for analysis of nature based tourism and to discuss the relative merits of particular options. A basic premise is the underlying need for nature conservation at all levels. Further, it is recognized that there is a great interest in nature-tourism as a way to achieve symbiosis between nature conservation and local development – such interest being expressed by both local communities and by conservation agencies (Young, 1986). The results of this review suggest not enough is known about nature tourism to express confidence that it might readily achieve either of these goals. Despite this uncertainty, or perhaps because of it, the experimental development of nature-tourism is seen as a valuable option for those communities with the resources and the inclination. This chapter is meant to be of practical value in better understanding the challenges inherent in nature-based tourism.

Defining Nature-based Tourism

There is a plethora of expressions for nature-based tourism already in the literature. Laarman and Durst (1987) use the term 'nature travel' (or sometimes 'nature-oriented tourism') to refer to a style of tourism which 'combines education, recreation and often adventure'. Boo (1990) in her major study of Latin America uses the title 'eco-tourism' as synonymous with 'nature tourism' which she uses throughout the work and defines as 'travelling to relatively undisturbed or uncontaminated natural areas with the specific objective of studying, admiring and enjoying the scenery and its wild plants and animals, as well as any existing cultural manifestations' (adopted from Ceballos-Lascurain). Lucas (1984) defines nature tourism as 'tourism which is based on the enjoyment of natural areas and the observation of nature' and further specifies that such tourism 'has a low impact environmentally, is labour intensive and contributes socially and economically to the nation'.

Nature-based tourism is also a subset of a larger class of tourism styles or developments much discussed by social analysts. Here the concepts of 'alternative tourism' (Gonsalves, 1987) and 'appropriate' tourism (Richter, 1987) encompass a critical concern about large scale mass tourism and its impacts on people and places. Other terms which have been applied to ecotourism and nature tourism include 'responsible' or 'ethical' tourism (Kutay, 1989), 'environment-friendly travel' (Borst, 1990), and 'green tourism' and 'sustainable tourism' (Lane, 1990). The evolution of concerns about the impacts of tourism on the environment has produced other perspectives also, for example the entire field of nature tourist ethics (Anon, 1989a, 1989b; Graham, 1979). Despite the complexity implicit in this array of terms, a useful starting point is the relatively simple definition:

> nature-based tourism is primarily concerned with the direct enjoyment of some relatively undisturbed phenomenon of nature.

For such tourism to be ecologically sustainable it must be appropriate for the specific location and should produce no permanent degradation of the natural environment.

Ecotourism Destinations and Activities

Examples of nature-based tourism help illustrate the diversity of activities, the range of destinations and the various styles of travel associated with it.

Table 9.1 Dimensions of nature-based tourism

	Dimension and variation
Experience	Nature-dependency (dependent, enhanced) Intensity of interaction (dedicated, casual) Social sensitivity (intra-group dynamics) Duration
Style	Level of infrastructure support (field, base) Group size and type Cultural interaction factor Willingness to pay Length of visit
Location	Accessibility (remoteness) Development contribution (city, village) Ownership (private, government) Fragility (sustainable, capacity)

In a study of nature-oriented tour operators, Ingram and Durst (1989) analysed the promotion of specific activities and their results show trekking and hiking the most commonly included activity in advertising (72 per cent of operators) closely followed by birdwatching, nature photography, wildlife safaris and camping (all over 60 per cent). Many quite specialist activities feature in the promotion including mountain climbing, botanical study, orchid study, butterfly collecting and river rafting.

The destinations are also very diverse. For this sample of USA operators, Kenya came in tops with Nepal, Tanzania and Puerto Rica providing high levels of 'activity-destination opportunities'. Other places included were India, China, Brazil, Costa Rica, Mexico, Paraguay and Ecuador. Some places are almost shrines for ecotourists of the 'environmental pilgrimage' type; for example the Galapagos Islands (Kenchington, 1989). The spatial spread of destinations of a single tour operator might be very great indeed. For example the 1990 tours for Peregrine Bird Tours (an Australian company) include Canada (northern), Israel, Nepal, Tibet, China, Kenya, New Zealand and Cape York Peninsula (northern Queensland). Other operators frequently offer similar geographic diversity in their nature tours.

Ingram and Durst (1989) also report the variety of accommodation style and their sample ranged from rural village through hostel, camping and luxury hotels. According to Laarman and Durst (1987) 'nature-oriented tourism has hard and soft dimensions in two senses' and these relate to the extent to which the tourism is dedicated or casual on the one hand and difficult or easy on the other. Thus a scientific study of butterflies is hard ecotourism while a casual (recreational?) interest in wildlife generally is soft. On the other axis if the nature tourist is 'roughing it' – by camping for example and preparing meals, this is seen as hard compared with the equally nature-based tourist who sleeps easy in a hotel with all meals provided – the soft option.

Understanding Diversity in Nature-based Tourism

It should be clear that nature-based tourists are not homogeneous and management agencies which act as though tourists are all alike create many problems for both tourists and themselves. Belief in the stereotypic tourist has also led to peculiar management practices such as access restrictions based entirely on numbers with no qualitative modifier. In classifying the range of tourists and operations which might be encompassed by the term 'nature tourism' it is apparent that there are many dimensions in which variation might occur. Initially it might seem that the most important element is the degree to which the experience depends upon nature. In a discussion on research needs for the management of recreation in tropical rainforest reserves, Cassells and Valentine (1991) discussed appropriate activities using a tripartite division:

- those activities (experiences) dependent on nature;
- those activities (experiences) enhanced by nature; and
- those activities (experiences) for which the natural setting is incidental.

For example, people seeking to observe animals in the wild (e.g. Hornbills) require natural environment (e.g. Khao Yai National Park) to enjoy their experience. Such birdwatching is clearly *dependent* on nature and that dependency is the basis of successful tour operators. Camping is an activity frequently *enhanced* by nature – people usually prefer to camp in a forest rather than a quarry. Preferences like this do depend upon nature but the activity might be possible with equal satisfaction for some users without a purely natural setting. If a person's primary interest is a cooling swim then the setting may be *incidental*, and relatively unimportant assuming the water is unpolluted! It is also true that there may be many activities which are ruined or at least degraded by nature – for example the presence of ants at a picnic or sharks at a beach. Nature-based tourism as a type of special interest tourism is mainly nature-dependent.

While this dimension of dependency is a very useful starting point, it is also clear that there are many other dimensions of value in studying nature-based tourism. Table 9.1 is a first approximation of some useful dimensions, divided into broad categories of experience, style and location. These will be of particular use in designing research programs or management plans and for most of these dimensions little is known.

An example might help illustrate the concepts outlined in Table 9.1. One class of nature-based tourism includes 'highly dedicated specialist birders', a market which is already well developed and expanding and can involve considerable cash flow (Valentine, 1984; Vardaman, 1982). Such birders ('twitchers' in some parts of the world – cf. Oddie, 1980) are frequently impatient with the presence of lesser skilled individuals and desire small group sizes of birders with a comparable experience base. Satisfaction comes almost entirely from nature observations, or related activities. By contrast a 'nature club tour group' would probably tolerate a wider variety of skills; would not focus simply on birds; and would be comfortable with a larger group and more variable individuals. A third example might be non-specialist tourists whose interest is in 'seeing somewhere different from home'. These 'exotica' tourists may also have an interest in nature and typically make up a high proportion of visitors to nature destinations accessible by road (e.g. national park front country). Satisfaction for this group comes mainly from the relatively superficial interaction with nature and the sense of discovery associated with it. These three examples illustrate a further point: that the impacts of the experience on both the participant and the environment will vary depending upon the dimensions outlined in Table 9.1. Certainly different groups would need very different support, and managers might need to design distinctive interpretation for each major group of users.

Although providing a potential area for future research, the immediate broad issue for many developing tourism destinations is the desirability or otherwise of nature-based tourism. What are the prospects and the problems?

Issues and Prospects for Nature-based Tourism

Social Carrying Capacity The dimensions listed in Table 9.1 draw attention to the possible characteristics of nature-based tourists. Wilson and Laarman (1987, p.1) point out that 'nature-oriented tourism usually is constrained by low social carrying capacity. The nature-oriented tourist tends to perceive crowding as a problem, not tolerating large numbers of other nature-related tourists'. The implications of this are clear – such nature-based tourism must be low volume and will have limited prospects for growth. It will also need very careful management if it is to be sustainable. There are very few tourist or resource management agencies with the skills and philosophy to address this issue. In this context it is instructive to note that the Great Barrier Reef Marine Park Authority has recently modified the management zones (Valentine, 1986) by adding a new category for 'wilderness'. Some areas will be permitted to have tourist fixtures and large numbers of visitors, but others will be free of them. This reflects the growing awareness of intergroup conflicts and the different reactions of visitors to built facilities on the reef. It is also important to recognize that different environments may have very different social carrying capacities; tropical rainforest for example is a very effective screening vegetation and may be able to accommodate many more wilderness users or ecotourists than an equivalent area of open woodland (Valentine, 1982).

Environmental Carrying Capacity Virtually every environment has the capacity to support nature-based tourism and there is growing interest in appraising the specific prospects in almost every country; partly due to a perception that this may well be a more sustainable form of tourism than any other. For example, in a discussion of the values of tropical rainforest it has been claimed that the tourist potential of rainforest equals that of the east African game parks (Allen, 1975) and the review by Boo (1990) gives detailed accounts of central and southern American prospects, many of which focus on rainforest. To a large extent the rainforest national parks of Costa Rica are the driving force behind tourism in that country. But even the Antarctic has seen a rapid increase in tourism over the past two decades, essentially based on the spectacular natural scenery and wildlife (Gell, 1989, p.82; Wace, 1990; Hall, forthcoming). In 1988 there were some 7,200 tourists, most via cruise ship from Chile and Argentina at a cost of between US$3,000 and US$10,000 each (Kutay, 1989). A rather more expensive tour was taken by eight tourists who paid US$35,000 each for a three hours Antarctic Airways flight and brief landing at the South Pole! Much concern has been expressed about the potential impacts on the Antarctic environment and an example of that can be seen in the decision of the Australian Conservation Foundation in July, 1990, to adopt a policy opposing all commercial tourism to the continent. One key element in the debate is the prospect that at least some tourists in Antarctica (carefully managed) might act as watchdogs on the activities of others who use the continent for geopolitical, resource or scientific reasons. On the other hand many people favour the notion that there may be at least one part of the planet not plagued by tourists.

Economic Impacts Peak nature experiences are extremely valuable and may command high willingness to pay values. For these kinds of nature-based tourism, the 'threshold' or 'excluvist' approach adopted by Bhutan may be valuable (Dixit, 1989, p.4). That country imposed a national quota (1988) of 2,400 visitors per annum, required US$200 per day per person expenditure and has minimal leakage of its 'rarity value' dollars. Some kinds of nature-based tourism undoubtedly share similar characteristics – exclusiveness and rarity dimensions. Most studies of nature-based tourism conclude that countries fail to collect the full potential income from such visitors (e.g. Brockelman, 1988). The other side of this issue is the tendency for societies to undervalue the worth of national parks and other protected areas (Valentine, 1989). Ecotourism represents an excellent mechanism for societies to recover some of the costs of a national park system.

In contrast to the environmental and social limits to nature-based tourism, the economic potential of nature-tourism may be extremely high. It is therefore often referred to as an example of 'low volume high value' tourism. This high value aspect can be seen in the kinds of costs usually associated with specialist nature tours. For example a bird-watching trip of three to four weeks in a developing country might cost around Aus.$5,000 per person. In 1990 Peregrine Bird Tours was running a 27 day trip to Nepal, Tibet and China for Aus.$7,572 (ex Australia). The 23 day Kenya trip was Aus.$7,313. In each case the ground content was just over 75 per cent of the total. Also in 1990, specialist nature trips to the Amazon with the Sierra Club (USA) cost around Aus.$3,700 for 14 days not including airfares while an African wildlife trip came in at over Aus.$4,000 ground costs for two weeks. These figures are fairly typical of nature-based group tours. An extreme example of high expenditure for nature-based tourism might be seen in the single Texan birdwatcher who in 1980 spent 10 days birding around the world (Valentine, 1984). This trip began in northern Queensland and planned to yield 1,000 different species of birds in just 10 days. After very rapid visits to Australia, Kenya, Germany and Peru the target was finally achieved (1,041 species). The same nature-tourist had earlier spent Aus.$50,000 seeing over 700 species in the USA in a single year.

But nature-based tourism may also be relatively inexpensive. The extreme thrills of tiger watching in the national parks of India is available at very moderate rates for western tourists, especially the backpacking style traveller. In Kanha National Park (Valentine, 1983) and in Bandhavgah National Park (both in Madhya Pradesh) either government or private facilities can provide a 10 day visit with ground costs between Aus.$20–$100 per day. There are few nature tourism experiences so intense and rewarding as stalking a tiger on elephant back and it is highly likely that consumer surplus remains very high. Another characteristic of nature-based tourism is that such tourists 'are generally more accepting of conditions different from home than are other types of tourists' (Boo, 1990, p.13). It is therefore likely that relatively low capital environments (i.e. developing countries) would experience less leakage from nature-based tourism than other kinds of tourism.

Political and Management Issues For many people the first example of nature tourism which springs to mind is the African wildlife safari. Such tourism may be seen as the 'soft' version of the big game safaris of earlier eras with cameras replacing rifles. Apart from the high economic values of African wildlife tourism (Western and Henry, 1979) there are interesting links between international ecotourism and nature conservation. It was Budowski (1976) who first articulated the idea of symbiosis between conservation and tourism, more recently expressed as 'wildlife pays so wildlife stays' (Kutay, 1989). In recent years one of the motivations for nations to nominate areas for World Heritage Listing has been a perceived link between that designation and the attraction of international ecotourists.

A related aspect is the view that ecotourists may be more desirable than mass tourists. In developing countries in particular there may be real advantages in attracting nature-based tourists but such policy-based discrimination is never easy (Richter and Richter, 1985; Richter, 1989). On the other hand ecotourists demand high quality information about nature – material not readily available, at least in most developing countries. Brockelman (1988, p.211), in his excellent review of nature conservation in Thailand, highlights the failure of managers to provide appropriate support for the 'very large and growing numbers of young affluent Western tourists interested in nature'. In this regard the World Wide Fund for Nature gave help in 1989 to the Conservation Data Center (Mahidol University) for the production of two excellent bird guides (for Doi Inthanon National Park and Khao Yai National Park) which are now sold in the parks.

Wilson and Laarman (1987, p.11) identify several beliefs about the characteristics of nature tourism (at this point there are too few studies to accept such beliefs as anything more than working hypotheses). The first, a kind of motherhood assertion, is that nature tourism is a 'wholesome kind of tourism' with a good type of tourist. Given the well known social problems of tourism in most parts of the world, this characteristic, if true, would be seen as highly desirable by host communities. A second hypothesis is that nature-based tourism disperses income more widely through the country (away from capital cities). This also may prove particularly valuable for some societies but of course will be constrained by the environmental resource. Finally, there is the belief that such tourists stay longer. The limited data presented by Boo (1990) suggests they may not stay longer but they might spend more. However, the extra expenditure may well be in high leakage areas (e.g. travel).

Nature-based tourism in its many forms frequently includes a strong educational component (Laarman and Perdue, 1988). There are numerous local and international nature-based education programs which develop links with nature conservation management agencies, or research institutes, and provide a service. Such ecotourists pay for the privilege of working as volunteers on nature-based projects and it appears this style of tourism is increasingly popular (e.g. Earthwatch, Sierra Club, Operation Raleigh). This might be one way by which managers can overcome the failure to use tourists enough to help conserve nature (Thorsell and McNeely, 1988).

Problems of Nature-based Tourism

Environmental Impacts Amongst the more popular discussions of nature-based tourism there is often a heroic assumption that it is inevitably environment friendly. This is far from the truth and, while it may appear ideal compared with many forms of mass tourism, there are significant problems. Many of these can be collectively identified as the need for high quality management. For example, an expression employed by United States Fish and Wildlife Service is 'non-consumptive wildlife use', which might imply no threat to the wildlife. Unfortunately, unintended negative effects of wildlife watchers have been well documented throughout the world (Webster, 1980; Duffie, 1981; Henry, 1982; Valentine, 1984). Even in the case of whales there are examples of harassment by watchers requiring the legal controls now in place in the waters off Hawaii and off Queensland, Australia. Very little is yet known about the tolerance levels of wildlife for human contact in the wild. There are numerous examples of tolerance failure amongst crocodiles, sharks, bears and tigers but little information about the less threatening and perhaps more threatened species. A useful account of the conflicts between bears and people will be found in Jonkel and Servheen (1977) and the unhappy story of grizzly bears in Canadian Parks is examined by Cottingham and Langshaw (1981). In North America, Ream has documented numerous examples of human–wildlife conflict (1978, 1980).

Apart from this aspect there is the more complex issue of environmental degradation. Cole has been quantifying some of the more significant human impacts on wilderness in a long series of studies (1989a, 1989b). How much damage can the environment take? How much degradation will the 'desirable' tourist accept? Both the ecological and experiential domains need careful study if nature-based tourism is to be sustainable. There is already evidence that as environments become damaged or use level and type changes, some tourists are displaced.

One of the greatest difficulties is to determine and maintain an appropriate level of tourism. How many people is enough? In an economic study of tropical forest tourism, Healy (1988, p.54) urges caution in expanding the volume of tourists at his study sites and suggests that increasing charges might be a more attractive alternative. The lure of expansion is very difficult to resist. One of the more poignant ironies in nature-tourism concerns the California over-wintering sites for the spectacular aggregations of the Monarch butterfly. Long the focus of a large nature-tourism industry, one of the local motels (Butterfly Trees Lodge) lost all its over-wintering clusters because expansion of units modified the area sufficiently that the butterflies have not returned (New, 1987, p.30).

There are many other examples of serious conflict between nature-based tourists and the particular aspect of nature they seek. Amongst the best known are the problems of interference with predator behaviour in the game parks of Africa (MacKinnon, et al., 1986, p.85). Henry (1982), discussing Amboseli National Park in Kenya, has identified a problem of potential conflict between nature tourists and the wildlife they love. By measuring the length of time visitor vehicles were stationary and identifying the animal species associated with the stop, he demonstrated that there were large variations in the focus of nature tourism on different animals. Six of the 56 species of large mammals in the park account for 80 per cent of the total stationary time – the six being lions, cheetah, elephants, rhino, giraffe and buffalo. The combined total of lions and cheetahs accounted for more than 50 per cent of all stationary time while lions alone produced 28 per cent of the stops! There are also reports of hyenas in Serengeti National Park using the presence of 'stationary minibuses as a means of locating and robbing cheetah families of their prey' (Edington and Edington, 1986, p.40). One point which was not made by Henry (1982), is that the decision on where and when to go and stop is made by the tour operators rather than the individual tourists. This suggests, given that the majority of visitors are in commercial operators' vehicles, the management agency must work with

Table 9.2 Negative impacts of nature tourists in national parks

Factor	Impact on nature	Effects on experiences
crowding	environmental stress, animals show changes in behaviour	irritation, displacement
development	built structures intrude on visual quality	reduced aesthetic values
roads and tracks	habitat loss, drainage change, barriers to animals	aesthetic scars
access – motor vehicles, powerboats, pedestrian	disturbance to animals, loss of quiet, trail erosion disturbs wildlife	noise pollution, loss of wilderness intergroup conflict, aesthetic impact
antisocial activity (noise, radios etc.),	interference with natural sounds, wildlife	irritation
litter	impairment of scene, habituation of wildlife to garbage	aesthetic loss, health hazard
vandalism	mutilation	loss of natural beauty
vehicle speeding	wildlife mortality, dust	aesthetic values, reduced safety concerns
driving – off-road and night	soil and vegetation damage, disturbance to wildlife	loss of wilderness, disruption of wildlife viewing
feeding animals	behavioural changes, poor diet	danger to tourists
souvenir and wood collection	removal of natural attractions, disruption of natural processes, loss of habitat	perceived inappropriate behaviour in national park
powerlines	destruction of vegetation, erosion	aesthetic impacts.

Source: based partly on Thorsell and McNeely, 1988.

the operators, as well as the tourists, to address the problem. Careful management is necessary to control this situation and to enable the wildlife to continue their normal lives.

Similarly, the presence of Mexican species of birds in the Chiricahua mountains of southern USA has prompted a concentration of birdwatchers which at times overwhelms the birds. A sign erected by the National Parks

Service warns birders to avoid disturbance to the birds but not everyone is careful (Valentine, 1984). Table 9.2 sets out a number of the types of potential impacts of nature tourists in national parks and other wildlife areas.

Community and Social Impacts Another dimension of concern is the impact on local communities (O'Grady 1990). Nature-based tourism is sometimes viewed with resentment by local people, especially in developing countries where the tourists tend to be affluent and not local while the local people may be very poor. Thus Mishra (1984, p.201) notes that most visitors to Chitwan National Park in Nepal are non-Nepalese and goes on to claim these 'are outsiders who have little interest in local problems'. Included amongst the local problems are human deaths inflicted by park wildlife (rhinos 3-5 per year and tigers 1 per year), as well as crop destruction from rhino trampling. Mishra also notes local price rises and little employment helps build local resentment against this nature tourism. In such circumstances the National Park may be viewed as being against the interests of the local people – as places for tourists only. Similarly, there is great resentment from the locals surrounding the management of Dudhwa National Park in India. This is not surprising when in four years 93 people were killed by tigers, and even more so when the government pays compensation of Rs5,000 per death but fines locals Rs50,000 if they kill a tiger! If the conservation is seen as primarily for tourism then it is likely problems will arise. 'One has to consider that pure tourism-based nature conservation is mainly for privileged visitors and usually outside the control and benefit of local people' (O'Grady, 1990, p.40).

Leakage of Benefits In his review of an African example, Lusigi (1984, p.141) points out 'little of that [tourism] money directly benefits the local populations surrounding the park' thereby leading to resentment, in this case exacerbated by a lack of resources to purchase the necessary bus to join the tourism industry and made more irksome for the people by a government-required permit to enter the land they have previously always used.

In developing countries in particular, there will be a need for novel skills amongst the local communities if they are to benefit from nature tourists. Language skills and natural history skills must be added to existing environmental skills and the necessary training programs are not in place. One consequence of the absence of such skills is the dominance in existing nature-based tourism of operators from outside the host country. This introduces higher levels of leakage and minimizes the scope for local control and benefits. As Boo (1990, p.36) points out, even if willingness to spend money is high amongst nature tourists, the extent to which this translates into more local dollars depends very much on the organization of the tourist industry. In principle, at least, nature-based tourism should perform well as a 'community tourism' candidate but in practice much local, regional and national skill will be needed.

Examples of Nature-based Tourism

There is an extraordinary level of interest in nature-tourism in developing countries and this seems particularly true throughout the Asian-Pacific region as well as in Central and South America. But nature-based tourism is also well established in the industrial nations throughout the world and although conditions vary, there may be many lessons to be learned which cross cultural and biogeographical boundaries. Despite the level of interest little is known about the appropriate styles of nature tourism, largely because so little research has been undertaken. In the following section some examples of nature-based tourism are given with brief comments on each as a way to identify some of the successful and some of the less successful elements. Note that many of these overlap with other types of special interest tourism such as adventure travel, sport tourism (see Chapter 11), and cultural tourism (see Chapters 5 and 7). But some of the more fascinating are very specialized, as for example attempts in Sikkim to focus on specialty ecotourists by organizing 'orchid treks' and 'bird treks', and the specialist tours to see the birds of paradise in Papua New Guinea.

Island Bird Sanctuary Bird concentrations are frequently spectacular and ocean islands provide some opportunities for limited tourism. Skomer Island off the Pembrokeshire coast of Wales is a Nature Reserve with access controlled by the daily ferry. A quota of 100 visitors per day has been established and a hardened walk path has been completed (about 3 km long) to which all visitors must keep. Both domestic and international travellers come to see the remarkably rich bird life (10,000 Puffins, 100,000 Manx Shearwaters and many other species). It is suspected that considerable consumer surplus exists due to the high quality of experiences. Local people (mainland) provide accommodation, food and the boat ride for the tourists. The island itself is uninhabited and access is strictly controlled. It is managed by the West Wales Naturalist Trust and provides an excellent model if the natural resources are available.

A different situation occurs at Michalmas Cay on the Great Barrier Reef. This National Park island is a breeding place for many sea birds and was originally subject to regular seaplane landings. These have been prohibited due to the disturbance to the birds and instead access is by boats including a large (300 passenger) power cat. The primary attraction at this location is the adjacent reef where people snorkel and dive, so this is an example of sport or adventure tourism, but most visitors go ashore on the Cay and experience the bird life. The island is segregated into a small strip of beach for tourists and the remainder preserved for the birds. Most of the benefits from the tourists go to the transport company and, given the mass tourism base in northern Queensland, a large local leakage occurs.

Underwater Guiding Program Although most of the Great Barrier Reef tourism in Australia does not fit the narrow definition of nature tourism there are segments within it which do. Most diving trips fall into the category of sport tourism (see Chapters 11 and 13), however some, including one with a snorkel guide service available at one of the offshore reef destinations, are particularly relevant to nature-based tourism. Here tourists pay for the professional services of marine biologists who lead them on discovery trips underwater. This has proved very successful despite the significant extra cost, demonstrating that many tourists who use the facilities of mass tourism have added willingness to pay for nature. As a proportion of total travel costs to this destination the extra cost is relatively minor. The recruitment of tourists for this opportunity usually occurs during the boat trip to the reef. A different style of nature-based tourism also uses the same reefs, but this is based on a fixed group of tourists from international origins who travel in a group with the local specialist nature guides who are expert marine biologists and photographers. The entire trip is packaged and all services are provided by the local operator who deliberately limits the quantity and emphasizes quality experiences. Selling is done by the operators during the low season and involves travel to the major centres of origin (USA, Europe) for personal recruitment through a network of contacts using highly sophisticated slide presentations. This style of operation requires very high operator skills and is very demanding personally, but also rewarding.

Whale Watching This classic wildlife observation style of nature tourism is increasing in importance throughout the Pacific. Whale watching is also developing as a nature-based tourism opportunity in the waters off Australia (Tucker, 1989), New Zealand, Chesapeake Bay and in the Ogasawama Islands of Japan – especially off Chichyima Island. The problem of avoiding disturbance to whales while allowing close up encounters is a major management issue and involves cooperation between operators and management authorities (with appropriate legislation in the case of Hawaii and Queensland). Within the Great Barrier Reef region whale sightings do occur frequently from day cruise vessels. The ability of nature to generate a dramatic response was evident on one cruise when a largely indolent boatload of visitors, returning home from the outer reef near the Whitsunday Islands, were galvanized into action with the appearance of whales. No other event on that trip came close to achieving the same unanimity of response or generated such excitement.

It is this intensity of experience which is frequently the hallmark of human-animal interactions provided by nature-based tourism. Shaw (1987) points out the cognitive element involved in whale-watching. Referring to the Cabrillo National Monument in California he notes that although the whale-watching activity seems neither aesthetically pleasing nor recreational 'nevertheless, the excitement of the participants is obvious… [and] the essence of this experience lies in the mind of the beholder'. The coastal presence of wild dolphins, as at Monkey Mia near Shark Bay in Western Australia (Doak, 1988), has also generated a large nature-based tourism program, sure to increase since a change in the area's status to World Heritage.

Navua River Wilderness Trips – Fiji Several operators use the Navua River for wilderness and ethnic tours (day trips). These include canoe trips down the river and powered long boat trips up. The river valley, beginning a few kilometres upstream from the town of Navua, narrows and the slopes and mountains are well vegetated. In places there is evidence of village gardens but generally the forest cover is extensive. Waterfalls and birdlife form part of the attraction. The power boats stop at one of two villages some 20 kms upstream, where the tourists meet the village people with appropriate ceremony. Although the operation is run by Fijians, they are from Suva and the local village people receive no return. The 'wilderness' is not interpreted for the tourists and the guides seem to have little or no interest in wildlife, and certainly no knowledge is shared. Despite being marketed as 'wilderness' these trips are of poor value for natural history tourists and the links with nature are slender. The potential exists for much more intensive nature-based tourism to be developed here, and for a better structure to support the local communities and environmental protection.

Cape York Wilderness Safaris (Queensland, Australia) This remote and wild part of Australia has rapidly gained large numbers of nature tourists in recent years. Despite the absence of sealed roads, and the impassable conditions of the roads for the duration of the wet season, by 1987 around 25,000 vehicles drove at least part way up the peninsula and about 16,000 vehicles (4 wheel drive) made it beyond the Archer River, implying at least 1,000 km of dirt 'road' travel. These adventure tourists are enjoying the 'wilderness on wheels' experience of the Australian outback but many are driven specifically because of wildlife. In a study of safari tourism on Cape York in 1987–1988 some 18 companies were operating with emphasis on adventure, remoteness and unique wildlife. These operators usually include several of the national parks and mostly follow a bush camping regime. Iron Range, a tropical rainforest area on the east coast, is especially important for nature-based tourists due to the many locally endemic wildlife species and the richness of the rainforests. Some companies offer a 'fly in fly out' option while others have 'fly-drive' or even 'ship-drive' by cruising up the waters of the Great Barrier Reef. People engaged in organized nature-based tours of Cape York are better educated, more affluent and better prepared than those travelling in their own vehicles. So far, however, little support in the form of interpretation has been made available in the national parks in the peninsula.

Strategies for Developing Nature-based Tourism

Ecological Sustainable Development

National parks and other protected areas form the basic resource for nature-based tourism throughout most of the world. One of the motives for international support to nature-based tourism is its potential to assist in nature conservation. It can only achieve this if certain conditions are met:

(a) a clear sustained and adequate benefit to the local community from the nature-based tourism venture;
(b) a clear link between the tourist choice of destination and locally protected nature; and
(c) appropriate local management and skills to provide satisfaction to both the visitors and the local community.

Even where state-owned and managed national parks are the primary resource, it seems likely that a similar set of conditions would add sustainability to nature-based tourism.

Returning to the parameters of nature-based tourism identified earlier, it is not possible to espouse any particular combination of location, style and experience as a preferred model. However, local communities and national governments will need to consider the implications of their choices very carefully. The unfortunate reality is that there are few properly documented case studies of nature-based tourism successes or failures which may help design new ventures. There are no doubt many potentially successful designs of nature-based tourism and different regions may benefit from a wide range of options, depending very much on local social and natural environments.

Guidelines for Integrating Nature-based Community Tourism and Conservation

Many parts of the world are just beginning to develop a nature-based tourist industry and the following principles may be useful in the absence of a formal manual. They certainly need testing but they are based on much international experience coupled with sensible caution. The guidelines suggested by McNeely and Thorsell (1987) for national parks should also be consulted.

A Small is beautiful principle: both the operation and the infrastructure should be small rather than large and considerable caution should be exercised before any increase in scale is attempted.

B High value – low volume may be best: capitalize on the highest quality elements of the natural environment and exploit the usually high willingness to pay values associated with these. Better to have the visitor numbers as a low proportion of the community numbers (5–10 per cent maximum?).

C Local control is better than overseas or capital city control BUT this must be based on adequate skills. Can a development program be designed to guarantee the transfer of any special skills not held and to refine existing skills? An external partner committed to eventual withdrawal is one possibility. A partnership with an international company might be valuable if it provides for local people to gain experience in other comparable settings. Alternatively such skills development might be the basis of a good aid program.

D Be cautious about allowing the nature-based experiences being offered to become too closely associated with cultural elements. A well-protected and managed natural resource will provide permanent opportunities for nature-based tourism but culture interests and cultures themselves are usually much more dynamic.

E Develop a careful monitoring program so that every step of the project development is recorded and its contribution to ultimate success or failure identified. Regular reports of progress will help in future decisions about nature-based tourism in the region. Association with concerned organizations such as IUCN or SPREP or WWF, may provide a valuable input of comment and support.

F Develop guidelines for operators. Recent examples include the Code of Environmental Practice developed in 1989 by the Australian Tourism Industry Association, the 1990 booklet prepared by the Tourism Council of the South Pacific, and a guide for maximizing nature tourism's ecological and social benefits produced by the World Resources Institute (Lindberg 1991).

G Develop guidelines for ecotourists. A good example is the Audubon Travel Ethic prepared by the Audubon Society, one of the largest USA conservation groups. This draws attention to the natural and social ethics which ought to be the hallmark of ecotourists. The seven point list is as follows:

1 The biota shall not be disturbed;
2 Audubon tours to natural areas will be sustainable;
3 The sensibilities of other cultures will be respected;
4 Waste disposal shall have neither environmental nor aesthetic impacts;
5 The experience a tourist gains in traveling with Audubon shall enrich his or her appreciation of nature, conservation, and the environment;
6 The effect of an Audubon tour shall be to strengthen the conservation effort and enhance the natural integrity of places visited; and
7 Traffic in products that threaten wildlife and plant populations shall not occur (Anon., 1989a).

Research Needs for Nature-based Tourism

Decisions about nature-based tourism are being made in a relative vacuum of research data and knowledge. As Boo points out (1990, p.4), 'despite rising expectations regarding the value of nature tourism in many fields of expertise, there are great gaps in the information necessary to manage the nature tourism industry'. In this final section some of the specific concerns about nature-based tourism which may be addressed by research are identified. It should be clear from this listing that there are great opportunities for researchers in a number of disciplines to make a valuable contribution to our understanding of eco-tourism. It is also clear that the jury is still out on the whole question of nature-based tourism and its role in both our economy and our ecology.

1 What are the attractive powers of nature? If a community sets up a nature-based tourism project what are the magnets and can the friction of distance be overcome?
2 What are the perceived and realized benefits for the tourist? In other words what are the components of satisfaction? How important is 'success' in nature tourism ('I saw a Crested Iguana, Spotted Cuscus, Little Penguin, Tiger, Humpback Whale, Bird of Paradise')? Evidence from hunting studies in North America suggests that actual success is less important for satisfaction than the nature of the search for the target. What are the expectations of such tourists, how are these developed and are they realistic? Understanding the role of 'rarity' in contributing to experiences and its interplay with status might help develop appropriate marketing emphases and activity programs.
3 What makes a particular destination popular for nature-based tourism and can a set of characteristics be generated which help in the selection of ecotourist locations? Is it biological diversity or some other characteristic (rarity, spectacular nature)?
4 What are the social and biological elements in developing ethical nature-tourism behaviour for a given site or species group?
5 What are the attributes of nature-based tourists and what demands do they impose on destination communities?
6 What skills are required for different roles in a community project in nature-based tourism? How can such skills be developed? Is there a role for aid programs in assisting the establishment of nature-based tourism projects and/or the provision of training needs?
7 Why do nature-based tourism projects fail and what are the main threats/problems affecting success?
8 How should nature conservation benefit from the commercial activities of nature-based tourism? Does nature-tourism protect or destroy nature? What are the limits to local, regional and national expansion of nature-based tourism?
9 What is the economic advantage/disadvantage of nature-based tourism compared with other styles of tourism? Who wins, who loses? How can the government agencies which manage the resources extract a reasonable share of the consumer surplus?
10 Are there useful regional or local 'bio-logos' which can draw attention to

special natural attributes of likely interest to tourists. For example, the Cassowary of northern Queensland's tropical rainforests, the Birds of Paradise of Papua New Guinea, and the Iguanas of Fiji. The ideal bio-logo would also be a carrier species – one of those highly attractive species which appeals to people and which saving from extinction would mean the salvation of a host of other lesser species. In order to save the cassowary from extinction we will need to conserve much tropical rainforest and by so doing will protect thousands of other organisms.

There is a clear role for research into this aspect of tourism and perhaps a need for a central repository to collate and disseminate the accumulated experience as more countries test the waters and walk the forests of nature-based tourism.

Endnote

1. The author wishes to express his gratitude to the East-West Center and particularly Dr. Larry Hamilton, for providing the opportunity to read and think about this topic during a period of sabbatical from my University in 1989 and 1990.

References

Allen, R., 1975, The year of the rainforest, *New Scientist*, 66: 178–180

Anon., 1989a, The Audubon travel ethic, *Elepaio,* 49 (12): 89

Anon., 1989b, Minimum impact code for the Annapurna Conservation area project, *Responsible Traveling*, 4 (3): 3

Australian Tourism Industry Association, 1989, *An environmental code of practice for the tourism industry, background, second draft*, Australian Tourism Industry Association, Sydney

Bateson, P., Nyman, S., Sheppard, D., eds, 1989, *National parks and tourism,* Royal Australian Institute of Parks and Recreation and New South Wales National Parks and Wildlife Service, Sydney

Berle, P.A.A., 1990, Two faces of eco-tourism, *Audubon,* 92 (2): 6

Boo, E., 1990, *Ecotourism: the potentials and pitfalls*, 2 Vols., World Wildlife Fund, Washington D.C.

Borst, B., 1990, Ecotourism: environment friendly international travel, *International Herald Tribune,* March 3–4: 9, 12–13

Brockelman, W., 1988, Nature conservation, 179–237 in A. Arkhabhirama, D. Phantumvanit, J. Elkington and P. Ingkasuwan, eds, *Thailand natural resources profile*, Oxford University Press, Singapore

Budowski, G., 1976, Tourism and conservation: conflict, coexistence or symbiosis, *Environmental Conservation,* 3 (1): 27–31

Cassells, D.S., Valentine, P.S., 1990, Recreation management issues in tropical rainforest, *Proceedings institute of tropical rainforest studies workshop no 1*, Institute of Tropical Rainforest, James Cook University, Townsville

Cole, D.N., 1989a, Recreation ecology: what we know, what geographers can contribute, *Professional Geographer,* 41 (2): 143–148

Cole, D.N., 1989b, Low-impact recreational practices for wilderness and backcountry, *USDA Forest Service General Technical Report INT – 265,* US Department of Agriculture, Forest Service, Intermountain Research Station, Ogden, Utah

Coleman, D., 1980, Conservation and tourism: harmony or conflict?, 73–79 in J.T. Griffin, ed., *Tourism and the future: coordination or chaos?,* Townsville College of Advanced Education, Townsville

Cottingham, D., Langshaw, R., 1981, *Grizzly, bear and man in Canada's mountain parks,* Summerthought, Banff

Dixit, K. M., 1989, An obsession with tourism, *Himal,* July/August: 3–12

Doak, W., 1988, *Encounters with whales and dolphins,* Hodder and Stoughton Ltd., Auckland

Duffie, J., 1981, Who will watch the birdwatchers? *Wildlife Review,* X (7): 23–24

Edington, J.M., Edington, M.A., 1986, *Ecology, recreation and tourism,* Cambridge University Press, Cambridge

Ferrario, F.F., 1982, Method approach for evaluating tourist resources: case of South Africa, 114–135 in T.V. Singh and J. Kaur, eds, *Studies in tourism and wildlife parks conservation,* Metropolitan Book Company, New Delhi

Gell, R., 1989, *Antarctica,* Houghton Mifflin, Melbourne

Gonsalves, P.S., 1987, Alternative tourism – the evolution of a concept and establishment of a network, *Tourism Recreation Research,* 12 (2): 9–12

Goudberg, N.J., Cassells, D.S., Valentine, P.S., 1991, The prospects for ecotourism in northern Queensland wet tropical rainforests, *Proceedings of the future research strategies workshop No 1,* Institute of Tropical Rainforest, James Cook University, Townsville

Graham, F., 1979, Case of the ugly birder, *Audubon,* 81 (4): 88–100

Hall, C.M., Tourism in Antarctica: activities, impacts and management, *Journal of Travel Research,* forthcoming

Healy, R.G., 1988, Economic consideration in nature-oriented tourism: the case of tropical forest tourism, *Forestry Private Enterprise Initiative Working Paper No 39,* Southeastern Center for Forest Economics, Research Triangle Park, North Carolina

Henry, W.R., 1982, Amboseli park: Kenya: problem of planning and resource management, 36–46 in T.V. Singh and J. Kaur, eds, *Studies in tourism and wildlife parks conservation,* Metropolitan Book Company, New Delhi

Ingram, C.D., Durst, P.B., 1987, Marketing nature-oriented tourism for rural development and wildlands management in developing countries: a bibliography, *USDA Forest Service general technical report SE44,* US Department of Agriculture, Forest Service, Asheville (North Carolina)

Ingram, C.D. and Durst, P.B., 1989, Nature-oriented tour operators: travel to developing countries, *Journal of Travel Research,* 27 (2): 11–15

Jonkel, C.J., Servheen, C., 1977, Bears and people: a wilderness management challenge, *Western Wildlands,* 4 (2): 21–25

Kenchington, R.A., 1989, Tourism in the Galapagos Islands: the dilemma of conservation, *Environmental Conservation,* 16 (3): 227–232

Kutay, K., 1989, The new ethic in adventure travel, *Buzzworm: The Environmental Journal,* 1 (4): 31–36

Laarman, J.G., Durst, P.B., 1987, Nature travel in the tropics, *Journal of Forestry,* 85

(5): 43–46

Laarman, J.G., Perdue, R.R., 1988, Tropical tourism as economic activity: OTS in Costa Rica, *Forestry private enterprise initiative working paper no 33*, Southeastern Center for Forest Economics, Research Triangle Park, North Carolina

Lane, B., 1990, Spreading the tourist load, *The Observer, Travelwatch*, 4 February: 4

Lindberg, K., 1991, *Policies for maximizing nature tourism's ecological and economic benefits*, World Resources Institute, Washington D.C.

Luard, N., 1985, *The wildlife parks of Africa,* World Wildlife Fund/Salem House, New Hampshire

Lucas, P.H.C., 1984, How protected areas can help meet society's evolving needs, 72–77 in J.A. McNeely, and K.R. Miller, eds, *National parks, conservation, and development*, Smithsonian Institution Press, Washington D.C.

Lusigi, W.J., 1984, Future directions for the Afrotropical realm, 137–147 in J.A. McNeely and K.R. Miller, eds, *National parks, conservation and development: the role of protected areas in sustaining society*, Smithsonian Institution Press, Washington, D.C.

Mackinnon, J., Mackinnon, C., Child, D., Thorsell, J, 1986, *Managing protected areas in the tropics,* IUCN, Gland

McNeely, J.A., Miller, K.R., Reid, W.V., Mittermeier, R.A., Werner, T.B., 1990, *Conserving the world's biological diversity,* IUCN, Gland

McNeely, J.A., Thorsell, J.W., 1987, *Guidelines for the development of terrestrial and marine national parks for tourism and travel,* IUCN, Gland

Marsh, J.S., 1987, National parks and tourism in small developing countries, 25–45 in S. Britton and W.C. Clarke, eds, *Ambiguous alternative,* University of the South Pacific Press, Fiji

Mishra, H.R., 1984, A delicate balance: tigers, rhinoceros, tourists and park management vs the needs of the local people in Royal Chitwan National Park, Nepal, 197–205 in J.A. McNeely and K.R. Miller, eds, *National parks, conservation and development: the role of protected areas in sustaining society*, Smithsonian Institution Press, Washington, D.C.

Neumann, M.S., Machlis, G.E., 1989, Landuse and threats to the parks in the neotropics, *Environmental Conservation,* 16 (1): 13–18

New, T.R., 1987, *Butterfly conservation,* Entomology Society of Victoria, Melbourne

Oddie, B., 1980, *Bill Oddie's little black bird book*, Methuen, London

O'Grady, R., ed., 1990, *The challenge of tourism*, Ecumenical Coalition on Third World Tourism, Bangkok

Ream, C.H., 1978, Human-wildlife conflicts in back country, possible solutions, 153–163 in *Recreational impacts on wildlands, conference proceedings October 27–29, Seattle, Washington, USDA Forest Service, R–6-001–1979*, US Department of Agriculture, Forest Service, Pacific Northwest Region, Seattle

Ream, C.H., 1980, Impact of back country recreationists on wildlife: an annotated bibliography, *USDA Forest Service general technical report INT–84*, US Department of Agriculture, Forest Service, Seattle

Richter, L.K., Richter, W.L., 1985, Policy choices in south Asian tourism developments, *Annals of Tourism Research,* 12: 201–217

Richter, L.K., 1987, The search for appropriate tourism, *Tourism Recreation Research,* 12 (2): 5–7

Richter, L.K., 1989, *The politics of tourism in Asia*, University of Hawaii Press, Honolulu

Shaw, W.W., 1987, The recreational benefits of wildlife to people, 208–213 in D.J. Decker, and G.R. Goff, eds, *Valuing wildlife: economic and social perspectives*, Westview Press, Boulder

Sheck, R.S., 1990, *Costa Rica: a natural destination*, John Muir Publications, Santa Fe, New Mexico

Thorsell, J.W., McNeely, J.A., 1988, Jungles, mountains and islands: how tourism can help conserve the natural heritage, in *First global conference tourism a vital force for peace*, Vancouver, Canada

Tisdell, C., 1984, *Tourism, the environment, international trade and public economics*, Asian–Australia Joint Research Project, Australian National University, Canberra

Tourism Council of the South Pacific, 1989, *Discover the South Pacific way: the 1989 South Pacific islands travel manual*, Tourism Council of the South Pacific, Suva

Tourism Council of the South Pacific, 1990, *Guidelines for the integration of tourism development and environmental protection in the South Pacific*, Tourism Council of the South Pacific, Suva

Tucker, M., 1989, *Whales and whale watching in Australia*, Australian National Parks and Wildlife Service, Canberra

Valentine, P.S., 1982, Tropical rainforest and the wilderness experience, 123–132 in V. Martin, ed., *Wilderness*, Findhorn Press, Scotland

Valentine, P.S., 1983, Conservation burning bright: progress in Indian national parks – the state of Madhya Pradesh, *Habitat Australia*, 11 (3): 8–1

Valentine, P.S., 1984, Wildlife and tourism: some ideas on potential and conflict, 29–54 in B. O'Rourke, ed., *Contemporary issues in Australian tourism*, Department of Geography, University of Sydney, Sydney

Valentine, P.S., 1986, Between the devil and the deep: parks in the water, *Park News*, 22 (1): 14–17

Valentine, P.S., 1989, How much is a park worth: economic and social benefits of nature conservation, *Proceedings fourth South Pacific conference on nature conservation and protected areas, Port Vila, Vanuatu, 4–12 September*, South Pacific Regional Environment Program, Noumea

Vardaman, J.M., 1982, Birding around the world: 1041 species in ten days, *Birding*, 14 (5): 182–191

Vickerman, S., 1988, Stimulating tourism and economic growth by featuring new wildlife recreation opportunities, 414–423 in *Transactions 53rd North American wildlife and natural resources conference*

Wace, N., 1990, Antarctica: a new tourist destination. *Applied Geography*, 10: 327–341

Webster, B., 1980, Are there too many birders? *National Wildlife*, 18 (4): 17–19

Western, D., Henry, W.R., 1979, Economics and conservation in third world national parks, *Bioscience*, 29 (7): 414–418.

Wilson, M.A., Laarman, J.G., 1987, Nature tourism and enterprise in Ecuador, *Forestry private enterprise initiative working paper no 27*, Southeastern Center for Forest Economics, Research Triangle Park, North Carolina

Young, A.M., 1986, Eco-enterprises: eco-tourism and farming of exotics in the tropics, *Ambio*, 15: 361–363

10 CASE STUDY

Fossickers and Rockhounds in Northern New South Wales[1]

John M. Jenkins

> The image of the old time fossicker–prospector is familiar to us all. His battered appearance, the gaggle of gear and the swag on his back are all automatically recognised as the mark of the searcher after nature's treasures. He has sometimes been looked down upon in the past but, with a general increase in leisure time, his pursuit has been copied by millions of enthusiasts world wide, who not only have come greatly to respect his calling, but have made it their own (Perry, 1982, p.7).

Introduction

The term fossick(ing) originated in the days of the 'Australian Gold Rush' in New South Wales and Victoria in the early 1850s. Several examples of the early use of the term fossicking have been recorded (Wilkes, 1978). In James Bonwick's (1852) *Notes of a Gold-Digger* it was observed that 'a good living may be got... by the newcomer, in a little tin-dish fossicking in deserted holes'. A fossicker was also described in 1867 by J. S. Borlase in *The Night Fossickers* when he spoke of: 'The night fossickers – miscreants who watched for the richest holes during the day, marked them, and plundered them at night'. Following this tradition, the present study defines fossicking as:

> the searching for artefacts and natural deposits such as gemstones and minerals, in or on the ground or in waterways primarily for enjoyment.

'Prospecting' and 'rockhounding' are terms also used to describe the activity of fossicking in countries such as the United States and Canada.

Fossicking is a popular special interest recreational and tourist activity in countries such as the United States of America, Australia and New Zealand. In fact, it comprises one of the world's largest single hobby groups (Perry, 1982). In Alaska gold fossicking is, for example, coupled with wilderness recreation at Paradise Valley, Bettles. The Valley contains over 6,000 mining claims and covers some 120 square miles. Activities available include viewing scenery and wildlife, hiking, cross country skiing, river float tours and, of course, fossicking. In New Zealand fossicking for gold is an important tourist attraction, especially on the

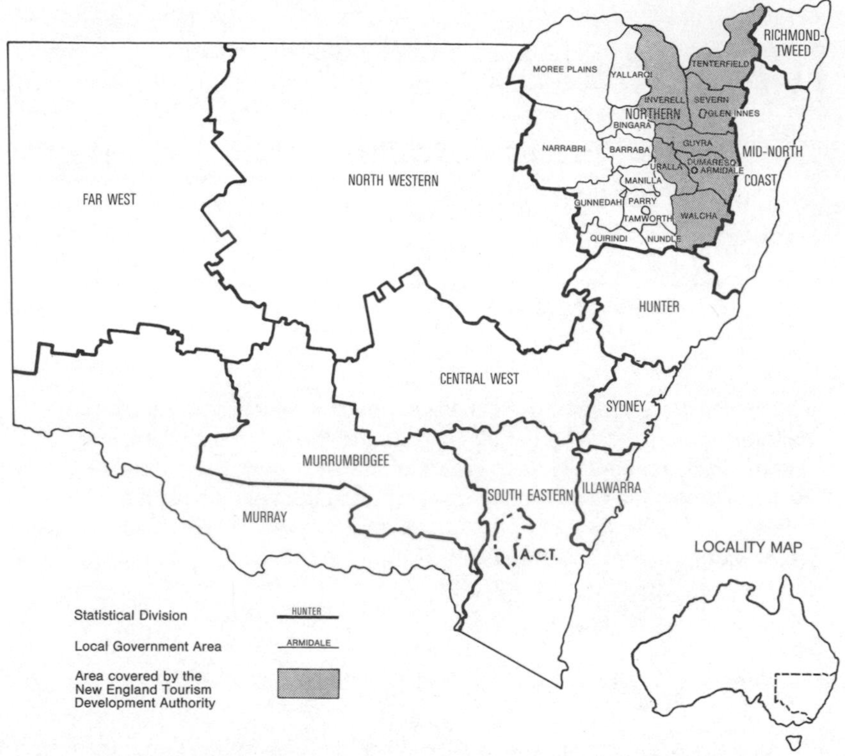

Figure 10.1 Map of New South Wales showing the area covered by the New England Tourism Development Authority

West Coast of the South Island (Heinz, 1972).

In Australia the types of gems and stones vary considerably at the national, regional and local scale to the extent that some places provide a single gem whereas others yield a range. For example, at Lightning Ridge, New South Wales, fossicking for opals is an important part of the town's economy. Despite its remoteness, tours of the opal fields have long been a popular tourist attraction. In the New England region of northeastern New South Wales (see Figure 10.1), sapphire, topaz, zircon, aquamarine, emerald, ruby, amethyst, diamond, quartz and gold are found. Given this wide range of gemstones, it is not surprising that fossicking has been promoted as a tourist attraction in the New England region for over twenty years. However, while there are many fossicking areas in the region, inadequate local knowledge, remote and inaccessible sites, and a lack of appropriate site settings, create many problems and frustrations for fossickers.

Fossicking in the New England Region of New South Wales

Recent figures indicate that the New England region is experiencing considerable tourism growth (New South Wales Tourism Commission, 1989). The region possesses a variety of cultural (Aboriginal sites and festivals), historical (nineteenth century homesteads and townsites), and natural (national parks, wild rivers and rainforest areas) features to which much of this growth is attributed by state, regional and local authorities. However, fossicking activities are also of great significance to the promotion and identity of the region.

This chapter presents a case study of fossicking in the New England region of New South Wales, Australia. It reports on interviews conducted at fossicking sites (90 respondents, 30 from each of three sites) (see Figure 10.1) and lapidary club meetings (37 respondents from the Glen Innes and Inverell lapidary clubs) during 1988. A survey was also conducted to assess visitor awareness of fossicking. Interviews were conducted at one hotel, one motel and one caravan park in each of Armidale, Glen Innes, Inverell and Uralla, and one motel and one caravan park in Guyra. Establishments in each category (hotel, motel or caravan park) were selected on the basis of, first, being close to the mean price for establishments within each establishment classification (i.e. hotel, motel or caravan park) in the respective city or town, and second, by a positive response by the manager of each establishment to participate in the survey.

Despite the importance of fossicking as a tourist attraction in the New England region, relatively little research has been directed towards the various aspects of its development and promotion. In particular, there had been no previous research on the motivations and management requirements of fossickers. This chapter therefore outlines research relevant to the future development of fossicking as a special interest recreational and tourist activity in the New England region and may also be of relevance to other destinations that use fossicking as a tourist attraction. The focus is on the predominant characteristics of fossickers in the New England region, their preferred settings and experiences. In line with this focus, potential strategies for the planning and development of fossicking in the region are presented. The results of this research have significant implications for the marketing of fossicking, and for visitor satisfaction and management of the recreational experience. While this study might appear to be a demand-based approach to improving recreational satisfaction, issues relating to the supply of fossicking opportunities are not neglected. Indeed, some of the most important factors in the supply and accessibility of fossicking areas in the New England region are the laws governing the designation, development and use of fossicking areas.

The Law Relating to Fossicking in New South Wales

The legal aspects of fossicking in New South Wales are important and need to be understood in order to provide a context for the study. Access to land to fossick is often difficult to obtain because of the extractive nature of the activity and also because there are laws as to how, when and where a person can fossick. In other words, it is an activity for which there are quite definite rules and regulations which must be followed even to the extent of purchasing licences to fossick on Crown Lands; to fossick on private lands a licence is not required (New South Wales Department of Mineral Resources and Development, 1980). There are a number of land types on which people can fossick:

- in designated fossicking reserves;
- on private land with the consent of the landholder or landowner;
- on vacant Crown Land with no need for consent; and
- on any Crown Land and land under titles (such as exploration licences) with the permission of the governing body.

Under the New South Wales Mining Act 1973, areas of Crown land and private land could be set aside as fossicking reserves by the New South Wales Department of Mineral Resources. The rules for fossicking reserves were set out in the Act and its accompanying regulations. In the Act, fossicking reserves were set aside for the exclusive use of holders of fossicking licences and no mining claims or leases could be pegged in designated fossicking reserves. However, The Mining (Amendment) Act 1980, and its accompanying regulations, made provisions for changes in fossicking laws. Fossicking areas designated in New South Wales under the Mining Act 1973 were retained in The Mining (Amendment) Act 1980, but the right to fossick was extended to include all areas of land except for certain categories specified in the Act.

Between 1976 and 1980 the New South Wales Department of Mineral Resources (NSWDMR) was very active in designating fossicking reserves. Each area proposed for designation was treated on its merits as to the availability, depth and type of minerals, and the accessibility of the site. Ultimately, the decision regarding designation rested on the opinion of the Minister for Mineral Resources. However, since 1980 the NSWDMR has given the dedication of fossicking reserves a very low priority because of cut-backs in financial and human resources. There is little likelihood that the priorities of the State Government and the NSWDMR will change in this respect. For example, the 1980 amendments to the 1973 Act were made by the Department partly in order to relinquish the responsibility of designating fossicking reserves. Indeed, it is now the duty of each fossicker to determine the status of the land on which he/she wishes to fossick and to obtain permission to enter upon that land for the purpose of fossicking. There are also questions regarding insurance and the legal liability of the Department of Mineral Resources for fossickers in designated reserves and these are likely to inhibit the expansion of such areas.

The designation of fossicking reserves relies almost solely on the attitude of the Minister for Mineral Resources and there is little likelihood that more areas will be designated. However, under the Mining Act, 1973, three avenues are available to local communities to create additional reserves. First, fossickers and interested parties can negotiate private investment and resources through well-organized and well-planned community groups. Community-based plans to develop and manage fossicking reserves could encourage the Department of Mineral Resources to devote more resources to designating fossicking areas. Local representatives and groups, such as lapidary clubs, could perform some of the initial research and documentation as they did in the early 1970s. To succeed, this approach would require considerable local community support. Secondly, interested groups can negotiate with those holding title over lands. For example, holders of Exploration Licences and private landholders could release areas of land for fossickers subject to certain requirements. Thirdly, individuals or groups can take out a mining lease and open that lease for public use. Fees can be imposed for use of the site.

Fossicking is, in short, an activity which has relied very much on public provision of opportunities. Considerable human and financial resources have been devoted to the designation of public reserves by the public sector as well as private groups and individuals, particularly in the early to mid-1970s. However, little research has been done to identify and set aside appropriate settings for fossickers. Such planning for special interest activities of course requires consideration of why people participate, particularly because different individuals and groups could have different reasons and motivations. In this regard it is important to note the phenomenon of latent participation. This is 'the unsatisfied component of demand that would be converted to participation if conditions of supply of recreation opportunities were brought to ideal levels' (Pigram, 1983, p.17). People might not be able to gain access to fossicking areas for various reasons (e.g. exclusion, inability to read maps) or they may simply not be aware of the existence of fossicking areas. Little is known about the extent of latent participation or about the extent to which ignorance impedes activity. The following section therefore examines visitor awareness of fossicking in the New England region.

Fossicking Awareness

As noted earlier, fossicking is one of several terms that can be used to describe the same activity. In the survey of accommodation establishments, 16 per cent of visitors to the New England region had not heard of the term 'fossicking', 40 per cent of visitors were not aware that they could fossick in the New England region, and 77 per cent had never fossicked in the region. Unfamiliarity with the term 'fossicking' was, excluding Inverell (100 per cent familiarity), evenly distributed throughout the sample. Inverell is the only town not located on the New England Highway and, interestingly, the only town other than Uralla (with second highest familiarity of 85 per cent), which is part of the 'Fossickers Way'. The 'Fossickers Way' is a widely advertised alternative North-South route for fossickers and other travellers (it is also the title of a widely distributed magazine for travellers). Given Inverell's more remote location for people travelling along the New England Highway, it might also be assumed that visitors would require more consideration of the town's attributes, and, therefore, perhaps a greater awareness of its fossicking potential prior to their visit. There were no significant differences in the awareness of (and participation in) fossicking according to age groups and gender.

From the survey, there appears to be a considerable element of latent demand for fossicking in the New England region, stemming from a lack of visitor awareness of fossicking as a recreational opportunity in the region. Those marketing special interest activities such as fossicking should not assume that the public understands the terminology directly associated with the activity. In the case of fossicking there are probably groups who might be more familiar with terms such as 'rockhounding' or 'prospecting'. One means of converting latent demand to effective participation might be to provide more information about fossicking to visitors.

Effective demand is of course more easily studied than latent demand. The following section identifies and evaluates aspects of the fossicking experience and the differences and similarities between lapidary club members and on-site fossickers so as to provide a picture of the nature of the current effective demand for fossicking in the New England region.

Reasons for Fossicking

Respondents were asked to indicate whether certain aspects of the fossicking experience were: very important, important, of some importance, or not important (see Table 10.1). Chi-square analysis revealed significant differences between on-site fossickers and club members. For example, peace and quiet were considered important to very important by only 44 per cent of club members compared with 91 per cent of on-site fossickers. Scenery was considered important to very important by 33 per cent of club members compared with 72 per cent of on-site fossickers. Finding gems and stones was considered important to very important by 78 per cent of lapidary club members; 47 per cent considered it very important to find gems or stones. This compares to 56 per cent of on-site fossickers who considered it as important to very important, and only 9 per cent of on-site fossickers who considered it very important to find gems and stones.

The quality of the rural landscape with regard to features such as peace and quiet and scenery are almost as essential to on-site fossickers as the activity itself (the fun of fossicking). However, for lapidary club members the features of the landscape are much less a consideration and more emphasis is given to finding gems and stones. Clearly, there appear to be at least two different types of fossickers.

Characteristics of the Fossicker

The Age Distribution of Fossickers Most fossickers are over thirty years of age. Excluding club members under 18 years of age, 92 per cent of club members are aged over 30 years and 87 per cent are over 40 years of age. For on-site fossickers (excluding those less than 18 years of age), 75 per cent were over 30 years of age and 48 per cent over 40 years of age. Lapidary club members indicated that they were having some difficulty in attracting young people to their clubs. The main reason offered as to why this difficulty existed was that ‘younger people’ were now more interested in team sports and home entertainment than they had been in the past. However, many fossickers from both groups commented that fossicking was a good way of introducing children to the outdoors and a welcome relief from home and social duties.

Gender Evaluation of the results in the survey of accommodation establishments identified gender as an important determinant of fossicking participation with women fossicking less than men. However, the results of the surveys of lapidary club members and on-site fossickers were inconclusive.

Table 10.1 Reasons for fossicking: on-site fossickers and lapidary club members

	Reasons for Fossicking: Degree of Importance			
	VI	I	SI	NI
On-site Fossickers				
To find gems or stones	9 (8)	47 (42)	33 (30)	11 (10)
Value of the gems or stones	6 (5)	8 (7)	34 (31)	52 (47)
Fun of fossicking	41 (37)	51 (46)	8 (7)	0 (0)
Peace and quiet	21 (19)	70 (63)	8 (7)	1 (1)
Scenery	12 (11)	60 (54)	22 (20)	6 (5)
Social reasons/friendship	11(10)	62 (56)	11 (10)	16 (14)
Lapidary Club Members				
To find gems or stones	47 (17)	31 (11)	19 (7)	3 (1)
Value of the gems or stones	19 (7)	6 (2)	39 (14)	36 (13)
Fun of fossicking	58 (21)	25 (9)	11 (4)	6 (2)
Peace and quiet	19 (7)	25 (9)	25 (9)	31 (11)
Scenery	14 (5)	19 (7)	31 (11)	36 (13)
Social reasons/friendship	36 (13)	31 (11)	25 (9)	8 (3)

Note : (a) numbers in brackets represent observed frequencies and numbers outside of brackets are the approximate percentage values of the observed frequencies.
(b) One response was not completed.

Key : VI: Very important;
I: Important;
SI: Some importance;
NI: Not important.

Accommodation Used by Visiting Fossickers Of the fossickers who were visitors to the New England region (59 respondents), none stayed in hotels, 32 per cent were staying in motels, 58 per cent were in caravan parks or were camping, and 8 per cent were staying with friends or relatives. No respondent indicated more than one type of accommodation. These results are markedly different from the latest figures regarding the type of accommodation used by visitors to the New England region. The New South Wales Tourism Commission (1989) estimated that 53 per cent of visitors to the New England region stayed with friends or relatives, with only approximately 7 per cent of total visitors to the region staying in a caravan park and only another 4 per cent camping outside a caravan park. These figures suggest that there is a greater use of commercial accommodation by fossickers, compared with the majority of people who visit and stay over in the New England region.

Length of Stay Fossickers who are visitors to the region frequently stay for at least one night in the region. In this case, 98 per cent spent at least one night in the region, 88 per cent spent at least two nights, 69 per cent at least three nights, 27 per cent more than five nights and 12 per cent more than eleven nights. These figures should only be regarded as an indication of the length of stay of fossickers because interviews were conducted on weekends only, and at times in the school-holiday period. Nevertheless, they are relatively favourable when compared with recent data (New South Wales Tourism Commission, 1989) which indicates that in 1987/88, approximately 74 per cent of all visitors to the region stayed at least three nights. One of the objectives of the New England Tourism Development Authority is to increase the length of stay of visitors in the New England region. One means might be to promote recreational activities such as fossicking which seems to facilitate a reasonably long length of stay by visitors.

The Origin of Visiting Fossickers On-site fossickers who reside outside the New England region came from the following areas:

- 15 (25 per cent) from the Sydney region (N.S.W.);
- 14 (24 per cent) from Queensland;
- 12 (20 per cent) from the Hunter region (N.S.W.);
- 7 (12 per cent) from the Mid-North Coast region (N.S.W);
- 4 (7 per cent) from the Richmond-Tweed region (N.S.W.);
- 4 (7 per cent) from Victoria;
- 1 (2 per cent) from each of Western Australia, South Australia, and the North-Western region of N.S.W.

In short, there is a strong concentration of fossickers from the Sydney region in New South Wales, and from Queensland. Of on-site fossickers who reside outside the New England region, 32 per cent were from the coastal regions north of Sydney. There appear to be similarities between the origins of fossickers and the origins of all visitors to the New England region.

Frequency of Activity

Chi-square analysis indicated a significant difference in the frequency with which lapidary club members and on-site fossickers (non-members) fossick; 87 per cent of lapidary club members fossicked 6–10 days or more in the twelve months preceding interview, compared with only 25 per cent of on-site fossickers.

Chi-square analysis revealed no significant difference in the frequency with which lapidary club members and on-site fossickers (non-members) fossicked outside the New England region. The analysis showed that 88 per cent of on-site fossickers and 82 per cent of lapidary club members fossicked two or fewer times a year outside of the New England Region. Of the 12 per cent of on-site fossickers who fossicked more than twice a year outside of the region, all were experienced fossickers. These figures indicate the importance of the New England region, as well as the generally high level of repeat visitation for fossickers.

Seasonal Preferences for Fossicking

The seasonal preferences of recreation participants can have widespread effects on destination areas. No doubt, the problems associated with demand peaks (such as overcrowding) and troughs (such as low revenue) are important considerations. For club members and on-site fossickers, autumn (March to May) is the most favoured fossicking season (61 per cent and 52 per cent respectively). This was followed by spring (September to November) 21 per cent and 27 per cent respectively. Some 83 per cent stated that climate determined their favourite season. The next most popular responses included the timing of school holidays (which is not within the control of the respondent) and annual leave.

Desired Facilities and Opportunities for Fossickers

In assessing the need for desirable site facilities and activities, on-site fossickers and club members were asked whether the following facilities or opportunities would attract them to fossicking sites:

(a) good road access;
(b) drinking water;
(c) a camping area;
(d) barbecue facilities; and
(e) bushwalking and hiking trails.

There were significant differences between on-site fossickers and lapidary club members with regard to the provision of drinking water, camping areas and barbecue facilities. In contrast to lapidary club members, 70 per cent of on-site fossickers (only 25 per cent of club members) said that fresh drinking water would attract them to a fossicking area; 41 per cent (only 11 per cent of club members) said that a camping area would attract them, and 47 per cent (only 17 per cent of club members) said that barbecue and picnic facilities were attractive. On-site fossickers favoured good road access slightly more than club members, and little interest was shown in bushwalking and hiking trails by either group.

Club members were found to fossick more regularly and be more likely to experience problems and conflicts in their use of the countryside for fossicking than most fossickers who were interviewed on-site. Several lapidary club members said that they do not require facilities and would not like to see them provided at their favoured fossicking areas. Many club members also considered that problems in maintaining fossicking areas (e.g. waste disposal, littering, and disruptive behaviour at camping sites) are associated with the provision of such developments.

Cross-tabulation of the observations of on-site fossickers revealed that, of the 47 per cent more experienced fossickers, 45 per cent desired good road access, 21 per cent drinking water, 14 per cent a camping area, 14 per cent barbecue facilities, and 5 per cent bushwalking/hiking trails. These results are similar to those of club members and perhaps support the relevance of the concept of recreational specialization and its implications for recreational planning. The pursuit of fossicking involves a continuum from the novice who fossicks for the fun of it and uses developed and easily accessible fossicking reserves, to the specialist fossicker who accepts and prefers the challenge of finding areas where stones are likely to be found.

These are important considerations for the planning and management of fossicking reserves. The Recreation Opportunity Spectrum (ROS) facilitates the development of recreational areas by providing for a range of opportunities. Given the variations in desirable facilities for fossickers, application of the ROS in the planning and management of fossicking areas would help create a range of sites with different attributes and qualities catering to different fossicking experiences.

Problems and Conflicts in the Fossicking Experience

Crowding was not an important problem at fossicking areas – only 6 per cent of club members and 18 per cent of on-site fossickers responded in the affirmative. However, the findings regarding on-site fossickers should be considered with caution as the majority of interviews were conducted in winter when the demand for fossicking is probably at its lowest. The low percentage of club members experiencing crowding at fossicking areas may be due to members fossicking at areas that are not well-known or publicized. Also, many club members are tolerant of the presence of fellow members, and/or avoid periods when crowding is likely (i.e. during school holidays and the vacation periods).

Access to fossicking areas was a problem for 36 per cent of club members and 40 per cent of on-site fossickers. The main reason put forward by lapidary club members was denial of access to private property and other areas of land, while on-site fossickers cited the poor quality of road access at many sites. Most lapidary club members had problems finding gems and stones and 54 per cent claimed that several public fossicking reserves 'have been fossicked out for many years'. However, club members also indicated that stones could be found at greater depths than it is feasible, and in fact legal, to dig (fossickers are only permitted to dig to a depth of two metres).

Access to Fossicking Areas in the New England Region Almost one-half of club members (47 per cent) said they had been denied access to areas where they would like to fossick in the New England region compared with only 19 per cent of on-site fossickers. Most fossickers were denied access either by private landholders (farmers), or by those holding mining leases. Access to private lands was limited because of problems of legal liability for landholders, the failure of many people to close gates, damage to fences and other property, and the disturbing of stock.

The Information Sources of Fossickers

Overall, word of mouth was the most widely acknowledged source of information for fossickers. However, there was considerable variation in the nomination of a further information source. In regard to the most important sources of information, 58 per cent of on-site fossickers noted word of mouth, 37 per cent referred to Tourist Information Centres, and 6 per cent to advertising pamphlets. Of the less experienced on-site fossickers, 60 per cent indicated that the most important source of information was a Tourist Information Centre. On the other hand, 71 per cent of club members indicated that their main source of information was word of mouth (some also noted the importance of mud-maps, which are rough but detailed diagrams of the location of private fossicking areas) and the remaining 29 per cent indicated lapidary club notes and newsletters.

The importance of word of mouth highlights the need for high levels of consumer satisfaction to increase return trips, and also to inform and motivate new consumers. The importance of tourist information centres for less experienced on-site fossickers (non-members of lapidary clubs) demonstrates the need for accurate information and its knowledgeable despatch to fossickers.

Conclusions

This case study has revealed a number of attributes of fossickers as special interest recreationists and tourists. Compared with the 'average' New England visitor, fossickers stay a relatively lengthy period of time, tend to make greater use of commercial accommodation and are more likely to return for a second or third visit. The New England Tourism Development Authority would do well to market to this segment of the population.

In the provision of fossicking areas, tourism promoters must realize that, ultimately, the final recreational experience is a function of the activity itself and the setting in which people fossick. By varying the types of settings and activity/ opportunity combinations at different fossicking areas, the manager can provide for the realization of different recreational experiences and outcomes. The ROS could be used to operationalize planning and management objectives for fossicking reserves in such a manner.

The New England Tourism Development Authority should also give serious consideration to the preparation of promotional material for fossickers. The material should describe the varieties and general characteristics of gemstones in the New England region, where to look for them and how to recover them. The dominant form of advertising is by word of mouth, but well-informed tourist information centres and well-designed brochures stressing local attractions would increase the information base and increase the likelihood of visitor satisfaction. In the preparation of such promotional material, the NETDA and other local organizations should work with the local community (e.g. local lapidary clubs and fossickers) to identify areas for development and promotion.

The recreational requirements of fossickers differ according to experience and enthusiasm, and there are people who are constrained by a lack of consideration of their needs. The frequency with which people fossick probably indicates the level of skill and degree of enthusiasm of the participant. However, several club members and on-site fossickers indicated that they would like to participate in fossicking more regularly, but are not capable of the effort necessary in their search for gems and stones. There is, in other words, a clear need for different facilities to be provided for fossickers on the basis of physical ability. Inappropriate management responses in providing information and developing facilities at fossicking areas have contributed to high levels of latent demand. Indeed, not all people need or desire facilities such as toilets, barbecues and picnic areas. The use of the Recreation Opportunity Spectrum would facilitate the development of fossicking areas with different attributes and so cater for different experiences for fossickers.

In summary, this study has highlighted the need for recognition of the needs and desired experiences of fossickers as a special interest travel segment. Fossicking provides economic and social benefits to the New England region. It also encourages appreciation of the cultural and natural environment, especially for the less experienced fossicker. The results of analysis of visitor profiles and preferences will hopefully contribute to better marketing and management of fossicking opportunities in New England and elsewhere.

Endnote

1. The author wishes to acknowledge the assistance of a New England Tourism Development Authority Scholarship in the undertaking of research into fossicking in the New England area.

References

Department of Mineral Resources and Development, 1980, *Notes on new fossicking laws*, New South Wales Government, Department of Mineral Resources and Development, Sydney

Heinz, W.F., 1972, Gemstone localities: New Zealand gold, in B. Myatt, ed., *Australian and New Zealand gemstones: how and where to find them*, Paul Hamlyn, Sydney

New South Wales Tourism Commission, 1989, *Tourism trends in New South Wales*, New South Wales Tourism Commission, Sydney

Perry, N., 1982, *Prospectors guide to gemstones in Australia*, Reed, Wellington

Pigram, J.J., 1983, *Outdoor recreation and resource management*, Croom Helm, London

Wilkes, G.A., 1978, *A dictionary of Australian colloquialisms*, Sydney University Press, Sydney

11 REVIEW

Adventure, Sport and Health Tourism

C. Michael Hall

Introduction

This chapter examines three significant segments of special interest travel: adventure, sport and health tourism. Although, at first glance, the topics may appear to bear little relation to each other, it should be noted that all three types of tourism are functionally related in terms of travel motivations and social values which emphasize improving an individual's quality of life, and which all involve relatively active participation, often in outdoor settings. In the 1980s and early 1990s, western society witnessed a marked trend amongst sections of the population toward more active, experientially oriented outdoor leisure activities (Lengfelder, 1988; Wright, 1988; Hall, 1989a). For instance, in North America in the 1970s and 1980s there was a marked increase in participation in camping, boating, water and snow skiing, and sailing, and a decrease in motorbiking and motorcycling (Halstenrud, 1980; Downing, 1985)

The growth of outdoor travel activities has sometimes been seen as part of national myth and culture:

> The magic of space is the taproot of the American character. The lure of the western horizon, the rightness of the land, and the sense of power of the wilderness were major elements in changing the Europeans who came to the United States and Canada into Americans. A reawakening of that sense of limitless potential is part of the reason for the tremendous interest in backpacking, canoeing, cycling, and other forms of self-contained travel in the past few years (Bridge, 1978, p.1).

However, despite the appeal or 'pull' of national values to individuals and promoters alike, the growth of outdoor activities is more likely to be in response to problems of urbanism and late twentieth century living than it is to the search for a new frontier. For instance, Mitchell (1983) has argued that much adventure oriented leisure is a reaction to the rationalism of everyday life in western society, particularly in the workplace. The present resurgence

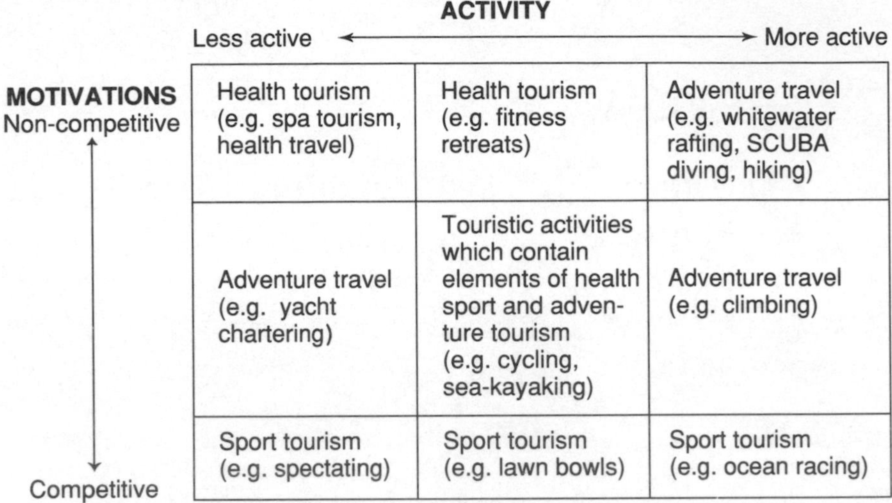

Figure 11.1 A conceptual framework of the motivations and activities of participants in adventure, health and sports tourism

of public interest in adventure, health and sport parallels the attention given to the physical, moral and spiritual 'damage' of urban living at the turn of the century in North America, Europe and Australia, and the resultant growth in national parks, sport, and physical education (Altmeyer, 1976; Nash, 1982; Hall, 1985). In the contemporary travel setting, the escape or 'push' from a mundane, alienating urban environment has been recognized as a major motivating force in tourism, while the physical activity possible in adventure or sport tourism provides the outlet for potential personal rewards (Crompton, 1979; Iso-Ahola, 1980, 1982). In addition, the desire for a healthy lifestyle, which is a significant intrinsic reward of travel, is a major component of all three categories of special interest tourism examined in this review chapter.

Figure 11.1 records the functional relationships between adventure, health and sports tourism in terms of the competitive–non-competitive motivations of participants and the active–passive nature of the activity. Each of the segments of the framework illustrate particular leisure social worlds (Devall, 1973) or recreational specializations (Bryan, 1977) which reflect sets of leisure value systems and behaviours (see Chapter 1). Therefore, while sets of sport tourists may be engaging in the same activity, such as sailing, they should be categorised as different special interest groups if one segment undertakes sailing on a competitive basis and another on a non-competitive basis (see section on sports tourism below).

The following discussion of the adventure, sports and health fields of special interest tourism examine the varying motivations and experiences of participants, and refer to some of the trends and management issues that arise in each segment. However, with the possible exception of spectator-oriented sports travel, it should be noted that the desire for an enhanced quality of life and participation in relatively active recreational pursuits in outdoor settings act as common denominators between all three areas.

Adventure Tourism

Adventure-oriented travel is a growing segment of the special interest tourism market. Since the late 1970s and early 1980s there has been a rapid growth of magazines, journals, equipment manufacturing, outfitters, retailers and commercial operators associated with adventure tourism throughout the western world, but particularly in Australasia and North America (Ewert, 1985a; McLellan, 1986; PCAD, 1987; Pybus, 1989). In addition, because adventure travel is closely associated with relatively undeveloped natural environments that lend themselves to outdoor recreation activities, adventure tourism has come to be promoted by many regions as a mechanism for broadening narrow economic bases previously dependent on agricultural products or extractive industries such as forestry and mining (Hall, 1990, 1991; Kearsley, 1990).

Adventure tourism is categorized by the deliberate seeking of risk and danger by participants in outdoor activities and is intimately related to the field of adventure recreation. Indeed, in distinguishing between adventure recreation and adventure tourism, the field of adventure tourism suffers from the same definitional difficulties as other areas of tourism. The distinguishing factor between adventure recreation and tourism is the degree to which participants have travelled from their home base and have engaged in formal, commercialized adventure-based activities. In adventure recreation activities, it is primarily the individual who creates and manages the adventure experience (Ewert, 1987), whereas as activities become commercialized, it is the tourist operator who manages and provides the adventure experience or package. However, this is not to downplay the significance of free independent travellers who may participate in adventure activities outside the domain of commercial operations. Indeed, there is some evidence to suggest that commercialized adventure activities serve as a safe introduction to certain fields of adventure travel following which the individual may act relatively independently (Hall and McArthur, forthcoming). Therefore, adventure tourism may be defined as:

> A broad spectrum of outdoor touristic activities, often commercialised and involving an interaction with the natural environment away from the participant's home range and containing elements of risk; in which the outcome is influenced by the participant, setting, and management of the touristic experience.

A wide range of tourism activities fall under the adventure tourism heading. These activities include:

backpacking (bushwalking, tramping)	bicycle-touring
cross-country skiing	fishing
hang-gliding	hot-air ballooning
hunting	mountain biking
mountaineering	orienteering
rappelling	river kayaking
rock-climbing	rogaining
sailing	SCUBA diving
sea kayaking	sky-diving
snowshoeing	spelunking
trekking	whitewater canoeing
whitewater rafting	

The varied activities which constitute adventure travel accommodate a number of different demographic segments. Demographic profiles suggest that the 'average' adventure traveller is more likely to be male, college or university educated, holding a professional position and be 25–40 years old (Mitchell, 1983; Hall and McArthur, 1991). However, it must be emphasized that the demographic profile will differ from activity to activity and from location to location, particularly in terms of the male–female participant ratio. In addition, it should be noted that the majority of studies of adventure travel, and hence, participant profiles, have been conducted in North America. Therefore, it would seem to be important to treat the generalization of North American profiles to other nations and cultures with a degree of caution.

Motivations

As Ewert (1987, p.5) observed, what distinguishes the above adventure-based activities from those more commonly associated with outdoor recreation 'is the deliberate pursuit of risk and uncertainty of outcome often referred to as adventure. While [traditional and adventure] forms of recreation involve elements of skill in specific settings, only in adventure-based recreation is there a deliberate inclusion of activities which contain threats to an individual's health or life' (also see case study by Johnston, Chapter 12). In adventure travel it is the activity which attracts the tourist, while in other forms of special interest travel, such as arts and heritage tourism, it is the setting which provides the dominant attraction. In this sense, adventure travel is primarily a non-consumptive activity which provides people with experiences rather than products, and with benefits such as reported for wilderness and Outward Bound programmes (Ewert, 1983; Kaplan, 1984). Exceptions to the generally non-consumptive nature of adventure travel are fishing, hunting, and, possibly, mountain-climbing (Vaske et al., 1982; Mitchell, 1983; Applegate and Clark, 1987).

Within adventure tourism the nature of the risk element has to be managed more directly than just the provision of an appropriate setting. From a tourism operator's perspective, injury to participants or loss of life will substantially affect business viability. Therefore, the adventure tourism experience must be carefully managed by operators to ensure that an appropriate balance is found between safety, the abilities and skills of participants, and real and perceived risk. As Anderson (1983, p.5) reported on the packaging of the adventure travel operations in Canada: 'This sense of "dangerous adventure" is achieved, in fact, with a high degree of safety. Staff are experienced; routes are carefully selected and tested in advance regularly; safety precautions are extensive. The trips present "danger in safety"'.

Motivations for participation in special interest activities can be examined at both the individual level and as broader social values. Adventure travel appears to have developed out of the broader growth of outdoor and wilderness recreation in western society during the twentieth century, but particularly during the post Second World War phase which was marked by greater leisure time, mobility, and spending power. The demand for forest oriented recreation has been well documented (Outdoor Recreation Resources Review Commission 1962a, 1962b; Erickson, 1964; Douglass, 1975), while wilderness activities have also been closely studied. However, in the case of adventure travel we are witnessing the trend towards participatory activity, rather than passive viewing (Kearsley, 1990), and the notions of recreation as constructive, rewarding and restorative are at least as important as the notion of recreation as fun (Hammitt and Cole, 1987).

In adventure travel the environmental setting is still important, but the setting only provides the backdrop for the activity. In adventure travel, by definition, the adventure experience derived from the product of the skill of the participant and the level of risk sought by engaging in a particular activity, is the focus of the activity and is one of the main outcomes desired by participants. Nevertheless, although it is only the stage upon which the adventure activity is set, the environmental setting must still be maintained as it is the resource on which the experience is dependent.

Although social group considerations may be of some importance as a motivating element in adventure travel, the primary motive for participation in adventure activities is the intrinsic psychological benefits to be gained by individuals from meeting recreational challenges. Challenge is an important motivation in outdoor recreation and is regarded as a particularly important factor in risk recreation (Iso-Ahola, 1980; Johnston, 1987; Johnston, Chapter 12). Indeed, Mitchell (1983) in his study of mountaineering noted that the dominant technocratic profile of many participants (e.g. engineering), reflected a lack of challenge and stimulation in the workplace.

The ability to meet a challenge is closely related to the concept of 'flow'. Flow is a special feeling that occurs when the abilities of the individual meet the demands of an activity or situation. Flow has seven aspects: a centring of attention; transitoriness; richer perception; forgetting oneself and being totally immersed in the requirements of the task at hand; disorientation with time and space; enjoyment; and momentary loss of anxiety and constraint (Csikszentmihalyi, 1977).

Although the experience of flow 'is not restricted to activities or situations that appear to involve a great amount of risk' and 'it can occur at any point where the individual's skills meet the demands, regardless of what those demands are' (Johnston, 1987, p.152), it may be argued that it is the desire to experience flow that provides the central motivation for individuals wanting to participate in adventure activities. For the tourism operator, the task is to match the competence of the participant with the risk associated with the activity in a manner which produces an appropriate adventure or peak adventure (flow) experience (Priest and Baillie, 1987; Carpenter and Priest, 1989).

Although attempting 'to combine a moderate level of sensation-seeking with a strategy of minimizing risk may be seen as a compromise which tourists make when participating in packaged, so called adventure tours' (Vester, 1987, p.244), the ability to control when and where stress and arousal can be experienced by participants could be vital in managing an adventure operation. Similarly, Csikszentmihalyi (1977) argued that novelty was an important facet of an individual's period of striving for optimum levels of stimulus or arousal. For instance, the timing of intense variation in whitewater rafting may well explain its significant growth, since the condensing of the adventure experience fits directly into the concept of a packaged commercial product (Hall and McArthur, 1991, forthcoming).

The presentation of different rafting obstacles and difficulties may meet participant demands for novelty in the touristic experience, which Ewert (1983, p.28) believed to be 'a major component in the growing participation in outdoor adventure activities'. Indeed, in the case of activities such as whitewater rafting, both operator and participant benefit from the manipulation of the adventure experience as the operator may anticipate the client's competence and manage the product accordingly. However, it should be noted that as adventure travellers gain more experience in their chosen activity then motivations may also shift. Ewert (1985b) in a study of mountain-climbers at Mount Rainier National Park, Washington, observed that although challenge was a consistent element in the adventure experience, motivations shifted from extrinsic reasons, such as escape, when the climber was inexperienced, 'to a more intrinsic, personally rewarding basis such as exhilaration, personal testing and being able to make decisions' (Ewert, 1985b, p.149), as experience grew. In contrast, in a study of Outward Bound participants, Ewert (1983, p.31) reported that 'adult participants came to programs such as Outward Bound not to experience any profound introspection or self-revelation, rather they chose to participate for the anticipated levels of adventure realized in a challenging outdoor environment'.

The relationship between participant expectations and the adventure experience was also examined in a study of commercial whitewater rafting in Australia by Hall and McArthur (1991, forthcoming). They noted that the majority of participants in commercial rafting were first-time rafters and that it was extremely rare for operations to have rafters who had gone on more than three commercial rafting trips. It was observed that participants were experiencing rafting as a one-off adventure activity, while those participants who wanted to continue whitewater rafting would either do so privately or join non-profit clubs, rather than use commercial operators. Indeed, the high ranking of safety over adventure expectations and motivations as factors determining participation in commercial rafting, supports the notion that packaged adventure tourism may serve as a 'safe' introduction to private adventure recreation or travel pursuits. Nevertheless, far greater research on the motivations of participants in adventure tourism packages is clearly required.

Sport Tourism

Sport tourism falls into two categories, travel to participate in sport and travel to observe sport. Therefore, sport tourism may be defined as travel for non-commercial reasons, to participate or observe sporting activities away from the home range. This section will briefly examine both aspects of sports tourism with particular attention being given to the management dimensions of sports tourism.

Sportspersons as Tourists

Travel to participate in sporting activities overlaps considerably with adventure tourism (often outdoors and involving elements of competency and risk), and health tourism (emphasis on a health and fitness lifestyle). Although there is as much dispute over the definition of 'sport' as there is of 'tourism', for the purposes of this chapter sport may be defined as, '...involving activities having formally recorded histories and traditions, stressing physical exertion through competition within limits set in explicit and formal rules governing role and position relationships' (Edwards, 1973, pp.57–58).

Sport has elements of competition, institutionalized patterns of activity, and the refinement of physical skills. Therefore, sport shares similarities with certain adventure activities, such as hang-gliding, cross-country skiing and climbing, with the degree to which formalized competition with other participants is involved probably being the distinguishing factor (Hamilton, 1979). However, despite difficulties in definition, travel to participate in sporting activities has its own distinct niche in any review of special interest travel.

Two types of tourists who travel to participate in sporting activities can be identified. First are *activity participants,* who pursue sport as a form of leisure for the development and expression of skills and knowledge, and for personal enrichment. Second are hobbyists who are competitive and who may be described as *players*. Players are amateurs whose participation in sporting activities is continual and systematic, and whose 'aim is to acquire and maintain the knowledge and skills enabling the individual to experience uncommon rewards from the endeavour' (Stebbins, 1982, p.262).

The differentiation between activity participants and players is well illustrated in the development of yachting as a sporting and travel activity (see Chapter 14). From being the domain of the rich in the nineteenth and early twentieth century, yachting achieved recognition as a family recreational activity in the mid-1950s with the development of one-design sailboats and family cruisers (Linskey, 1986). Aversa (1986, p.53) reported that those sailors who entered yachting through sailing schools and older, established, upper-class yacht clubs tend to perceive sailing as 'a "product-oriented" activity concerned with winning sailboat races, rather than a "process-oriented" activity which highlights the aesthetic experience of moving through the water noiselessly by the force of wind and current'. In contrast, those sailors who enter yachting through interest created by the commercial marketing activities of boat dealers, commercial marinas, and less-prestigious yacht clubs tend to perceive yachting as a recreational activity rather than as a form of competitive sport.

The implications of these observations for the marketing of sail travel are substantial. From the perspective of activities such as yacht chartering discussed by Richins in Chapter 14, yachting or cruising is a relatively *passive* or less active and non-competitive activity providing personal enrichment although it may well have a high status level attached to it (see Figure 11.1). However, for a great many travellers to sailing schools, yachting is a competitive activity and 'an *active* sport, one which requires many of the requisites needed to participate in other "main-line" competitive sports. Indeed, the same physical and psychological attributes cultivated by athletes involved in competitive sports – strength, agility, endurance, and most importantly, a competitive spirit – are also recommended to student sailors by their instructors' (Aversa, 1986, p.53).

Skiing has probably been one of the most prominent of sports associated with tourism development and a substantial set of literature on ski-field development exists (Barbier, 1978; Pearce, 1989). While skiing has had high prominence in the tourism market, particularly in such locations as The Rocky Mountains of North America, the European Alps, and the New Zealand alpine resorts, ski resorts have increasingly had to diversify their activities in order to cater for a broad range of consumer interests and to operate as year round destinations. One mechanism to counter the seasonal nature of skiing has been the establishment of sports vacation resorts such as that operated by *Sports Illustrated* in Colorado, which caters to a wider range of sports than just ski activities. Alternatively, relatively non-seasonal sports, such as tennis, may be able to offer a sport resort experience all year round, in which the consumer arrives to receive coaching, and general advice on training and lifestyle with a high standard of service and accommodation. For instance, tennis ranches or resorts are already well-established destinations in California, Florida, Spain, and

Australia. Indeed, training camps for various sport activities are a significant attraction to people who wish to improve their skill and fitness levels.

Golfing is also a major sports tourism activity both as a direct form of special interest travel and as an adjunct to other forms of travel. The vast majority of golf courses in Spain have been constructed to meet the demands of the North American and north European holiday market and are able to take advantage of year-round mild weather in order to attract clients during the northern winter. The cost and social status of golfing in Japan has also led to the redevelopment of golf courses in Australia and New Zealand specifically for the Japanese market and golf has featured heavily in promotion campaigns in Japan. For instance, in 1991 Australian airline QANTAS was offering specific packages for Japanese golfers in Australia which enabled them to play on a number of courses in different cities.

Sports tourism activities may also be designed around more individual, athletic pursuits. For instance, there is a Boston travel agency which deals exclusively in organizing tailor-made vacations to marathons around the world. As Toohet (1988, p.22) commented 'As the market continues to expand, the travel consumer can look for continued specialization of this sort, as travel agencies and tour-packagers discover the tastes and preferences of increasingly narrower segments of the population'.

'Going to the ball game': Sports Events as Tourist Attractions

Whereas travel to participate in sport may be regarded as 'serious leisure', travel to watch sporting events may be characterized as unserious or casual leisure (Stebbins, 1982). Nevertheless, the economic significance of spectating for the tourism industry is substantial. Sports events, from the Olympics to little league games, may have a major impact on regional economies, and on the prestige and image of destinations. For instance, Scottsdale, Arizona, the winter home of the San Francisco Giants, receives substantial economic spin-offs from Giants' games. Total expenditures in Scottsdale of fans who attended Giants home games in 1988 was estimated at US$7,137,499. The home attendance figure of 61,971 was generated by an estimated 29,662 spectators, with nearly 21,950 of these fans being out of state tourists. 'Scottsdale-resident fans spent US$3,283,793 in the city. The other 18,220 tourists spent an estimated US$22,582,898 while in Arizona, of which US$3,226,128 went directly into the Scottsdale economy. Cactus League game-related expenditures in Scottsdale totalled US$627,588 (Diffendererfer, 1989, pp.61–62). At the other end of the scale, sporting events such as the America's Cup, World Cup soccer, and major athletic events such as the Olympics have economic impacts measured in the hundreds of millions (Burns, Hatch and Mules, 1986; Hall, 1989b) and may also contribute significantly to positive resident attitudes towards tourism, sport and sporting events. For instance, in a post-event study of the 1988 Calgary Olympic Winter Games, Ritchie and Lyons (1990, p.23) reported that the 'visitation levels have jumped dramatically for the pleasure travel market and efforts to attract high profile conventions have already met with success'.

The high profile attached to many one-off (i.e. an Olympics) or regular (i.e. a major league club) sporting events, has led to many governments and municipalities subsidizing the construction and operation of stadia, arenas and associated sporting infrastructure (Lipsitz, 1984). For instance, in an attempt to improve the tourist profile of Beijing, the Chinese Government injected over US$500 million into the hosting of the 11th Asian Games held in September, 1990 (Knipp, 1990). Okner (1974, pp.327–328) has noted several reasons why government involves itself in sports in this way:

- prestige and 'big-town' image;
- may lead to generation of new industry through relocation and establishment, and may add to the marketing power of locations;
- the possible generation of additional employment, consumer sales, and tax collection which result from sporting events;
- additional recreational opportunities for community residents, especially if attendance at sporting events replaces other activities which are socially disruptive;
- beneficial effects on the morale of the citizens resulting from the presence of a successful sports team in the city; and
- encouragement of interest in sports among young.

The construction of stadia and sports facilities to promote tourism and assist in urban redevelopment is not new. The 1932 Summer Olympics and the associated construction of the coliseum in Los Angeles were designed to promote tourism (Reiss, 1981), while American college football games such as the Orange Bowl (Miami) Sugar Bowl (New Orleans) and the Cotton Bowl (Dallas) were established to help revive ailing cities during the great depression (Reiss, 1989, 144–145). Similarly, racing was legalized in the United States (Michigan, Ohio, California, Texas, Florida) to help establish tourism (Reiss, 1989, p.188).

In the 1990s sports tourism has reached new heights in the development of large-scale stadiums not only for sporting clubs but also for major, one off events. Sporting events which create favourable impressions are believed to encourage follow-up visitation by spectators in which the spectator will return to sample the non-sporting delights of a city. For instance, 47 per cent of a sample of visitors to the Calgary Olympic Games reported that they would visit the city again within the next two years (Kolsun, 1988). However, the growth of sport tourism through visitation to sporting events is also influencing the nature of professional sport. Vanderzwang (1988) noted that the growth of golf as an industry has led to the concept of stadium golf whereby courses are designed as much for the spectators as the players on the US PGA circuit.

Sports tourism has evolved to occupy a significant niche within the special interest travel market. Both as participants and as observers sports tourists may contribute substantially to the economic impacts of tourism at specific locations and at certain times of the year. The continued growth of mega-events will see sports tourism become increasingly important as a justification for urban development, while certain sports markets such as golf and tennis may well witness the development of increasingly specialized resort destinations.

Health Tourism

Health and tourism share a number of relationships. The taking of waters at mineral spas and hot springs has occurred since Roman times and the 'taking to the waters' of the élites of seventeenth century Europe provided one of the foundations for the modern pleasure resort concept (Lowenthal, 1962). In addition, the use of travel to improve an individual's health, for instance through cruising or a change in climate, has long been a motive for travel (Mathieson and Wall, 1982; Wright, 1988). However, in an increasingly health and fitness conscious western society, health tourism has developed as a small, yet extremely significant special-interest market segment in some countries, such as Austria (Ender, 1989), France (Guignand, 1989; Mesplier-Pinet, 1990), Germany (Carone, 1989; Godau, 1989), Hungary, Israel (Bar-On, 1989; Niv, 1989), Italy (Becheri, 1989) and Switzerland (Lanquar, 1989).

Health tourism has been defined by IOUTO (1973, p.7) as 'the provision of health facilities utilizing the natural resources of the country, in particular mineral water and climate'. Van Sliepen (in Goeldner, 1989, p.7) defined health tourism as '(1) staying away from home, (2) health [as the] most important motive, and (3) done in a leisure setting'. A narrower definition is provided by Goodrich and Goodrich (1987, p.217) who defined health-care tourism as 'the attempt on the part of a tourist facility (e.g. hotel) or destination (e.g. Baden, Switzerland) to attract tourists by deliberately promoting its health care services and facilities, in addition to its regular tourist amenities'. Five components of the health tourism market can be recognized, each identifying a more specific market segment (after Van Sliepen in Goeldner, 1989, p.7):

1. Sun and fun activities;
2. Engaging in healthy activities, but health is not the central motive (adventure and sports tourism activities such as hiking, cycling, or golf);
3. Principle motive for travel is health (e.g. a sea cruise or travel to a different climate);
4. Travel for sauna, massage, and other health activities (spa resort).
5. Medical treatment.

For the purposes of this review, segments 3 to 5 will be regarded as constituting the specialty travel market as it is in these categories that health is the primary motive for travel.

From Spa Tourism to Health Tourism

Balneotherapy and spa tourism has long been an important component of European travel motivations (Witt and Witt, 1989). Mesplier-Pinet (1990) reported that 1 per cent of the population of France, 2 per cent of the population of Italy, 2.5 per cent of the population of West Germany, and 3 per cent of the population of Poland engaged regularly in visits to traditional thermal resorts. The costs of many domestic visitors to European spas is borne by the state as a component of national health delivery (Bar-On, 1989; Mesplier-Pinet, 1990). For instance, in Italy approximately 85 per cent of domestic thermal spring tourists are government financed. However, in 1987 so many employees were exploiting their ability to take time off work to have thermal spring treatment, that the Italian high court acted to contain health service expenditure, labour costs, and reduce the abuse of government sponsorship of thermalists (Becheri, 1989).

Government involvement in spa tourism is not confined to Europe. According to Niv (1989, p.30), Israel is endowed with four basic characteristics which can transform it into a leading centre for health tourism:

1. Good natural resources
2. Stable, comfortable climate all year round
3. One of the world's most progressive medical systems
4. Attractive scenic locations which have a calming effect on patients.

Israel has established health resorts in the Dead Sea, Tiberius and Kinneret regions. The Tiberius hot springs have been used as a spa area since Roman times. Indeed, Israel in recognizing the 'promotion of health tourism as an issue of national importance' has passed a special law regulating health tourism and has established a Health Spa Authority (Niv, 1989, p.32). 'The law regulates all aspects of developing and promoting health tourism, and guarantees priority for the advancement and marketing of sites endowed with the necessary features. The law emphasizes that in regions clearly suited to health tourism, only projects directly or indirectly related to this sphere will be approved for development' (Niv, 1989, p.32). Israel has developed a network of vacation balneological centres for the treatment of non-contagious diseases which do not impose limitations on daily living, such as dermatological ailments, particularly psoriasis, and rheumatic conditions. The Health Spa Authority has a variety of tasks including health spa development, classification of land and services, research, encouragement of visitation, publicity, 'to initiate and encourage the search for therapeutic springs', and 'to encourage, plan and promote the production and sale of mineral water and similar products' (Niv, 1989, p.32).

The traditional notion of spa tourism has changed substantially in the 1980s with the rapid expansion of what Becheri (1989, p.17) described as 'thermal spring tourism of well being', which broadens the traditional image of health tourism to include massage centres, health clubs and centres, fitness, marine therapies, diet therapies and physiotherapies, beauty treatments, detoxicating treatments, sports and exercise, steam bath, hydrotherapies, health education, and relaxation techniques. Health tourists may also combine health motivations with other interests. For instance, at the Hamat Gader site in northern Israel, 'vacationers combine a visit to this ancient archeological site with independent bathing in the thermal pool' (Niv, 1989, p.31).

In the United States, the traditional spa concept has been modified to take account of the broader interest in health and fitness. America's fitness spas constitute a service industry that is presently riding the crest of the recent strong interest in physical conditioning (Blair, 1984; Robey, 1985; Rea, 1987). Spa participants are younger persons who are concerned about their appearance, confident in their own state of conditioning, and active in a number of both active and passive pursuits (Olsen and Granzin, 1989). Similarly, Becheri (1989) argued that the broader concept of health tourism, including the pursuit of a healthy lifestyle in the general population, could provide a basis for the relaunch of traditional thermal spring tourism in Italy. Nevertheless, he also noted that the health tourism market is made up of different groups:

> The average customer of health clinics could be thought of as an independent, self-employed professional or a high level manager, 35, 40, 50 years of age, who has achieved economic success in life and who, now, turns his thoughts to the restoration of the body.
>
> The thermal spring patient is on average older, with very little or no motivation and with a considerably lower income. On the plus side, he shows a certain habit towards the treatments which he repeats every year (Becheri, 1989, p.17).

The evidence from Europe and North America suggests that the health tourism market is developing into two distinct yet related segments: the health resort in which the emphasis is on improving overall health and fitness, and the spa resort which is specifically targeted at providing medical services to clients suffering from disease. However, it should be noted that these segments will have considerable overlap and their respective popularities will depend as much upon medical and social trends as it will upon successful advertising and promotions. Nevertheless, the diversification and redevelopment of traditional spa resorts in Europe and North America would appear to indicate that health tourism will remain a small yet significant component of specialty travel for many years to come.

Conclusions

The three special interest segments examined in this chapter exhibit significant commonalities in terms of emphasis on quality of life issues and, to a lesser extent, dependence on outdoor activities as expressions of specialized leisure preferences. However, while quality of life may be a dominant factor in adventure, sports and health tourism, there may be several changes in activity preference which occur with age and education, and which may offer a guide to public and private sector abilities to cater to the special interest market.

According to Mercer (1981, p.26), 'age is the single most important variable influencing participation in outdoor pursuits'. Given the significance of age for the nature of travel activities it may be hypothesized that the special interest tourism groups examined in this chapter will demonstrate a trend to participate in active adventure and sport tourism in youth and early adult stage, and health travel as they get older. Quality of life is still a dominant motivation but the manner in which it is expressed changes according to the age of the participant. Unfortunately, there is a lack of longitudinal data to fully support the hypothesis. However, some evidence for changing patterns of specialization in outdoor activities may be found in the work of Hendee, Gale and Catton (1971) who observed that there was 'an apparent tendency for well educated individuals to gradually transfer their allegiance from active 'appreciative-symbolic' activities such as bushwalking and mountain climbing in their youth' (Mercer, 1981, p.27), to more sedate activities in later life. Nevertheless, substantial research still needs to be conducted on the pattern of involvement that an individual will have in specialized travel activities over time and the degree to which activity displacement occurs given various functions of age and education.

Research on special interest tourism is still in its infancy. Nevertheless, the present chapter and the case studies of yacht chartering and mountain risk recreation which follow, highlight the rich mosaic of activities which comprise adventure, health and sport tourism. The challenge for the researcher and for the operator is to discover the patterns that lie behind specialty travel activities in order to predict future trends and appropriate management responses.

References

Altmeyer, G., 1976, Three ideas of nature in Canada, 1893–1914, *Journal of Canadian Studies*, 11 (3): 21–36

Anderson, D.N., 1983, Packaging of outdoor/wilderness experience: does it hold implications for national parks, *Park News*, 19 (1): 5–7

Applegate, J.E., Clark, K.E., 1987, Satisfaction levels of birdwatchers: An observation on the consumptive–nonconsumptive continuum, *Leisure Sciences*, 9: 129–134

Aversa, A., Jnr., 1986, Notes on the entry routes into a sport/recreational role: the case of sailing, *Journal of Sport and Social Issues*, 10 (2): 49–59

Barbier, B., 1978, Ski et stations de sports d'hiver dans le monde, 130–146 in K.A. Sinnhuber and F. Jülg, ed., *Studies in the geography of tourism and recreation*, Wiener Geographische Schriften 51/52, Verlag Ferdinand Hirt, Wien

Bar-On, R., 1989, Cost-benefit considerations for spa treatments, illustrated by the

Dead Sea and Arad, Israel, *Revue de Tourisme*, 44 (4): 12–15

Becheri, E., 1989, From thermalism to health tourism, *Revue de Tourisme*, 44 (4): 15–19

Blair, S., 1984, Sports permeates all lifestyles – it may be our lifestyle, *The Journal of Physical Education and Program*, 81 (April): 12

Bridge, R., 1978, *High peaks & clear roads a safe and easy guide to outdoor skills*, Prentice Hall, Englewood Cliffs

Brown, I., 1989, Managing for adventure recreations, *Australian Parks and Recreation*, 25 (Summer): 37–39

Bryan, H., 1977, Leisure value systems and recreational specialisation: the case of trout fishermen, *Journal of Leisure Research*, 9: 174–187

Burns, J.P.A., Hatch, J.H., Mules, F.J., ed., 1986, *The Adelaide Grand Prix: the impact of a special event*, The Centre for South Australian Economic Studies, Adelaide

Carone, G., 1989, Pour un thermalisme différent – considérations sur le cas de l'Italie, *Revue de Tourisme*, 44 (3): 23–26

Carpenter, G., Priest, S., 1989, The adventure experience paradigm and non-outdoor leisure pursuits, *Leisure Studies*, 8: 65–75

Crompton, J.L., 1979, Motivations for pleasure vacation, *Annals of Tourism Research*, 6: 408–424

Csikszentmihalyi, M., 1977, *Beyond boredom and anxiety*, Jossey-Bass Publishers, San Francisco.

Devall, B., 1973, The development of leisure social worlds, *Humboldt Journal of Social Relations*, 1 (Fall): 53–59

Diffendererfer, P., 1989, The economic expenditure of fans attending cactus league games in Scottsdale, Arizona, *Visions in Leisure and Business: An International Journal of Personal Services, Programming and Administration*, 8 (3): 61–75

Douglass, R.W., 1975, *Forest recreation*, Pergamon Press, New York

Downing, K.B., 1985, Visitor demands and services: the western United States experience, 177–183 in P.J. Dooling, ed., *Parks in British Columbia, symposium on parks in British Columbia February 17–19, 1984, University of British Columbia, Vancouver*, Parks, Recreation and Tourism Program, Department of Forest Resources Management, Faculty of Forestry, University of British Columbia,Vancouver

Edwards, H., 1973, *Sociology of sport*, Dorsey, Homewood

Ender, W., 1989, Diversifikation des kurörtlichen Angebots, Möglichkeiten und Grenzen, *Revue de Tourisme*, 44 (3): 16–22

Erickson, R.B., 1964, Urbanization and the shooter, *The American Rifleman*, 112 (12): 26

Ewert, A., 1983, Perceived importance of outdoor adventure activities, *Recreation Research Review*, 10 (2): 28–34

Ewert, A., 1985a, Risk recreation: trends and issues, *Trends*, 22 (3): 4–9

Ewert, A., 1985b, Why people climb: the relationship of participant motives and experience level to mountaineering, *Journal of Leisure Research*, 17: 241–250

Ewert, A., 1987, Recreation in the outdoor setting: a focus on adventure-based recreational experiences, *Leisure Information Quarterly*, 14 (1): 5–7

Godau, A., 1989, Das kur- und bäderwesen der DDR – bestandteil des tourismus und des sozialistischen Gesundheitsschutzes, *Revue de Tourisme*, 44 (4): 20–22

Goeldner, C., 1989, 39th Congress AIEST: English workshop summary, *Revue de*

Tourisme, 44 (4): 6–7

Goodrich, J.N., Goodrich, G.E., 1987, Health-care tourism – an exploratory study, *Tourism Management*, 8: 217–222

Guignand, A., 1989, Thermalisme et remise en forme dans les villages de vacances familiaux, *Revue de Tourisme*, 44 (4): 23–25

Hall, C.M., 1985, Outdoor recreation and national identity: a comparative analysis of Australia and Canada, *Journal of Canadian Culture*, 2 (2): 25–39

Hall, C.M., 1989a, Special interest travel: a prime force in the expansion of tourism?, 81–89 in R. Welch, ed., *Geography in action*, New Zealand Geographical Society Conference Series No.15, Department of Geography, University of Otago, Dunedin

Hall, C.M., 1989b, The definition and analysis of hallmark events, *Geojournal*, 19: 263–268

Hall, C.M., 1990, From cottage to condominium: recreation, tourism and regional development in northern New South Wales, 73–99 in D.J. Walmsley, ed., *Change and adjustment in northern New South Wales*, Department of Geography and Planning, University of New England, Armidale

Hall, C.M., 1990, *Introduction to tourism in Australia: impacts, planning and development*, Longman Cheshire, South Melbourne.

Hall, C.M., McArthur, S., 1991, Commercial whitewater rafting in Australia: history and development, *Leisure Options: Australian Journal of Leisure and Recreation*, 1 (2): 25–30

Hall, C.M., McArthur, S., forthcoming, Commercial whitewater rafting in Australia, in D. Mercer, ed., *New perspectives on Australian leisure and recreation*

Halstenrud, R.J., 1980, Trends in participation sports during the decade of the 70's, 195–202 in *Proceedings 1980 national outdoor recreation trends symposium*, vol.II, General technical report NE–57, USDA Forest Service, Northeastern Forest Experiment Station, Broomall

Hamilton, L.C., 1979, Modern American rock climbing, *Pacific Sociological Review*, 22: 285–308

Hammitt, W.R., Cole, D., 1987, *Wildland recreation ecology and management*, John Wiley and Sons, New York

Hendee, J.C., Gale, R.P., Catton, W.R., Jr., 1971, A typology of outdoor recreation activity preferences, *Journal of Environmental Education*, 3: 28–34

Iso-Ahola, S.E., 1980, *The social psychology of leisure and recreation*, William C. Brown, Dubuque

Iso-Ahola, S.E., 1982, Toward a social psychology theory of tourism motivation: a rejoinder, *Annals of Tourism Research*, 9: 256–261

IUOTO, 1973, *Health tourism*, United Nations, Geneva

Johnston, M., 1987, Risk in mountain recreation: challenge or danger?, 148–153 in R. Le Heron, M. Roche and M. Shepherd, eds, *Geography and society in a global context*, New Zealand Geographical Society Conference Series No.14, Massey University, Palmerston North

Kaplan, R., 1984, Wilderness perception and psychological benefits: an analysis of a continuing program, *Leisure Sciences*, 6: 271–290

Kearsley, G.W., 1990,Tourism development and users' perceptions of wilderness in southern New Zealand, *Australian Geographer*, 21 (2): 127–140

Knipp, S., 1990, A long hard march ahead, *PATA Travel News*, October: 22–23

Kolsun, J., 1988, The Calgary Olympic visitor study, *The Operational Geographer*, 16 (September): 15–17

Lanquar, R., 1989, La filière du tourisme de santé, *Revue de Tourisme*, 44 (4): 25–30

Lengfelder, J., 1988, Hi tech rec: are we losing the real pleasures of life, *Visions in Leisure and Business: An International Journal of Personal Services, Programming and Administration*, 7 (2): 50–60

Linskey, T., 1986, One-design sailing: what it is and could be, *Sail*, 17 (6): 62–65

Lipsitz, G., 1984, Sports stadia and urban development: a tale of three cities, *Journal of Sport and Social Issues*, 8 (2): 1–18

Lowenthal, D., 1962, Tourists and thermalists, *Geographical Review*, 52 (1): 124–127

Mathieson, A., Wall, G., 1982, *Tourism economic, physical and social impacts*, Longman Scientific and Technical, Harlow

McLellan, G., 1986, The future of outdoor recreation: what the trends tell us, *Parks and Recreation*, 21 (5): 44–48, 63

Mercer, D., 1981, Trends in recreation participation, 24–44 in D. Mercer, ed., *Outdoor recreation: Australian perspectives*, Sorrett Publishing, Malvern

Mesplier-Pinet, J., 1990, Thermalisme et curistes: les contraintes, *Revue de Tourisme*, 45 (2): 10–17

Mitchell, R.G., 1983, *Mountain experience: the psychology and sociology of adventure*, The University of Chicago Press, Chicago

Nash, R., 1982, *Wilderness and the American mind*, 2nd. ed., Yale University Press, New Haven

Niv, A., 1989, Health tourism in Israel: a developing industry, *Revue de Tourisme*, 44 (1): 30–32

Okner, B.A., 1974, Subsidies of stadiums and arenas, 325–348 in R.G. Noll, ed., *Government and the sports business*, The Brookings Institution, Washington D.C.

Olsen, J.A., Granzin, K.L., 1989, Life style segmentation in a service industry: the case of fitness spas, *Visions in Leisure and Business: An International Journal of Personal Services, Programming and Administration*, 8 (3): 4–20

Outdoor Recreation Resources Review Commission 1962a, *Outdoor recreation for America, ORRRC report to Congress*, Government Printing Office, Washington, D.C.

Outdoor Recreation Resources Review Commission 1962b, *Projection to the years 1976 and 2000: economic growth, population, labor force and leisure, and transportation*, ORRRC Study Report No.13, Government Printing Office, Washington, D.C.

Pearce, D., 1989, *Tourism development*, 2nd. ed., Longman Scientific and Technical, Harlow

President's Commission on Americans Outdoors (PCAD), 1987, *Americans and the outdoors*, US Government Printing Office, Washington D.C.

Priest, S., Baillie, R., 1987, Justifying the risk to others: the real razors edge, *Journal of Experimental Education*, 10: 6–22

Pybus, V., 1989, *Adventure holidays*, 12th ed., Vacation Work, Oxford

Rea, P.S., 1987, Using recreation to promote fitness, *Parks and Recreation*, 22 (July): 32–36

Reiss, S.A., 1981, Power without authority: Los Angeles' elites and the construction of the coliseum, *Journal of Sport History*, 8: 50–65

Reiss, S.A., 1989, *City games the evolution of American urban society and the rise of sports*, University of Illinois Press, Urbana

Ritchie, J.R.B., Lyons, M.M., 1990, Olympulse VI: a post-event assessment of resident reaction to the XV Olympic Winter Games, *Journal of Travel Research*, 28 (3): 14–23

Robey, B., 1985, Life on a treadmill, *American Demographics*, 7: 4–5

Stebbins, R.A., 1982, Serious leisure a conceptual statement, *Pacific Sociological Review*, 25 (2): 251–272

Toohet, W.D., 1988, The future of travel, *Employee Services Management Journal of Employee Recreation Health and Education*, 31 (50): 20–24

Vanderzwang, H.J., 1988, *Policy development in sport management*, Benchmark Press, Indianapolis

Vaske, J.J., Donnelly, M.P., Heberlein, T.A., Shelby, B., 1982, Differences in reported satisfaction ratings by consumptive and non-consumptive recreationists, *Journal of Leisure Research*, 11: 195–206

Vester, H-G., 1987, Adventure as a form of leisure, *Leisure Studies*, 6: 237–251

Witt, C., Witt, S.F., 1989, Does health tourism exist in the UK?, *Revue de Tourisme*, 44 (3): 26–30

Wright, C., 1988, *The global guide to health holidays*, Christopher Helm, London

12 CASE STUDY

Facing the Challenges: Adventure in the Mountains of New Zealand

Margaret E. Johnston

Introduction

Adventure tourism is a thriving activity in many parts of the world. In New Zealand, the 1980s was a key decade for the growth and promotion of the commercial provision of adventure tourism opportunities for not only international visitors but also domestic participants (see Jebson, 1983; Kearsley, 1985; Dale, 1987). This expansion encompassed activities as diverse as white-water rafting, heli-skiing, mountain climbing and bungy-jumping. Recognition of the popularity of adventure tourism in the country was given in the New Zealand Post Office's special issue of six commemorative stamps in 1987 which depicted jetboating, flightseeing, camper-van travel, windsurfing, climbing and rafting.

Much of this type of tourism takes place in mountain environments. This reflects the country's extensive endowment of mountain landscapes (see Smith, Davison and Geden, 1980) which, through features such as height, slope, snow, valleys and fast flowing rivers, provide tremendous recreation resources. This use of the mountains for adventure recreation is not a new phenomenon in New Zealand. There is a long history of individual, club and more recently, public agency organization of adventurous activities. 'Facing the challenges of their wild and very beautiful country has always been a part of the New Zealanders' self-image' (Kearsley, 1985, p.133). For over one hundred years both domestic and international visitors have pursued the types of adventure recreation that are possible only in mountain environments.

Travel to the mountains for the specific purpose of pursuing adventurous recreation can be considered adventure tourism. Many mountain tourists might be seeking experiences additional to adventure recreation, particularly if their journey is an extended one or if they are international visitors. Indeed, focussed travel to mountain areas or national parks can be in itself a special interest. However, insofar as travellers make a specific focus of their trip travel to the mountains to participate in adventure they can be considered as tourists pursuing adventure as a special interest.

The focus of this chapter lies not in touristic phenomena such as travel patterns or amenity development, but rather with the recreation experience itself that motivates, and is the result of, this travel. This chapter explores adventure recreation as it is carried out in the mountains of New Zealand. It discusses the views of recreationists regarding the place of risk in their recreation in order to gain an understanding of adventure as a motivating force in special interest tourism. First, however, it is necessary to clarify the nature of the activities under consideration.

Adventure Recreation in the Mountains

'For both domestic and international markets the major *raison d'être* of New Zealand as a tourist destination is its landscape' (Shultis, 1989, p.329). Two themes which feature strongly in tourism promotional material are mountain landscapes and outdoor recreation (Dilley, 1986; Shultis, 1989). The mountain environment is itself a destination for many tourists, only a small proportion of whom are pursuing adventure activities (Johnston, 1989a). The popularity of mountain landscapes particularly for passive pursuits relates not only to the physical resource itself, but also to the access and publicity accorded to the national park or protected area status which covers much of the mountain lands. Pearce and Booth (1987) outlined the activities undertaken by park users, revealing that for both domestic and international visitors passive and semi-active pursuits such as sightseeing, flight-seeing, picnicking and walking are popular. 'Certain active pursuits tend to have a very high profile but involve comparatively few users compared to the total number of visitors to the parks concerned' (Pearce and Booth, 1987, p.69). This is particularly evident for the traditional adventure activities like climbing.

Surveys of recreation participation over the past 20 years suggest that about 10 per cent of the New Zealand population regularly participates in the active mountain land recreations of tramping, climbing, hunting and downhill skiing (see Jorgenson, 1974; Aukerman and Davison, 1980; New Zealand Council for Recreation and Sport, 1985). These four, along with day walking, are the traditional mountain recreation activities in New Zealand.

Although a few adventurous tourists did climb mountains prior to the 1880s, most travel in the mountains was undertaken in search of natural resources or in aid of exploration and surveying. However, in the 1880s, recreation in the hills and mountains began to grow. Mountain climbing as a distinctive form of recreational endeavour began in 1882 when an Irishman and two Swiss came to within 60 metres of the summit of Mt Cook, New Zealand's highest mountain. The 1880s also saw the official advent of recreational hunting and the increased popularity of day walks in the local bush and hills, aided by the development of huts and tracks. Both trophy hunting and mountain climbing attracted international visitors in these early days, most of whom pursued these activities in the company of professional guides.

The sport of downhill skiing appeared briefly at Mt Ruapehu in 1913 (reaper blades had been used as makeshift skis at Mt Cook in 1890), and reappeared in several locations around 1930. Tramping (known in North America as backpacking) began to develop after World War I. These traditional activities have surged in popularity at various times, particularly tramping and downhill skiing. In the 1930s climbing and tramping increased dramatically through a large influx of university students and others who did not hire professional guides. Following World War II, all mountain recreation increased as New Zealanders sought adventure and freedom from everyday constraints. In the 1970s much of the rise in popularity of mountain recreation can be attributed to the easier access to downhill skiing and to mountain walking tracks provided by commercial operators (Johnston 1989b; Pearce, 1978).

Commercial provision of adventure recreation has always been part of mountain recreation in New Zealand, but the best examples are the great popularity of commercial skifields and the recent boom in adventure tourism which relies most heavily on a variety of non-traditional activities. Both types of commercial endeavours have taken over the role previously fulfilled by the mountain clubs as providers of access to the mountains and recreation experiences. Professional mountain guiding has been revived after a long hiatus in which amateur self-organized trips were the rule in mountain travel. Alongside the present day commercial element is a strong public agency presence in the form of school mountain programmes and specialist training courses. Included here are courses provided by the New Zealand Mountain Safety Council, a government organization which, according to the business card of its Executive Director, 'promotes safer enjoyment of mountain recreation'. The pro-adventure position of the Council is part of a comprehensive system reflecting government and societal recognition of mountain recreation as a healthy, desirable activity for New Zealanders (Johnston, 1989b). This philosophy is exemplified in a speech prepared for the 1986 Adventure Tourism Seminar, in which the New Zealand Minister for Tourism and for Recreation and Sport stated: 'Adventure Tourism helps New Zealand to become a nation of calculated-risk takers. If we take all the risk out of life we will become a nation of followers with a sedentary lifestyle rather than a dynamic nation of leaders' (Moore, 1987, p.7).

Mountain recreation involves travel to a certain type of environment in order to undertake a particular activity, an experience which might be unavailable elsewhere. The pursuit of their preferred activity draws people from around the world and from within New Zealand, as evidenced in the results of many studies of mountain recreationists and park users, and in the intentions' and visitors' books found at park headquarters and in mountain huts. The specialist nature of this tourism is manifest, but it is not yet clear the ways in which such pursuits involve adventure and can thereby be classified as adventure tourism.

Various definitions of adventure recreation, risk recreation and adventure tourism exist (e.g. Allen and Meier, 1982, p.48; Yerkes, 1987, p.10; Ewert, 1989, p.6), and have been discussed in Chapter 11. Ewert (1989, p.8) states: 'What distinguishes [outdoor adventure pursuits] from those more commonly associated with outdoor recreation is a deliberate seeking of risk and uncertainty of outcome often referred to as *adventure*'. Ewert lists 21 different activities considered as outdoor adventure pursuits, which include backpacking and mountaineering. He notes that 'the concept of risk taking is central to outdoor adventure activities as the absence of risk may result in a decrease in satisfaction as well as a decrease in the desire to participate' (Ewert, 1989, p.8). Risk is an important and integral element in outdoor adventure activities, but is not necessarily sought in other outdoor pursuits which are not adventure-based.

> People seeking outdoor adventures through recreation are specifically interested in participating in activities that feature risk and potential danger. This danger ... can be translated into actual or perceived threats of physical or emotional harm. While the outdoor recreationalist may occasionally experience similar circumstances, these types of occurrences are not deliberately sought out (Ewert, 1989, p.66).

Given this distinction it is necessary to explore the nature of adventure in mountain recreation as perceived by the participants. Is risk a sought-after component or is it merely tacitly accepted as part of the mountain experience? Of course, it cannot be denied that there is real danger in all mountain recreation activities. From 1890 to 1987 there was a total of 751 fatalities during land-based mountain recreation in New Zealand (Johnston, 1989b). The majority of these occurred during climbing activities; however, recreationists also died on family day walks, guided tramping tracks and commercial skifields. Fatal and non-fatal injuries and close call events are a feature, albeit infrequently occurring, of mountain recreation in New Zealand.

Clearly, however, risk in recreation involves more than the possibility of injury. The experience of risk features the potential not only for negative outcomes, but also for positive ones. Indeed, pursuit of the positive outcomes can be seen as the motivation for undertaking activities involving risk (Allen, 1980; Mitchell, 1983; Johnston, 1987; Ewert, 1989). This relationship between positive and negative outcomes is clarified by Allen's (1980) 'structure of risk'. From the perspective of the recreationist, this structure distinguishes challenge (risk which is under personal control) and danger (risk which is not under personal control). Such a distinction can be seen as context-based, relating to the skills of the recreationist and the particular demands of the situation (see Csikszentmihalyi [1975] on the flow construct). Sense of control and personal competence are two significant components in adventure recreation (e.g. Mitchell, 1983; Carpenter and Priest, 1989; Ewert, 1989), which assist the recreationist to experience the thrill of challenge while avoiding danger.

In order to explore views and experiences of risk in recreation, a questionnaire survey of 915 individuals, and personal interviews with a further eighteen were undertaken (Johnston, 1989b). Taking place in New Zealand from 1986 to 1988, the survey and interviews sought information on meanings of risk, experienced outcomes of risk and personal approaches to risk. The information thus obtained can be used to examine further the role of adventure in mountain recreation in New Zealand.

The Recreationists

On the basis of the activity in which they participated most often, respondents to the questionnaire survey were categorized into one of five main activity groups: trampers (n=309), skiers (n=442), hunters (n=25), climbers (n=49) and day walkers (n=62). A total of 28 respondents were unable to be classified in this way because of non-response to this question, or responses which indicated activities outside the main focus of this study (e.g. photography, birdwatching).

The focus of activity groups as the unit of participation, rather than on the place of recreation or the activity being pursued on the day of the survey, is based on the assumption that it is these activity groups that have most significance. It is assumed that the activity in which the individual is most involved is of greatest importance to the person. It is primarily through this main activity that the recreationist faces the types of physical challenges and achievements that are potentially available, developing views about risk during such experiences. Furthermore, activity group distinctions indicate the subcultural context in which behaviour and attitudes appropriate to an activity, including those with respect to risk, are learned and shared by participants (Pearson, 1977; Brannigan and McDougall, 1983). (Recognition of the larger societal context to recreationists' views toward risk is necessary as well, see Klein, 1980; Mitchell, 1983; Robbins, 1987.)

The population characteristics of the questionnaire respondents generally fit the established patterns for mountain recreationists. As a group, recreationists in the mountains are younger and better educated than the general population. Males dominate in the hunting (100 per cent) and climbing (86 per cent) groups, but there is a significant female component for most activities with walking, tramping and skiing groups comprising 30 to 60 per cent female participants. Unmarried people, students and employed persons are found in greater proportion in the recreationist group than in the general population. While these characteristics are features of mountain recreationists as a whole, differences between the activity groups are evident (see Aukerman and Davison, 1980; Johnston, 1989b).

Personal interviewees included five female and thirteen male recreationists, the majority of whom were students and unmarried. Ages ranged from 21 to 55 years. Eight of these interviewees were climbers, four were trampers, three were hunters, one was a skier, one was a day walker and one was a tramper-climber.

Risk and Enjoyment in Mountain Recreation

What role does risk play in the enjoyment of mountain recreation? This question was approached first by an examination of mountain recreation enjoyment in general terms in order to clarify the place of risk in relation to other sources of enjoyment. Both questionnaire respondents and personal interviewees were asked open-ended questions about enjoyment in mountain recreation.

Several interesting patterns are immediately evident. Generally, the climbers mentioned risk elements in a greater proportion than did other groups, suggesting that these recreationists are indeed seeking adventure more so than the others. Negligible differences were noted between females and males, and between segments on the basis of age and experience. Most importantly, risk-related elements (e.g. challenge, adventure, excitement) are much less frequently mentioned than are other sources of enjoyment such as fun, physical fitness, scenery and social atmosphere. Does this mean that risk has no place in the enjoyment of mountain recreation? It is necessary to examine risk in a more direct fashion in

Table 12.1 Meanings of risk selected by recreationists

Meaning	Total Sample %	Trampers %	Skiers %	Hunters %	Climbers %	Walkers %
challenge	33.6	29.1	35.6	56.0	32.7	30.6
danger	28.7	31.4	27.2	20.0	30.6	35.5
uncertain outcome	20.5	19.1	22.4	12.0	16.3	17.7
danger and challenge	5.0	6.1	4.6	0	10.2	1.6
uncertain outcome and danger	3.7	3.6	3.7	4.0	4.1	6.5
uncertain outcome and challenge	2.4	2.3	2.3	4.0	2.0	4.8
all of the above	1.5	2.3	0.7	0	4.1	1.6
other	3.0	5.2	1.6	0	0	0
no response	1.5	0	2.1	4.0	0	1.6

Source: Survey data

order to determine the role, positive or negative, it plays in actual situations.

Results from the questionnaire survey show the meanings associated with risk by these recreationists (Table 12.1). Three possible meanings, developed from definitions of risk, were listed: uncertain outcome, danger and challenge. 'Challenge' and 'danger' proved to be the most popular meanings associated with risk, but 'uncertain outcome' was also important. Some respondents selected more than one of the meanings provided, while others responded with an entirely different meaning (e.g. steep rocks, calculated risk). With categories combined, 'challenge' featured in the responses of 42.5 per cent of the sample, and 'danger' was reported by 38.9 per cent.

Some differences between activity groups are evident. What appears remarkable is that climbers and trampers, the recreationists who are taking part in the outdoor adventure pursuits listed by Ewert (1989), do not stand out from the other groups in their views of risk. Several possible reasons exist. One is that there are no major differences between these groups. Another is that these recreationists, as risk-seekers, have a well-defined understanding of risk which was not catered for in this simple list of meanings. Thirdly, as a group of recreationists who are often considered as death-obsessed by the general public (Mitchell, 1983; Walter, 1984), climbers in particular might attempt to downplay the positive motivational role of risk, for fear of being misperceived.

Discussion with the personal interviewees indicated that most of them saw risk as having elements of both challenge and danger. Most also stated that they previously had not thought consciously about a definition of risk. This underlines the importance of asking about risk specifically in order to develop an understanding of its place in recreation.

In the course of these discussions on the meaning of risk, several interviewees stated that risk was important in their mountain recreation. For example, one climber stated: 'Yes, it is [important]. Otherwise I'd wonder what I'm doing here'.

Table 12.2 Effect of risk on enjoyment of recreation

Effect	Total Sample %	Trampers %	Skiers %	Hunters %	Climbers %	Walkers %
increases it	31.8	34.0	31.3	48.0	28.5	24.2
decreases it	23.1	22.7	23.3	12.0	26.5	25.8
does both	38.1	35.3	40.9	40.0	40.8	29.0
does neither	4.4	4.5	3.2	0	0	12.9
no response	2.6	3.5	1.3	0	4.1	8.1

Source: Survey data

However, the more common response that risk was not necessary is typified by this comment from a tramper. 'For me, the risk is not a particularly important factor in my mountain recreation. I go into the mountains to feel good basically, and I don't feel that I need to take major risks to get a big adrenalin flow'.

The impact of risk on enjoyment was explored further in the questionnaire survey (Table 12.2). The majority of the sample considers risk to have some degree of a positive impact on their enjoyment, while less than 30 per cent found risk as negative or having no impact. The dual nature of risk was evident for the 38.1 per cent of the respondents who said that risk both increased and decreased their enjoyment.

Differences in respect of the views of the role of risk in enjoyment were noted as well on the basis of self-assessed experience levels. A greater proportion of those with more experience saw risk as challenge, and as increasing their enjoyment. Similarly, a greater proportion of respondents in the higher participation group viewed risk in this way than did those in the low and medium participation groups. An increased importance of risk with greater participation and experience is hypothesized in a number of adventure recreation models (e.g. Schreyer and White, 1979; Ewert and Hollenhorst, 1989).

Although there appeared to be no differences in the importance of risk elements as sources of enjoyment generally in mountain recreation between males and females, there were considerable differences in respect of the more specific questions regarding the effect of risk on enjoyment. This reinforces differences noted in the meanings of risk: while 37.2 per cent of the males viewed risk as challenge, only 27.7 per cent of the females responded in this way. Regarding the effect of risk on enjoyment, 20.1 per cent of the female respondents reported that it increased their enjoyment, 30.2 per cent that it decreased their enjoyment and 41.7 per cent that it had both effects. For males, the comparable figures are 39.2 per cent, 19.0 per cent and 35.5 per cent respectively. This suggests that there are some quite important differences between these two groups in the extent to which risk is viewed as positive and is pursued as a vital component of mountain recreation. Such behaviour distinctions might be reflected in the outcomes of risk that are experienced.

This possibility is reinforced by the differences evident in the statistics on mountain recreation fatalities between 1890 and 1987. There is an overwhelming domination by males in the fatality statistics (92 per cent) completely out of proportion to their rates of participation. Furthermore, the activities with the highest numbers of fatalities (climbing and hunting) are also the activities the least popular with women. However, even in the activities which attract women, males still account for proportionally far more fatalities than could be expected on the basis of the participation ratio. These results raise interesting questions regarding differences in the role of risk for men and women, particularly in relation to the effects of socialization on participation in certain activities, and risk-seeking in recreation generally (see Miranda, 1985; Warren, 1985; Hargreaves, 1986; Gilroy, 1989).

While these figures indicate the extent of various views and important distinctions between recreationist groups, they give no sense of the ways in which risk affects enjoyment. Respondents were asked to explain why risk had the stated effect on their enjoyment of mountain recreation. For those who indicated that risk increased their enjoyment, this was because it was seen as either an essential part of the experience or providing an important added dimension. One person responded, 'If there is no element of risk there is no spark', while another stated: 'It adds to the situation and once one has faced that risk and overcome it one has an unsurpassed sense of achievement'.

Responses from those who stated that risk both increased and decreased their enjoyment stressed the dual nature of risk as challenge and danger, or the idea that a certain amount of risk was positive, but beyond that point it was negative. One recreationist wrote: 'It adds excitement and represents a challenge – a buzz. It depends on the amount of risk – too much may become dangerous'.

A sense of achievement clearly was part of the challenge of risk and frequently respondents reported this as having a positive impact on enjoyment, relating this to their skill level. One recreationist declared: 'To move ahead in your activity usually entails for me some degree of risk'. Another concurred: 'I want to improve, so by taking small risks I can do so, but only when I achieve them'. This chance to progress was not without negative components, as outlined by this respondent: 'A risk situation generally means you are close to the limit of your ability. However, too much risk has a negative effect on your performance'.

For the majority of the questionnaire respondents and the personal interviewees risk comprised, in part, positive elements which added enjoyment to the experience. Other than to a small proportion of the respondents, risk was not stated as a central focus. Yet responses demonstrate that risk can indeed be significant, particularly in relation to achievement and skills development where challenge clearly heightens enjoyment. Risk plays such a role, however, mountain recreation is experienced in a holistic way in which elements relating to the environment, social atmosphere, and active participation are all important. Thus, for most of the participants surveyed, mountain recreation does not strictly fit the special interest tourism model as they do not pursue adventure as a central focus. However, given that the majority of the sample viewed risk as having a positive impact on their enjoyment, it is clear that adventure can be a component of varying importance in mountain tourism.

Conclusion

This chapter set out to explore the role of adventure in mountain recreation in New Zealand and to determine the special interest nature of such tourism. The clear distinction noted by Ewert (1989) between outdoor recreation and outdoor adventure pursuits has not been overwhelmingly evident here. Climbers mentioned risk-related sources of enjoyment more frequently than did other groups; however, with respect to the meaning of risk and the impact of risk on enjoyment, neither climbers nor trampers stand out.

One difference noted was that between the recreationists with greater experience and with more frequent participation, and those recreationists who had less experience and less frequent participation. This finding ties in with the expectation that risk will become increasingly important to participants as they develop their involvement. This raises questions as to the role of risk, and the outcomes experienced, for those who cease participation. A further difference is evident between the responses of males and females, with the former more frequently replying in a positive manner toward risk. The role of socialization in determining attitudes to risk-seeking, as well as access to risk activities needs study. This is particularly important given the domination by males in the fatality statistics, demonstrative of differences in the final outcomes of risk for male and female participants, and suggestive of distinctions in the ways in which risk is experienced during recreation.

Although the expected differences between outdoor recreation and outdoor adventure pursuits did not arise, it is clear that an element of adventure might, in fact, be a part of all the traditional mountain recreation activities in New Zealand. The majority of respondents in each activity group experience risk as a positive influence. Not all these people are actively seeking risk, yet they enjoy it and it is an important part of their recreation experience.

The role of adventure in motivating special interest tourism ranges from being central to being peripheral. Tourists pursue the types of experience they desire in respect of environment, social setting and activity. Clearly, the substantial range of interest is manifest in the great variety of adventure tourism opportunities organized by commercial operators, public agencies, mountain clubs and individuals themselves.

References

Allen, S., 1980, Risk recreation: a literature review and conceptual model, 52–81 in J.F. Meier, W.T. Morash, G.E. Welton, eds, *High adventure outdoor pursuits: organization and leadership*, Brighton Publishing Company, Utah

Allen, S., Meier, J.F., 1982, Let's take a risk with adventure recreation!, *Parks and Recreation*, 17 (2): 47–50

Aukerman, R., Davison, J., 1980, *The mountain land recreationist in New Zealand*, Tussock Grasslands and Mountain Lands Institute, Lincoln College, Canterbury, New Zealand

Brannigan, A., McDougall, A., 1983, Peril and pleasure in the maintenance of a high risk sport: a study of hang-gliding, *Journal of Sport Behaviour*, 6 (1): 37–51

Carpenter, G., Priest, S., 1989, The adventure paradigm and non-outdoor leisure pursuits, *Leisure Studies*, 8: 65–75

Csikszentmihalyi, M., 1975, *Beyond boredom and anxiety*, Jossey-Bass Publishers, San Francisco

Dale, P., ed., 1987, *Adventure tourism seminar: current issues and future management*, Vol. 2, *South Island seminar*, Hillary Commission for Recreation and Sport, Wellington

Dilley, R.S., 1986, Tourist brochures and tourist images. *The Canadian Geographer*, 30 (1): 59–65

Ewert, A.H., 1989, *Outdoor adventure pursuits: foundations, models and theories*, Publishing Horizons, Inc., Columbus

Ewert, A., Hollenhorst, S., 1989, Testing the adventure model: empirical support for a model of risk recreation participation, *Journal of Leisure Research*, 21 (2): 124–139

Gilroy, S., 1989, The emBody-ment of power: gender and physical activity, *Leisure Studies*, 8 (2): 163–171

Hargreaves, J., 1986, *Sport, power and culture*, Polity Press, Cambridge

Jebson, R.M., 1983, Administration of commercial recreation in the South Island mountain lands, Unpublished MSc thesis, Centre for Resource Management, University of Canterbury, Christchurch

Johnston, M.E., 1987, Risk in mountain recreation: challenge or danger?, 148–153 In R. Le Heron, M. Roche, M. Shepherd, eds, *Geography and society in a global context, proceedings of the fourteenth New Zealand geography conference, Palmerston North, New Zealand, January 1987*, New Zealand Geographical Society, Palmerston North

Johnston, M.E., 1989a, Accidents in mountain recreation: the experiences of international and domestic visitors in New Zealand, *Geojournal*, 19 (3): 323–328

Johnston, M.E., 1989b, Peak experiences: challenge and danger in mountain recreation in New Zealand, Unpublished PhD thesis, Department of Geography, University of Canterbury, Christchurch

Jorgenson, G.M., 1974, *Recreation and leisure: a bibliography and review of the New Zealand literature,* New Zealand Ministry of Works and Development, Wellington

Kearsley, G., 1985, Wilderness images and national park management, in D.F. Marks and D.G. Russell, eds, *Imagery 1, Proceedings of the first international imagery conference, Queenstown, 1983*, Human Performance Associates, Dunedin

Klein, D., 1980, Work, leisure and recreational risk, 18–31 in R.L. Bury, ed., *Risk and accidents in outdoor recreation areas – selected papers*, Texas A & M University, College Station

Miranda, W., 1985, 'Heading for the hills' and the search for gender solidarity, *Journal of Experiential Education*, 8 (2): 6–9

Mitchell, R.G., 1983, *Mountain experience: the psychology and sociology of adventure,* The University of Chicago Press, Chicago

Moore, M., 1987, Opening speech (presented by Sir Ron Scott), 5–10 in P. Dale, ed., *Adventure tourism seminar: current issues and future management*, Vol. 2, *South Island seminar*, Hillary Commission for Recreation and Sport, Wellington

New Zealand Council for Recreation and Sport, 1985, *Policy for outdoor recreation in New Zealand*, Government Printer, Wellington

Pearce, D.G., 1978, Skifield development in New Zealand, 91–94 in *Proceedings of the ninth New Zealand geography conference, Dunedin, New Zealand, August 1977*, New Zealand Geographical Society, Dunedin

Pearce, D.G., Booth, K.L., 1987, New Zealand's national parks: use and users, *New*

Zealand Geographer, 43 (2): 66–72

Pearson, T.K., 1977, Surfing subculture: a comparative analysis of surf livesaving and surfboard riding in Australia and New Zealand. Unpublished Ph.D. thesis, Department of Sociology, University of Queensland, St. Lucia

Robbins, D., 1987, Sport, hegemony and the middle class: the Victorian mountaineers, *Theory, Culture and Society*, 4: 579–601

Schreyer, R., White, R., 1979, A conceptual model of high risk recreation, 191–194 in *Proceedings of the first annual national conference on recreation planning and development, Snowbird, Utah, April, 1979*, American Society of Civil Engineers, New York

Shultis, J.D., 1989, Image and use of New Zealand's protected areas by domestic and international visitors, *Geojournal*, 19 (3): 329–335

Smith, J., Davison, J., Geden, B., 1980, *The public mountain land resource for recreation in New Zealand*, Tussock Grasslands and Mountain Lands Institute, Lincoln College, Canterbury

Walter, J.A., 1984, Death as recreation: armchair mountaineering, *Leisure Studies*, 3: 67–76

Warren, K., 1985, Women's outdoor adventures: myths and reality, *Journal of Experiential Education*, 8 (2): 10–14

Yerkes, R., 1985, High adventure recreation in organized camping, *Trends*, 22 (3): 4–9

13 CASE STUDY

Scuba Diving Holidays[1]

Raymond S. Tabata

Scuba diving has become one of the fastest-growing sports in the world. The annual expenditures on scuba equipment, lessons and travel are increasing rapidly and expenditures on scuba travel are growing at the fastest rate of the three, according to industry experts (Dignam, 1990).

Introduction

Snorkeling and scuba diving are now among the most popular activities for tourists travelling to the tropics and subtropics. According to Bill Gleason, editor of *Skin Diver* magazine, dive travel is the fastest growing interest in diving today (Klemm, 1984). Even in places far removed from the ocean, divers enjoy their sport in quarries, lakes, streams, ice ponds, kelp beds, and underwater caves. This chapter provides an overview of important dive destinations, origins, and demographic profiles of dive travellers, and some insight into the preferences and activities of divers. This is followed by a case study of the recreational diving industry in Hawaii.

Dive travel is a significant part of international and domestic travel in certain regions. The popular 'sunspot destinations' in the global 'sunbelt' near the Equator include the Mediterranean, Pacific islands, Gulf of Mexico/Caribbean, and Florida (Matthews, 1978). Divers travel extensively to view wrecks, coral reefs, caves, 'walls', 'blue holes', and sleeping sharks. Major diving destinations such as the well known Truk Lagoon are banking on dive travel as a primary means of developing tourism (Pacific Area Travel Association [PATA], 1977). Places such as the Caymans, Bonaire, and U.S. Virgin Islands depend on dive travel to support their tourism industries which have been promoted as 'sun, sea, and surf' destinations. According to *Skin Diver* (1989), the top ten diving destinations in the world were:

1. Bahamas
2. Caymans
3. Cozumel
4. Hawaii
5. Bonaire
6. U.S. Virgin Islands
7. Cancun
8. British Virgin Islands
9. Jamaica
10. Bay Islands, Honduras

Plate 13.1 Great Barrier Reef Marine Park, Australia (courtesy of TraveLearn)

The United States alone is estimated to have about 85 per cent of the world's diving travellers (PATA, 1977). In 1975, it was reported that there were 474,000 active divers (U.S. Dept of Commerce, 1975). Since then, the sport has grown con-siderably. Monaghan (1988a, b) reported an industry consensus that there were between 1.7 and 2.0 million divers in the United States. The Professional Association of Dive Instructors (PADI) (1990) reports increasing numbers of scuba certi-fications in the United States, increasing from 107,000 in 1980 to 422,000 in 1989.

Japanese divers are also of interest due to their extensive travel in the Pacific and relatively high personal expenditures. Perusal of Japanese diving magazines reveals numerous dive shops, dive clubs, and tours to exotic places such as Truk, Palau, Philippines, and the Red Sea. Japan certified 33,000 divers in 1988, second only to Australia which certified 39,000 (PADI, 1988). This places Japan in the position of being an important source of dive travellers, especially in the Pacific Basin.

Economic Importance of Dive Travel

Dive travel in the United States contributes significantly to local economies. A Michigan study documented diver activity in the Great Lakes region, including travel and expenditure patterns (Peterson and Sundstrom, 1987; Peterson, Sundstrom and Kinnunen, 1987; Peterson, Sundstrom and Stewart, 1987). The study found that divers travel considerably and contribute significantly to local economies for non-diving goods and services – including lodging, dining, entertainment, and shopping.

In the Pacific, tourism in general has been growing at a phenomenal rate. For example, Hawaii's arrivals grew from 243,000 to nearly 7 million in 1990; visitor expenditures now exceed US$11 billion annually, making tourism Hawaii's foremost industry. Diving is an important aspect of tourism in that a significant number of tourists engage in scuba diving or snorkeling. A survey of 23 dive shops in Hawaii (out of 44 shops) revealed that they grossed nearly US$7 million in 1982 (van Poollen, 1983). A subsequent study found that 47 dive shops generated an estimated US$20 million in 1986 (Tabata, 1989).

A Demographic Profile of the Dive Traveller

Diving is an important form of special interest travel. Divers seek a wide variety of experiences and are willing to travel extensively to pursue their hobby. Many destinations in Florida and the Caribbean that offer dive resorts and dive yachts cater solely to recreational divers. A wide variety of people participate in diving, ranging from novices trying scuba diving for the first time to experienced open-water scuba divers seeking new challenges.

Skin Diver magazine (1989) provides some of the best available data on U.S. divers, their interests and travel characteristics. Their biennial readership surveys indicate that divers comprise a distinct group of consumers. Subscribers have an average household income of US$64,300 compared to the U.S. average of US$35,000; 84.2 per cent attended college or beyond, compared to 35.6 per cent for the U.S. as a whole; 73.1 percent of subscribers have occupations as owners, or in managerial, technical, professional or sales positions, compared to the U.S. average of 29.5 per cent; 65 per cent of readers are male while 58.4 per cent are married. The median age in the 1989 survey was 35.3 years, compared to 30.8 years in the 1987 survey. Another survey conducted by *Underwater USA* (1988) indicates very similar demographics for their subscribers.

In summary, divers are generally well-educated, young, and financially secure. The sport is also male-dominated, although there are increasing numbers of women becoming scuba divers. Also, due to advances in technology, scuba diving is less physically demanding, allowing older or less fit individuals to take up the sport (Dignam, 1990). The diverse interests and skill levels of divers present a major challenge to resource managers in accommodating their varied recreational needs in underwater environments.

Motivating Factors for Dive Travel

Rice (1987) described three general types of divers: (1) 'hard core'; (2) 'tourist'; and (3) 'potential'. The 'hard core' diver chooses a destination for its flora and fauna or the challenges of local diving conditions. The 'tourist' diver includes scuba diving as part of a vacation. The 'potential' diver is a novice who wants to try scuba diving. This typology suggests that there is a range of interests among

Table 13.1 Factors affecting selection of dive site characteristics

	Questionnaire Item	Keyword
1.	outstanding marine life	life
2.	good underwater visibility	clear
3.	good for underwater photography	photo
4.	generally calm waters	calm
5.	no strong currents	current
6.	close to harbour or dive shop	close
7.	caves, lava tubes, arches	cave
8.	enjoyable ride to site	ride
9.	presence of pinnacle or wall	wall
10.	not crowded	crowd
11.	diveable wreck or plane	wreck
12.	drift dive possible	drift

dive travellers as far as their educational motivation is concerned. Another way to classify divers would be along an 'adventure' – 'educational' spectrum: 'adventure' divers seek excitement (i.e. wall dives, drift dives) while 'educational' divers really want to see unique marine life or interesting underwater geology.

The literature on diver preferences for various environmental attributes is very limited. The *Skin Diver* magazine (1989) subscriber surveys show that divers are attracted by features such as reefs, wrecks, lobsters, abalones, shells, walls, 'drifts', and caves (Table 13.1). In a Great Lakes area study, Somers (1979) found that nearly 40 per cent of respondents enjoyed coral reef diving; they also enjoyed wrecks, underwater photography, ice diving, spearfishing, treasure hunting and cave diving. Another study by Holecek and Lothrop (1980) suggests that divers with special interests, such as wreck diving, are willing to travel farther to enjoy their sport. A New Zealand study (New Zealand Department of Lands and Survey, 1984) examines diver usage of marine parks with respect to environmental features. In the Cape Rodney – Okakari Point Marine Reserve, observation of fish and other marine life was reported in this study to be the most popular activities among divers while fish feeding and photography were also somewhat popular.

Matheusik (1983) compared preferences of sports divers in the British Columbia and Ontario Provinces of Canada. Of 36 resource attributes examined, seven were found to be reliable indicators. For the resource setting scales, both populations of divers (in the two provinces) on the average placed more importance on good water quality, natural geological formations, diversity of marine life, and safe and easy access than they did on low dive trip costs, boat facilities and other services. Among the four most preferred resource setting attributes, good water quality had the highest mean for Ontario divers, while diversity of marine life had the highest mean for British Columbia divers. Finally, O'Reilly (1982) provides some insights into dive site preferences among recreational divers. Of 24 listed attributes, the five most frequently mentioned were expected clarity, marine life/lots of fish, cost, accessibility, and underwater scenery.

Meeting the Needs of the Dive Traveller – a Hawaii Case Study

This case study attempts to better define resource requirements for recreational diving as viewed by dive tour operators. As tourism grows in areas with popular dive sites, such as along the southern coast of Lanai or the Kona coast of the Big Island, there will be increasing pressures on the marine environment. Water pollution, fresh water runoff, litter, siltation, anchor damage, trampling, and specimen collecting can cumulatively destroy the natural resource base used by the dive shop industry. Better understanding of dive operators' needs and preferences is important to managing popular dive areas, as well as for developing dive travel as a form of special interest travel.

The general approach used in the 1987 Hawaii Sea Grant study was to ascertain dive site preferences and choices from the viewpoint of commercial dive operators. This contrasts with studies of the environmental preferences of individual divers. The operator is an 'intermediary' decision-maker between the resource and the user; the operator generally decides what sites will be visited by their customers who are unfamiliar with specific dive sites. Presumably, an experienced dive operator will know what dive site features would be attractive and satisfying to customers – that is, what 'sells'. Therefore, it is assumed that the operators' preferences generally reflect the desires and expectations of customers.

Definitions

The term 'dive operator' in this study includes (1) dive shops which have a retail store offering a variety of services, including tours; and (2) dive tour operators who principally offer shore or boat dives, without necessarily having a 'shop' or office. A 'dive site' is defined as a specific nearshore location where tour customers are taken for either boat or shore dives; dive sites are usually given a colorful nickname (e.g. 'Cathedrals', 'Turtle Canyon', or 'Rainbow Reef') commonly used by dive operators in an area.

Data Collection

A survey was conducted using personal interviews. Of the 47 dive operations interviewed, half belonged to Destination Hawaii, a statewide association of dive businesses (now called Dive Hawaii). The questionnaire was reviewed by the Destination Hawaii executive director and board of directors, then field tested over several months prior to the actual field interviews which were conducted during Summer and Fall 1987.

Hawaii's Recreational Dive Industry

Recreational diving is big business in Hawaii. Dive operators interviewed reported gross sales of US$19.8 million in 1986. Maui accounted for 57 per cent of the total with Oahu (25 per cent), Hawaii (Big Island) (13 per cent), and Kauai (6 per cent) making up the remainder. The reported US$19.8 million is about 7.4 per cent of

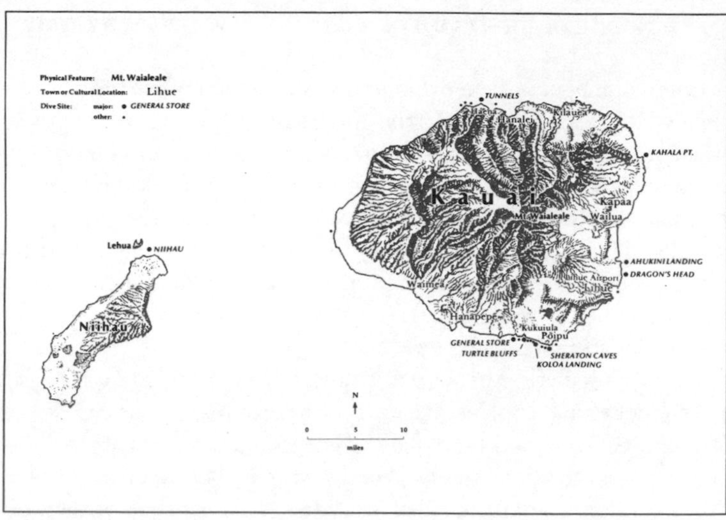

Figure 13.1 Popular sites used by Kaua'i dive operators

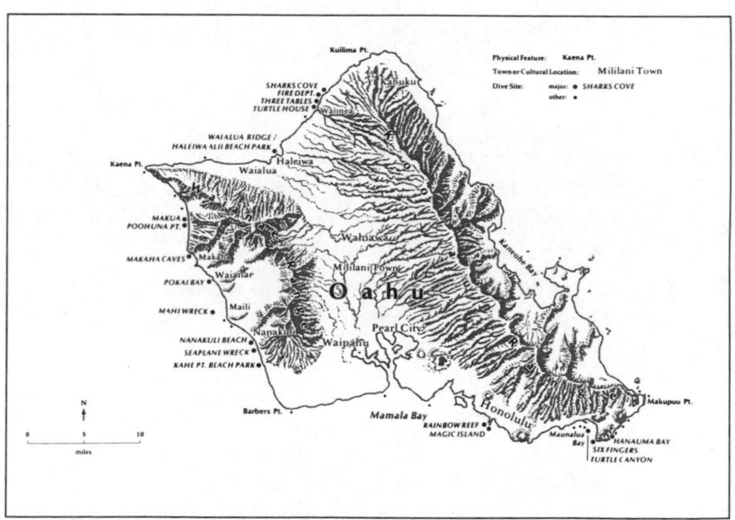

Figure 13.2 Popular sites used by Oahu dive operators

the estimated US$269 million in 1986 revenues for Hawaii's ocean recreation businesses (MacDonald and Deese, 1988).

The operators sold nearly 250,000 scuba and snorkeling tours in 1986. Of this total, about 54,000 were introductory dive tours, 68,000 were certified dive tours, and another 128,000 were snorkeling tours. Many of the 128,000 snorkeling tours were sold by a few operators interviewed, but did not include about 100 sail/snorkel operators statewide which reportedly rival dive operators in gross sales.

Fifty-seven per cent (27 of 47) of the operations interviewed had been in

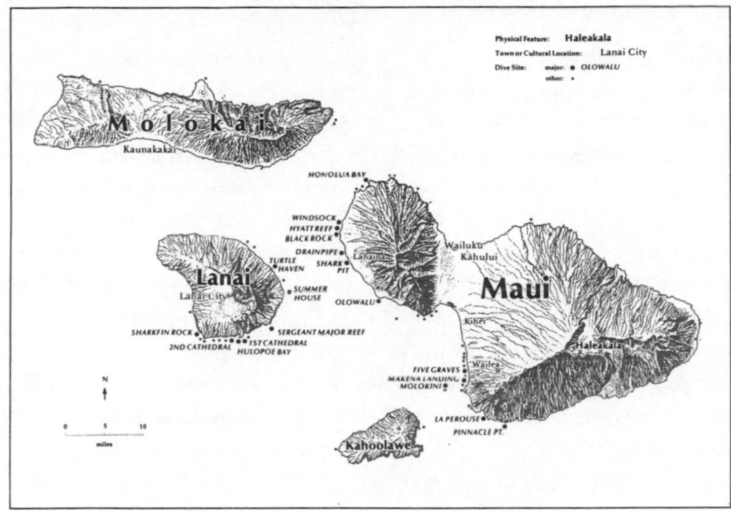

Figure 13.3 Popular sites used by Maui dive operators

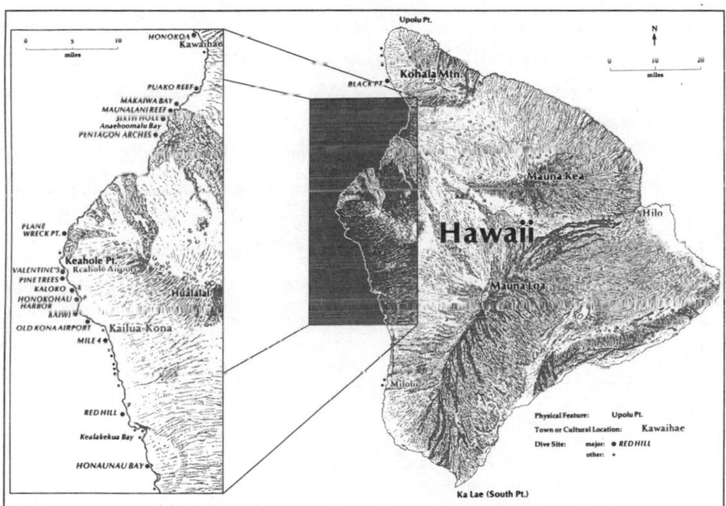

Figure 13.4 Popular sites used by Hawaii dive operators

business less than six years, mostly on Oahu and Hawaii (Big Island). Maui operations were seven years old on the average, while Oahu and Hawaii averaged 4.4 years. The number of new operations might help account for the three-fold increase in reported gross income between 1982 and 1986. In 1982, a Sea Grant study (van Poollen, 1983) of dive shops reported gross sales of US$6.7 million, compared to US$19.8 million in 1986. The 47 operators employed 300 people full-time and 95 part-time, with another 145 individuals on contracts.

Seasonal Use of Dive Sites

Interviewees were presented with a list of known dive sites and asked to check off all sites used for dive tours during 1986. Site names were compiled from several diving guides (Hoffman, 1984; Thorne, 1984; Thorne and Zitnik, 1984; Wallin, 1984) and listed in clockwise geographic sequence for each island. Interviewees were also able to add other sites to the list. Respondents indicated that they used a total of 196 individual sites in 1986. Interviewees were then asked to select the three sites they used the most during 1986; they were also asked to rank the three sites from 1 to 3 (1= used most). Of the 196 total sites, 69 were selected among the top three sites by at least one respondent (see Figures 13.1–13.4).

The most popular dive sites for tours, as indicated by dive operators, generally are located in leeward areas of the various islands (i.e. Poipu on Kauai, Waianae and Maunalua Bay on Oahu, Southern Lanai and Molokini in Maui County, and the Kona-Kohala coasts of Hawaii). These areas are generally sheltered from the prevailing tradewinds most of the year and, therefore, water conditions are well-suited to diving.

Site Usage for 'Intro' and 'Certified' Dives

Dive tours can be classified as 'intro' or 'certified' tours. 'Intro' tours are designed for uncertified divers. 'Certified' tours, on the other hand, are intended for divers certified by a recognized agency such as PADI or the National Association of Underwater Instructors (NAUI). In 1986, respondents reported selling 54,000 'intro' tours, compared to 68,000 'certified' tours. Most of the dive sites were used by certified divers, and to a lesser extent, for novices on introductory dives. In general, more popular sites tended to be rated by more operators as being suited to certified dives. Operators seem to favour sites which are attractive to both experienced and new divers. For the former, the sites must offer interesting features or animals to observe, while for the latter, the sites should be relatively calm and safe. Because many dive tours take on both 'intro' and certified divers, operators probably prefer sites which can satisfy both groups.

Site Usage for Boat and Shore Dives

Access to dive sites is critical to dive tour operations. Most of the respondents relied heavily on boats for access to their favourite sites while a few specialized in shore dives, especially on Oahu where harbour facilities are relatively limited. Boats are needed to reach desirable areas inaccessible from shore (e.g. Kona-Kohala coastline, Southern Lanai). On Kauai and Oahu, there seems to be an even split between use of sites for shore and boat dives. On Kauai, sites such as 'Koloa Landing' are easily reached from shore, while others such as 'Sheraton Caves' and 'General Store' require a boat. On Oahu, 'Shark's Cove' is a shore dive for most, while the 'Mahi' is some distance offshore. One factor favouring shore dives is the convenience and low capital cost involved in shore dives, only a van is needed to reach dive sites, another might be the unavailability of harbour space and launch ramps on Kauai and Oahu. Maui and Hawaii operators, in contrast, use predominantly their favourite sites for boat dives. On Maui, this is probably the case since most of their favourite sites are offshore (i.e. Molokini) or off another island (i.e. Lanai). On Hawaii, operators have a large number of sites along the Kona-Kohala coast which can be easily reached from the main harbours at Keauhou Bay, Kailua Bay, and Honokohau Harbor; in addition, much of the coastline lacks public access at the shoreline, therefore favouring boat access.

Travel Time to Boat Dive Sites

Interviewees were asked to estimate travel time to their favourite boat dive sites from their particular operating port. Maui appears to be the exception among the islands in terms of typical travel times. Maui operators reported considerably longer travel times from port to dive sites. Various respondents explained that the longer trips were due to several factors: (1) availability of high quality dive sites at nearby islands (i.e. Lanai, Molokini); (2) the scenic boat ride to other islands, particularly during the winter humpback whale season; (3) relatively poor condition of nearshore waters around Maui island due to siltation, runoff, and resulting murky conditions and poor reefs. Maui operators have the greatest variation in travel times with a standard deviation of 29.5. Coupled with their highest average travel time of 46.0 minutes (compared to 19 for the other islands), it seems clear that Maui dive tours also take advantage of sites fairly close to operations (i.e. near resorts, harbours, or shops) while also using sites farther away, especially off Lanai and Molokini.

Maximum Diving Depths and Bottom Times for Popular Dive Sites

In planning each dive trip, dive operators must continually balance a number of factors: experience levels and desires of customers, weather and water conditions for a given day, and 'bottom time'. Recommended bottom time for a single dive is determined by the maximum depth reached on that dive; for a series of dives, allowable bottom times are based on maximum depths on preceding dives and 'surface interval' times between dives. Various dive tables produced by the U.S. Navy and diving agencies (i.e. PADI, NAUI) help divers plan dive sequences to maximize bottom time. Ideally, operators attempt to keep maximum depths to less than 18 metres (60 ft.); this normally allows nearly an hour of bottom time while accommodating normal depth limits for divers with 'open water' (i.e. basic) scuba certification. Also, to reduce the risk of decompression sickness (i.e. 'bends'), operators generally allow considerable safety margins for diver error and individual susceptibility.

The survey results verify that most popular sites accommodate dives under 18.3 metres in depth and 30–60 minutes in dive time. Certain sites have operating depths exceeding 18.3 metres but are used primarily for advanced certified divers. For example, the 'Mahi' wreck on Oahu can be dived at about 21.3 metres (70 ft.) at deck level, but at 27.4 metres (90 ft.) on the ocean floor. 'General Store' on Kauai is generally dived between 15.2 – 27.4 metres (50 – 90 ft.) permitting basic

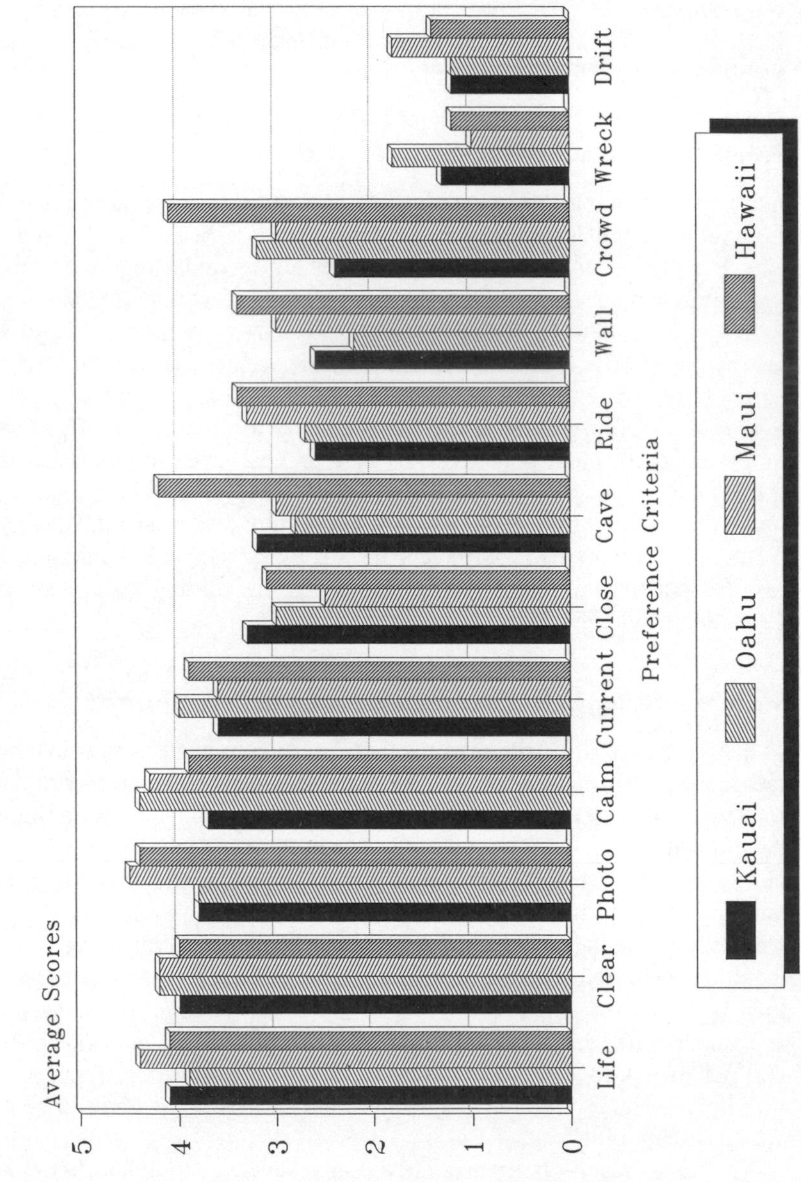

Comparison of average preference scores for all popular sites by island

divers to dive on the lower end and more advanced divers on the higher end. The 'Kaiwi' site and 'Pine Trees' area in Kailua-Kona can be dived as shallow as 4.6 meters (15 ft.) but as deep as 39.5 metres (130 ft.). The range of diving depths will, in turn, affect the bottom time available during tours.

Bottom Times for Favourite Dive Sites

For a given dive, 'bottom time' (i.e. time elapsed between beginning of descent and surfacing) is inversely related to maximum diving depth. Deeper dives generally mean less diving time. Dive operators attempt to trade off depth, bottom time, and adequate safety margin to lessen the risk of diving accidents. Because the bulk of certified divers have only 'open water' (i.e. basic) level certification, their diving depth is usually limited to 18.3 metres; at this depth, bottom time is normally planned for 45–60 minutes on the first dive. The results indicate that average bottom times are very similar among the islands, except for Hawaii where the average bottom time is about 10 minutes more. Compared to the other three islands, this could suggest that: (a) their dives are generally in shallower waters; or (b) their customers are generally less experienced, thereby necessitating shallower dives. Another possible interpretation is that many Big Island dive sites are relatively close to operations (i.e. shop or harbour), allowing more time during dive tours for actual diving.

Dive Site Characteristics

For each of their favourite sites, interviewees were asked to rate how important 12 factors (Table 13.1) were in their decision to use the site on a scale of 1 to 5 (1 = not important; 5 = very important) (see Figure 13.5). When average scores for all sites by island are examined, slight differences can be seen. Preference 'profiles' are somewhat similar among the four islands. The top five items (i.e. 'life', 'clear', 'photo', 'calm', and 'current') generally rated higher than the remainder of the list. 'Wreck' and 'drift' rated the lowest in general. Closer examination, however, shows interesting differences. 'Caves' (i.e. caves, lava tubes, arches) rated much higher among Hawaii operators – an average score of 4.2 compared to 2.8 to 3.2 for the other islands. This could be explained by the Big Island's abundant geologically 'young' lava formations along the shoreline. For Maui and Hawaii operators, an enjoyable ride to the dive site seems to be more important than for Kauai and Oahu operators; this may be due to relatively short boat rides on Kauai and the relative importance of shore dives on Oahu. Interestingly, Hawaii operators seem to prefer sites that are not crowded (4.1 compared to 3.2 for Oahu operators and 3.0 for Maui). This could be due to the larger number of relatively small dive operators on the Big Island who specialize in personalized tours and seek uncrowded spots.

Implications for Developing and Managing Special Interest Travel

University of Hawaii Sea Grant's study helped to identify the various factors which influence dive operators' selection of dive sites throughout the year. Hawaii's recreational diving industry, composed of about 60 operations (of which 47 were interviewed in 1987), generated US$19.8 million in gross revenue in 1986. The 47 respondents reported selling 250,000 diving and snorkeling tours to nearly 200 sites statewide; about 70 of these sites were considered 'favourite' sites. The bulk of 'tour-days', however, were reported from relatively few sites on each island. Selection of sites appears related to wave and wind conditions which are largely determined by the season and sheltering by large mountains. Some sites were better suited for beginners (i.e. for 'intro' dives) while others were better for certified divers; many popular sites were suitable for both types.

Boat dives were especially popular on the neighbor islands of Kauai, Maui, and Hawaii; shore dives were more popular on Oahu. Maui operators generally travelled much farther to reach popular sites; Maui respondents attributed this to better diving conditions offshore from neighboring islands, especially Lanai. Desired diving depths and bottom times reflect the needs of divers with basic 'open water' certification. Finally, ratings of 12 dive site characteristics indicate some differences among the different islands in how operators select sites.

Better understanding of why operators favour certain sites will help resource managers and tourism development agencies provide a range of diving opportunities that will attract dive travellers. Clearly, maintaining the diversity of marine life will require that consumptive activities (e.g. fishing, spearing) and habitat destruction (e.g. anchor damage) need to be carefully controlled. The importance of clear water indicates the need to minimize siltation and runoff in areas important for diving.

The attractiveness of certain sites due to geological features or presence of a wreck suggest that divers can be enticed to dive sites lacking spectacular reefs and abundant fish life. For example, a program of developing artificial reefs (e.g., sunken ships and planes) for non-consumptive diving could increase the number of sites available to recreational divers. The fact that divers can be attracted to specific sites based on particular features (i.e. tame eel, fish feeding, sleeping shark, and boat wrecks) provides an opportunity to develop new diving attractions and distribute diving to more areas. It is clear that a popular dive site does not require pristine conditions nor biological diversity. Promotion of less sensitive dive sites, or even creating artificial attractions, could reduce the environmental impact of recreational diving. Finally, measures such as installation of day-use moorings will help reduce anchor damage at popular sites.

Development of diving as a form of special interest travel needs to recognize that travellers have a range of preferences and perceptions as well as skill levels. A challenge for planning and managing dive tourism will be to:

1. identify the range of opportunities for activities in a given area;
2. identify and manage the key resources to ensure long-term sustainability;
3. inform visitors about the range of activities suitable for given sites; and

4. educate visitors about marine conservation to minimize adverse impacts to the resource resulting from inappropriate behaviour such as collecting and trampling.

By understanding both resources and users, and the delicate relationship between them, we can, perhaps, better provide memorable experiences for the special interest traveller while protecting the very same resources that attracted them to an area.

Endnote

1. This study was sponsored by the Sea Grant Extension Service project A/AS-1 which is funded by the University of Hawaii Sea Grant College Program under Institutional Grant no. NA85AA-D-SGO82 from NOAA Office of Sea Grant, Department of Commerce.

References

Brundage, B., Tabata. R., 1986, *Dive Hawaii*. University of Hawaii Sea Grant College Program, Honolulu

Dignam, D., 1990, Scuba gaining among mainstream travelers, *Tour & Travel News*, March 26, 1990: 1, 44–45

Hoffman, P., 1984, *Comprehensive guide to scuba diving in Hawaii*, Press Pacifica, Honolulu

Holecek, D.F., Lothrop, S.J., 1980, *Shipwreck vs. nonshipwreck scuba divers: characteristics, behavior, and expenditure patterns*, Michigan Sea Grant Program, Publication MICHI-SG-80-205, Ann Arbor.

Klemm, R., 1984, Have reefs, want divers, *Makai Newsletter*, 6 (12): 1, 4

MacDonald, C.D., Deese, H.E., 1988, A typology and portfolio model of Hawaii's ocean industries, in *Oceans '87 proceedings*, Vol.2, Marine Technology Society, Washington, D.C.

Matheusik, M.E., 1983, Sport divers and underwater parks: a market segmentation analysis, Unpublished M.S. thesis, Texas A & M University, College Station

Matthews, H.G., 1978, *International tourism: a political and social analysis*, Schenkman, Cambridge

Monaghan, R., 1988a. Just how many active divers are there? – 3.5 million… or 700,000?, *Undercurrent,* 13 (1): 9–12

Monaghan, R., 1988b, How many divers, how safe the sport? – the debate continues, *Undercurrent*, 13 (6): 9–12

New Zealand Department of Lands and Survey, 1984, *The Cape Rodney to Okakari Point Marine Reserve visitor survey, 1983–1984 (prepared for the Cape Rodney to Okakari Point Marine Reserve Management Committee)*, New Zealand Department of Lands and Survey, Auckland

O'Reilly, M.B., 1982, Sport diving in Texas: a study of participants, their activity, and means of introduction, Unpublished M.S. thesis, Texas A & M University, College Station

Pacific Area Travel Association [PATA], 1977, *Truk: a study of tourism development*,

Pacific Area Travel Association, San Francisco
Peterson, J.P., Sundstrom, T.C., 1987, *A profile of 1986 diver activity in the Thunder Bay Bottomland Preserve*, Michigan Sea Grant College Program, Ann Arbor
Peterson, J.P., Sundstrom, T.C., Kinnunen, R.E., 1987, *1986 recreational diving activity in Michigan bottomland preserves*, Michigan Sea Grant College Program, Ann Arbor
Peterson, J.P., Sundstrom, T., Stewart, S. 1987, *A profile of Great Lakes diver activity, travel, and expenditure patterns*, Michigan Sea Grant College Program, Ann Arbor
Professional Association of Dive Instructors [PADI], 1981, *The retail dive store: management and operation*, Professional Association of Dive Instructors, Los Angeles
Professional Association of Dive Instructors [PADI], 1988, *The 1988 Year-End Report – PADI*. Professional Association of Dive Instructors, Los Angeles
Professional Association of Dive Instructors [PADI], 1990, *Fact Sheet*, Professional Association of Dive Instructors, Los Angeles, 19 January
Rice, K., 1987, Special report: scuba diving – dive market requires specialized skill, information, *Tour & Travel News*, February 9: 24–27
Skin Diver, 1989, *Skin Diver magazine 1989 subscriber survey*, Petersen Publishing, Los Angeles
Somers, L.H., 1979, *Profile of a Great Lakes diver*, Michigan Sea Grant Program, Ann Arbor
Tabata, R.S., 1989, The use of nearshore dive sites by Hawaii's recreational dive industry. Unpublished M.A. thesis, University of Hawaii at Manoa, Honolulu
Thorne, C., 1984, *The divers' guide to Maui*, Maui Dive Guide, Kahului
Thorne, C., Zitnik, L., 1984, *The diver's guide to Hawaii*, Hawaii Divers' Guide, Kihei
Underwater USA, 1988, *Subscriber survey 1988*, Underwater USA, Inc., Beach Haven
United States Department of Commerce, National Oceanic and Atmospheric Administration, 1975, *An analysis of the civilian diving population of the United States*, United States Department of Commerce, National Oceanic and Atmospheric Administration, Washington D.C.
van Poollen, H.W., 1983, Recreational scuba diving industry survey and business analysis, State of Hawaii, 1982, *Working paper no. 52*, University of Hawaii Sea Grant College Program, Honolulu
Wallin, D., 1984, Diving and snorkeling guide to the Hawaiian Islands, Pisces Books, New York

14 CASE STUDY

Yachting Holidays, an Experience with Island Adventures

Harold Richins

Introduction

'The gods do not deduct from man's allotted span those hours spent in sailing' (Ocean Voyages, 1986). For those people who have the desire to explore some of the world's oceans, seas and islands, this ancient Phoenician proverb expresses the special feeling of chartering a yacht.

Yachting is a rapidly growing special interest tourism activity. Though it is often perceived as adventurous and exotic, there has been a misconception as to the 'élitist' nature of yachting holidays (Rogers and Thomas, 1986, p.94). In the last 15 years, yacht chartering has also become accessible to many middle income earners with discretionary dollars. An advertisement by Valef Yachts S.A. of Greece illustrates this trend:

> For less than the price of checking into a hotel room, you can check out the thousands of hidden islands, the tucked-away beaches and the quaint fishing villages of the Greek Isles in your own, fully crewed, luxury yacht. Snorkel in a secluded cove, water ski from your yacht's private ski boat, explore the remains of an ancient civilisation or just relax ... If it sounds like a vacation fit for a millionaire, it is ... (Valef Yachts S.A., 1988).

Yachting selections range from the 'luxury' expense of a 50 metre motor yacht for almost US$80,000 per week to a 'stripped down' 7.5 metre yacht for four people with sailing experience at US$100/day. For example, Valef Yachts offers the *Christina I*, which includes six double staterooms with private baths and a crew of nine. It has a sun deck, outdoor bar, speed boat, windsurfer, small sail boat, large lounge and dining room with leather chairs and a cruising range in the Mediterranean of 9,500 kilometres. All of this is offered at 'just' over US$50,000 per week not including the extra US$10,000–$30,000 for fuel, air and land transportation, dock fees, tips, tax, food and drink! On the other hand, for approximately US$1,300 per person, the company Windjammers can take the adventurous individual on a 50-60 passenger schooner for an all inclusive (food, drink, numerous water and land activities and return air fare from the United States) cruise through various islands of the Caribbean. Daniel and Sally Grotta offer this explanation of the popularity of chartering:

> Charter yachting, once the domain of the rich and famous, is quickly becoming the newest of the 'in' vacations, replacing African safaris, hot-air ballooning and excursions into mainland China as the most prestigious adventure for the money. The burgeoning popularity of chartering can be attributed to the fact that it's an easy and affordable way to explore – in civilized comfort — all the uninhabited atolls, secluded coves and pristine islands that most tourists miss (Grotta and Grotta, 1986, p.67).

The following review will elaborate on the numerous aspects of yachting holidays as a special interest tourism activity. Beginning with an historical and experiential understanding of this enterprise activity, the chapter will also include a case study of Island Adventures Holidays, which the author spent five years developing and operating as a company specializing in yachting vacations. The chapter will conclude with discussions of the various changes in the yachting vacations 'industry'.

The Scope and Definition of Yachting Holidays

The Context of Special Interest Tourism

Yacht chartering is an experience that has unique characteristics shared by a subset of people with specific interests. It normally combines rugged adventure and relative luxury in a package of beautiful surroundings, participatory challenge and small group involvement. These holidays may also offer distinctive historical, cultural and/or environmental experiences, and often involve travelling to 'exotic' out-of-the way waters and island destinations.

Through the development of the yacht chartering concept, people today are able to see islands and explore remote coastlines the world over without having to sail a month or more across the Pacific to get there. This is primarily due to improvements at numerous remote airports, which have enabled most of the world's coastlines to be accessible by yacht within a day's flight. Sailors and others are thus able to utilize their time exploring areas of choice rather than spending most of their time just getting to their destination.

Different Types of Yachting Holidays

A yachting vacation (or yacht chartering) can be defined as hiring a sail or motor propelled vessel for a period of one day or more to cruise in various locations throughout the world. The typical profile is of four to six people chartering a yacht for a period of one week or more, however, the number of participants may vary from one to more than twenty depending on the size of the yacht. Travellers interested in yachting holidays may choose from a variety of holiday plans. There are bareboat, skippered, crewed, or flotilla holidays as explained below.

A *bareboat* cruise normally requires that the person renting the yacht have sailing experience. Often many of his/her crew will also have some open water experience, but this is generally not a requirement unless the yacht is of a size large enough to require experienced assistance. The yacht skipper is generally required to present a sailing résumé, show completion of at least a basic sailing course and undergo an operational check out prior to being allowed to depart for his/her holiday.

A second type of chartering holiday involves *skippered* cruises, for those with little or no sailing experience. The client pays to rent the yacht and pays an extra fee (generally US$60–90 per day) to engage the services of a skipper to sail the yacht. The skipper normally reviews charts of the area with the client and enables him/her to choose the course prior to departure while giving information and recommendations about the area, as well as interesting historical, cultural and geographic details, consistent with the client's interests.

The third type of chartering holiday is the *crewed* yacht. This is very similar to the skippered yacht option except that there is not only a skipper, but a few other crew members along to ensure smooth sailing and provide 'gourmet style' meals complete with before and after meal cocktails. This type of charter may be regarded as: ' ...the ultimate in luxury on your own "floating villa" at prices that will compete with land-based holidays, but with experiences that give you the most personal service, the most delicious food and drink, and the ability to explore historical and cultural sites that few are able to see. No experience is necessary!' (Island Adventures, 1988).

Finally, the fourth type of chartering holiday is the *flotilla*. This particular holiday choice was the fastest growing portion of Island Adventures' business due to an extensive marketing effort by the company and increased demand. Flotillas are similar to bareboats in that clients are on their own yacht without a hired skipper, however, they sail in groups of from 10 to 12 similar yachts. Included with each flotilla is a lead boat with a skipper who conducts morning briefings of the charter area and an engineer who is able to make any necessary repairs to yacht equipment and assist with yacht operation. A hostess is also on board the lead boat providing information and suggestions about special needs and social activities.

Additional options of special cruising holidays are also offered to address particular markets such as singles' holidays, diving charters, combination hotel and yachting holidays, wedding charters, fishing charters (Mermon, 1983, p.3), corporate incentive charters and even scientific expeditions. In the future other alternatives may develop as the popularity of these special interest holidays continues to increase.

Who goes on Yachting Vacations

People of diverse backgrounds choose yachting charters for their holidays. From the author's experience, bareboat charterers are typically middle to higher income people, aged 35–50, with some sailing experience, who choose 'bareboating' to meet up with friends and enjoy a bit of adventure on their own.

Flotilla charters are generally taken by couples and families who desire the experience of sailing their own yacht while enjoying the security of a lead boat for guidance and extra service. Flotilla charterers are also attracted by the social aspects of this kind of holiday, looking forward to the scheduled regattas and group barbecues. Flotillas, due to the larger groups that travel on each yacht, are also more affordable and do not require as much experience as bareboats charters.

Crewed yachts normally attract a higher income group of people, with little or no yachting experience. Due to the great diversity in the kinds of yachts available for crewed charter, they may attract small groups, singles, families and couples in twos and threes at various levels of luxury and price (US$400–$10,000 per day per yacht). Crewed yachts may attract the adventurous with 'rustic' old sailing vessels marginally equipped, having basic bunks, shared toilets and no electricity. Crewed yachts may, on the other hand, give the charterer the comfort, accommodations and special treatment that are similar to the best suites in five star hotels. The attraction of adventure that is often experienced by charterers is described in the following Galapagos Island promotional material:

> Travelling from island to island is sheer bliss as the ship slides gently over the broad Pacific swell. Whether one is on … one of the schooners or an even smaller yacht suitable for fewer than half a dozen people, the sense of adventure in the wide open spaces is breathtaking. The sea is full of marine life and one has the startling experience of seeing a Manta Ray surface with huge black 20 ft wings spread out as it leaps from the water (Swinglehurst, 1982, p.149).

Providers of Yacht Chartering Services

There is today a large assortment of companies offering yachting holidays. These range from the actual owners of individual yachts who may market the charters directly, to large scale operations that own hundreds of their own yachts and have multinational booking operations. Potential clients may often be confused and a bit frustrated by the variety of special interest yacht companies from which they can choose. Though these companies may have vastly different roles and objectives, they may be indistinguishable to the unknowledgeable customer. The assortment of yacht charter providers may be seen in Table 14.1.

History of Yachting Vacations

Of the early pioneers, Julie Nicholson may have been the first to formalize the business of yachting vacations after she and her husband and son sailed for Australia in 1949. Following a visit to the Caribbean island of Antigua, they stayed and eventually started a company, Nicholson Yacht Charters. Nicholson (in Hartman, 1986, p.65), expresses those early days of yacht chartering:

> A few travel agents from the States were making the move into the world of charter yacht brokering. They'd come down here and we'd sail to various islands and get ashore and call out for the captains to fetch us and take us out to get a first hand look at their charter yacht. … We were few in number in those days [as charter yacht brokers] but we were very supportive and fiercely loyal to each other.

Commercial yachting vacations began in the late 1950s and early 1960s. The concept of a yacht with a skipper or crew was developed first in the Caribbean, followed a decade later by the hiring of yachts similar to the hiring of automobiles (bareboating). Bill Robinson wrote of his experiences in the early 1960s:

Table 14.1 Yachting holiday providers

Provider Type	Description of Provider Type
Yacht charter owners	Actual owners of individual yachts who may market the charters directly
Yacht charter owner associations	A consortium of individual owners who have grouped together to operate and market charters
Bareboat companies, Crewed yacht companies, Flotilla companies	Companies that operate exclusively for bareboat, crewed or flotilla
Yacht charter management companies, Yacht charter marketing companies	Organizations that are in the business of managing and marketing a charter boat operation
Bareboat associations, Crewed yacht associations	Associations of bareboat or crewed yacht companies who assist in assuring optimum service and cooperative marketing
Charter yacht brokers	Charter brokers who represent specific yachts and who can pass on certain discounts or commissions to regular travel agencies or market direct to customers on behalf of yacht owners
Specialty travel agencies	Specialty travel agencies who concentrate on different types of special interest tourism including yachting
Tour operators	Tour operators who may group a week on a yacht with other tourism activities (i.e. air travel, hotel accommodations and ground transportation)
Travel agencies	Common travel agencies who may have sporadic client interest in taking a yachting holiday
Combined companies	Some combination of the above

> When we first chartered a Nicholson yacht out of Antigua in 1961, there were eleven yachts in the trade. Now there are hundreds and hundreds, spread around many harbours. Some forty to fifty thousand people a year come into the Caribbean to charter bareboats out of the British and American Virgins [Virgin Islands], through many of the … Caribbean islands … (Robinson, 1986, p.26).

Bareboating was first introduced in the Virgin Islands which is still today the world's most successful chartering area (Scott and Scott, 1986, p.7). A small marina operator on the island of St. Thomas named Dick Avery convinced a few sailboat owners to try putting their boats out for hire in the early 1960s. An informally run operation began with over a dozen yachts being allowed for

Table 14.2 Pioneers and their contributions to the development of the yachting holiday concept

Pioneer Name and Company	Primary Contribution to the Yachting Holiday Concept
Jack Van Ost (Caribbean Sailing Yachts (CSY))	After chartering one of Avery's boats in the early 1960s, Jack Van Ost envisioned the possibility of developing a more standardized fleet of sailing yachts, and thus started Caribbean Sailing Yachts (Robinson, 1986, p.27).
Nancy Stout (Blue Water Cruises)	Nancy Stout started in the yacht chartering (yacht charter broker) business in 1965 and purchased Blue Water Cruises from Francie Henry who retired in 1973 (Anonymous, 1985, p.64). Blue Water Cruises is still in operation today.
Dick Jachney (Caribbean Yacht Charters (CYC))	With his wife Lynn, Dick Jachney owns a bareboat business named Caribbean Yacht Charters, which has catered to approximately 80,000 people since 1968 (Anonymous, 1987, p.4).
Mary Crowley (Ocean Voyages)	Mary Crowley has offered unique yachting experiences, first with Oceanic Expeditions, then with her own company Ocean Voyages. She initiated more adventurous, expedition style chartering on shared one to two week trips to some of the most remote water locations on earth (Herron, 1982, p.58).
Ginny and Charlie Cary (The Moorings)	Ginny and Charlie Cary have built one of the world's largest and most effectively marketed charter businesses, The Moorings, which started in 1968 with the establishment of a charter yacht type resort in the British Virgin Islands and now have spread to the Pacific and Mediterranean (Shepard, 1985, p.63).
Christopher Clode (Island Sailing Ltd and others)	After the company Yacht Cruising Association (YCA) expanded their business in the mid 1970s by offering a grouped bareboat approach to sailing in waters, far away from the comforts of home, the modern concept of 'Flotilla' was born (Jennings, 1986, pp.20, 21). Today, Island Sailing (now owned by Sunsail, Inc. which also purchased YCA), has a fleet of over 600 yachts operated throughout the Mediterranean, primarily utilising the Flotilla approach. Additional ideas that have been successful

	include: singles cruises, stowaway shared cruises and beach-villa-sailing combination holidays (Sunsail, 1989).
David Halsey	David Halsey, as early as 1960, at the age of 19, did research for a client while working at a travel agency and discovered a potential for crewed charter yachting. He later started Halsey Marine in the early 1970s and is now offering charters in all areas of the Mediterranean, the Caribbean and the South Pacific (Hartman, 1985, p.54).

bareboat by 1966 (Robinson, 1986, p.27). By the late 1970s, many larger yachting charter companies managing the operations were successful at selling yachts to private owners and then leasing back the use of the yachts for charter purposes. These owners then were able to take advantage of the tax benefits of small incomes as well as the use of their yachts on holiday for a few weeks per year.

Some of the additional pioneers who had significant impact on the charter yacht field are included in Table 14.2. The concept of flotilla sailing was born in 1974 when Eric Richardson and 'a few cruising friends' purchased 10 similar small sailing yachts, based them in Greece, and waited for people to book bareboat trips. Though English yachting enthusiasts love the exotic nature of sailing in Greece, they were quite leery of 'doing it alone'. A suggestion from one of the group was made to sail together and for someone who had a bit more experience to lead the yachts during their sailing holiday (Jennings, 1986, p.20). This concept became popular and was effectively developed and marketed over the following 17 years through such companies as Yacht Cruising Association, Seven Seas and Island Sailing Ltd, all of Great Britain.

A good example of the flotilla concept's phenomenal success is Island Sailing, which started its Greek Sailing operations in 1976 with close to a dozen small sailboats. In 1989 with assistance from Managing Director Chris Gordon and its parent company Sunsail Ltd, Island Sailing owned and operated over 600 yachts, offering approximately 40 separate 9–12 yacht flotillas to locations throughout the Mediterranean (Sunsail, 1989, p.2).

Case Study of Company Island Adventures

How Island Adventures Started

Island Adventures was conceived in late 1983 after founders Harold and Kathy Richins experienced the excitement of sailing a yacht in the Greek Isles and foresaw the possibilities for North Americans. After limited market research (which consisted of reviewing various secondary advertising reports from consumer travel magazines), it was decided that there was indeed an American market niche that was scarcely being tapped for not only sailing holidays, but flotilla sailing holidays in particular. Broad based reports were understood to have

Figure 14.1

Figure 14.2

Figure 14.1 Cooperative display advertisement placed in *Chartering* magazine

Figure 14.2 Island Adventures' display advertisement placed in *Cruising World*, *Sail*, *Chartering* and *Yacht Vacations* magazines

indicated that Americans spent a good proportion of their discretionary dollars on travel with most overseas travel going to Western Europe. With this in mind, a 'non-scientific conclusion' was reached (like many small businesses who have little or no funds for research) that there would be a market opportunity for sailors and their families to travel to the Mediterranean and participate in a flotilla.

In late 1983, Island Sailing Ltd, a British company, was formally approached and an agreement was reached for the newly-formed Island Adventures Sailing Holidays to represent them as a charter broker in the United States and Canada. This was a mutually beneficial business relationship since Island Sailing was certainly interested in improving its limited North American sales.

Island Adventures increased its sailing and motor yachting offerings over the years by continued investigation in the field and by visiting other chartering organizations, finding those that could offer the high standards and quality Island

Figure 14.3 Island Adventures' display advertisement placed in *Cruising World*, *Sail*, *Chartering* and *Yacht Vacations* magazines

Figure 14.4 Island Adventures' logo design and business card

Adventures required for its clients. These exploratory travels took the owners to Turkey, Yugoslavia, Great Britain, Greece, Italy, the Caribbean, the San Juans, and other areas in the United States including Hawaii.

Island Adventures specialized in selling flotilla, bareboat and crewed yachting holidays direct to customers, through common travel agencies and through individual agents. In addition, it offered accommodations, airline tickets, special tours and other services to its clients. Primarily, however, Island Adventures was a specialty travel agent or broker-representative working for the managing yacht companies it selected and was chiefly involved with direct marketing to its customers. After five years of steady growth, challenges, and many exciting experiences in the travel world that would otherwise not have been possible, Island Adventures was sold in the Spring of 1989.

Marketing the Business

Island Adventures started quite conservatively, learning by nominal mistakes and steady successes, and utilizing a deliberate method of lowered risk through a measured infusion of funds and an accompanying delayed growth in business. With a sizable number of word-of-mouth recommendations and the use of local promotions and slide presentations to local groups, most of the first year's charterers came from the Oregon area. This regional approach broadened in scope the following year to advertisements in large scale, national special interest magazines (see Figures 14.1–14.4). Work with regional, national, and international clients was effectively continued throughout the first five years of Island Adventures' operations.

Dealing with Clients

Effectively addressing clients needs is one of the most time-consuming, challenging, and important aspects of any business. Island Adventures was no exception. Fast, friendly, personalized and flexible service with a little extra thrown in was the strength of the company. Strict guidelines were set up to achieve this success with clients. Extra services such as destination advice, communication of local knowledge, charts and maps delivered to the potential clients and a computerized booking, filing and information system were offered with favourable response. Quality and service guidelines were developed to accommodate the potential yacht charterer:

> We have strict standards for the professionals with whom we work: All bareboats are three years old or newer, and are well maintained and equipped... All yachts with crew are ... in beautiful, hotel-like conditions. We have the lowest prices available, without skimping on quality and service. We go out of our way to please our clients ... the most important aspect of our business! We can advise you on the best area, the boats, what to bring, what to watch out for and where to go (Island Adventures, 1988).

Dealing with Companies

Companies offering yachting holidays vary considerably, and in choosing the correct companies to work with, considerations had to be made in such areas as the quality of operations, discounts and commissions passed on to the broker, types of holidays and selection of yachts being offered, credibility, and reliability of service. Yacht owner/operators varied from one person 'old salts', who have a creaky old yacht offering a truly 'rough' experience, to companies such as Island

Sailing or The Moorings, both of which operated extensive fleets of yachts with large numbers of staff, high tech booking and communications systems, and standards of quality and service well above the average.

Understanding the 'Industry'

One of the major shortcomings in many unique niche type businesses such as Island Adventures is the failure to fully understand the industry. Island Adventures undertook preliminary research (e.g. travel to destinations and company locations, discussions, association meetings, familiarization trips to observe foreign charter enterprises, client questionnaires, acquiring competitor information) during the development process.

Pitfalls and Headaches

A small business can have a difficult time making ends meet if major events beyond its control have an effect on business. Emerald Yacht Charters, which only offered sailing charters to the small island group of Fiji, was severely impacted by the political unrest in that country. After a decent business start in 1984 and 1985, Island Adventures, which had been concentrating on the Eastern Mediterranean during those years, also suffered with the rest of the European travel companies during the terrorist attacks of 1985 and 1986. A number of groups who had already booked and paid large deposits cancelled or postponed their trips. In order to minimize future risk, Island Adventures expanded its offerings to locations in other parts of the world.

Travel/tourism businesses need to take measures to address potential down turns due to major world, political or financial events beyond their control. This is particularly so with special interest travel which has a very narrow market niche.

Changes Within the Yachting Holidays Industry

Since the early days there have been a number of major changes that have occurred in the yacht chartering industry. Some of these changes have included an increased number of companies offering chartering vacations, the increased professionalism of the industry, improved marketing techniques, improved quality of service and more use of specialty travel agents for increased charter sales.

In the last ten years, a change in demand has resulted in the building of sleeker and more high performance yachts for chartering, an expansion of the diverse offerings both in the higher and the lower end of the market, the recognition of new customer markets such as Japan, Germany and Brazil and an expansion of chartering offerings into newer and more exotic destinations such as the South Pacific, Thailand, the Seychelles, Alaska, Brazil, Australia and the Galapagos Islands (Robinson, 1984, p.9).

Yachting holidays will continue to be offered through innovative approaches and enhancements for the clients. Though there is currently little understanding and standardization of the industry, general travel agents may eventually have the skills to represent and market small yacht holidays in a somewhat similar way to how they currently offer large cruise ship packages (Deland, 1985, p.xi). Due to the diversity and lack of any real central control and regulation of the charter yacht industry, these skills are presently reserved for specialty charter agents, owner/operators and brokers.

The Enticement of a Yachting Holiday

Yacht chartering has attracted great enthusiasm from its customers and among the companies offering these enchanting holidays. From being available to only a select few, chartering a yacht has become an exciting and rewarding holiday option for an increasing number of experienced and inexperienced yachts-people. Advertising for the yacht *Ovation* illustrates the emphasis on luxury and service:

> From the moment you step aboard, and we greet you with our official Standing Ovation drink, Ovation will surround you with leisure and luxury … and a style of hospitality you won't find anywhere else. The dining is superb—every meal is abundant, delicious, and expertly prepared and a selection of wines and champagnes are always in stock …. Try the windsurfer, picnic on the beach, go exploring in the dinghy … take a turn at the wheel … breakfast in bed, fresh flowers in your stateroom … we're thinking of you from sun up to sunset … experience luxury on a very personal scale (Ovation, 1989).

The above discussion has tried to give the reader a better understanding of the nature of chartering a yacht as a special interest tourism activity. Through a brief review of a small company specializing in yachting holidays, the reader should have gained insights of various unique aspects of this 'industry'. By providing the kind of relatively low impact tourism discussed in this chapter, the yachting 'industry' can assist in bringing tourists into a destination in smaller numbers while minimizing the negative effects of large scale tourism development.

The hiring of a yacht allows people to enjoy a small private group, experience distant cultures, see areas not usually touched by tourists, and, at the same time, be involved in a fulfilling holiday that is participative, dynamic and personal in nature. Yachting holidays are a growing segment of special interest tourism that, in future years, will continue to provide enjoyment and satisfaction to a wider cross-section of the travelling public. In providing for the diverse needs of these additional clients, pioneering yacht chartering companies will continue to enhance and expand their offerings to newer, more remote, and more 'exotic' locations throughout the world.

References

Anonymous, 1985, Nancy Stout: specializing in the Caribbean, St. Thomas' blue water cruises began with five boats and has developed a worldwide charter network, *Chartering*, February, 64–5

Anonymous, 1987, Dick Jachney, CYC's founder is a detail man, *Chartering*, May, 4–5

Deland, A., 1985, Fielding's worldwide cruises, William and Morrow, New York

Grotta, D., Grotta, S., 1986, Island odysseys by charter yacht, *Islands*, September/October, 67–72

Hartman, T., 1985, David Halsey: with a mainstay of yacht charter vacations, Halsey Marine has evolved as a chronicle to today's charter industry, *Chartering*, February, 54–98

Hartman, T., 1986, Julie Nicholson, charter yacht pioneer Julie P. Nicholson was introduced to the business of yacht chartering when she gazed into the eyes of her eventual husband after sailing onto the island of Antigua in the British West Indies, *Chartering*, March, 65–86

Herron, M., 1982, Voyaging to a small obsession: Mary Crowley and her ships, *Sail*, February, 58–63

Island Adventures, 1988, *Sailing holidays brochure*, Island Adventures

Jennings, G., 1986, The yacht cruising association: villa flotillas are added to the Mediterranean menu, *Chartering*, June/July 20–1

Mermon, D., 1983, *An angler's virgin territory*, Charter World International, July 4 (2): 3–5

Ocean Voyages, 1986, *Promotional brochure*, Ocean Voyages

Ovation, 1989, *Promotional brochure*, Ovation

Robinson, B., 1984, *Where to cruise*, W.W. Norton, New York

Robinson, B., 1986, *The Caribbean cruising handbook: a planning guide for charterers and private owners*, Dodd, Mead & Company, New York

Rogers, B., Thomas, A., 1986, The dollars and sense of it!, *Chartering*, February, 94–5

Scott, S., Scott, N., 1986, *The cruising guide to the Virgin Islands*, Cruising Guide Publications, Clearwater

Shepard, M., 1985, Ginny and Charlie Cary: caring and hard work are qualities which Ginny and Charlie Cary bring to the charter yacht industry, *Chartering*, April, 63–85

Sunsail, 1989, *Brochure on Sardinia, Corsica, Elba, Greece, Turkey, Yugoslavia*, Sunsail

Swinglehurst, E., 1982, *The world's greatest adventure holidays: a guide to the best climbing, trekking, safari, railway, winter, river and sea adventures in the world*, Proteus, London

Valef Yachts S.A., 1988, *Advertisement*, Valef Yachts S.A.

15 CONCLUSION

Special Interest Tourism: In Search of an Alternative

Betty Weiler and C. Michael Hall

Summarizing a collection of tourism market segments and products as diverse as those encompassed within the rubric of 'special interest tourism' is indeed challenging. The differences between the various types of special interest tourism at times appear to be more numerous than the similarities. Moreover, the limited amount of research that has been done seems to raise more questions than answers. Notwithstanding these observations, this chapter examines some of the commonalities that can be identified in the special interest tourism literature from the perspective of the tourist, the host population and environment, and the tourism industry, in order to provide a comprehensive perspective on the phenomenon. Implications for the future and suggestions for further research are discussed throughout the chapter.

The Scope of Special Interest Tourism

The topics of the review chapters in this book were selected to give a broad overview of special interest tourism. They do not constitute an exhaustive list of special interest tourism markets and products. For example, farm tourism, working vacations, religious holidays and pilgrimages, and wine/gourmet tours are further examples of well-established special interest tourism products (Hall, 1989; *Specialty Travel Index*). The range of topics for the case studies is even more limited, being restricted by availability of research, expertise on the topic, and space in the book.

Trying to compartmentalize particular types of special interest tourism is not without its risk. Clearly, there are overlaps between the main categories such as heritage, arts and ethnic tourism, which might easily be seen to come under the umbrella of cultural tourism. There is overlap between ethnic and adventure tourism, and adventure tourism also includes some sport and nature-based travel. Educational travel is sometime nature-based, sometimes culture-based.

Rather than quibble over terminology and categories, it is perhaps of more value to reiterate the rationale for the inclusion of each. A special interest tourism experience is always motivated primarily by that particular interest. As noted in the introductory chapter, 'it is the hub around which the total experience is planned and developed' (Read, 1980, p.195). Sometimes, the particular activity or experience might serve more than one purpose, such as being both educational and outdoor activity-based. Regardless, it is the special interest that motivates the trip and influences other decision-making by the tourist.

The Tourist

> To [people] of taste and intelligence, the standard holiday trip has frequently become, at best, a crushing bore, at worst a horror, a nightmare (Frommer, 1989, p.xiii).

From the point of view of the traveller, the trips and travel experiences described in this book are anything but boring. In fact, although there are significant differences between the various types of special interest tourism, there seems to be a common thread in that much of it is novelty-seeking, and all of it is quality-seeking.

What is novelty? The examples in this book illustrate that novelty-seeking comes in many forms, but mainly relates to the two foci of 'activity' and 'destination' discussed in the introductory chapter and illustrated in Table 1.3. The special interest *activity* itself may be a novel one to the tourist, such as a tourist trying fossicking or visiting a foreign culture for the first time. A slightly different type of novelty-seeking is the pursuit of a new variation to a familiar activity, such as birdwatching in a different season in the hope of seeing a different species. Often, however, the special interest is a familiar one, but the tourist seeks a novel location, environment or *destination* in which to pursue the activity. This is evident in activities such as scuba diving, mountain climbing and yachting. Finally, novelty may simply be in the social environment, for example in the company of a high-quality tour leader and/or other tourists with similar interests, such as on an educational tour. In every case, novelty-seeking does seem to be an important component of special interest tourism.

What is quality? Within all service industries, quality has become a major concern, and it is a theme often heard in conventional mass tourism. However, its intangible, subjective nature makes quality elusive and difficult to achieve. According to Read (1980), quality travel is Rewarding, Enriching, Adventuresome, and a Learning experience – or REAL travel. While this may be a catchy and laudable objective, it provides limited insight as to how it might be achieved.

In the case of special interest tourism, quality is achieved partly through a participatory or experiential dimension. While not necessarily physically demanding, special interest tourism has an active component that demands the commitment of the traveller either mentally (e.g. educational travel), physically (e.g. sport tourism), emotionally (e.g. ethnic tourism), or some combination of these. In cases where a tour leader is present, this person can play a critical role in facilitating active participation and thus enhancing the quality of the experience.

The pursuit of quality may be closely related to the concept of authenticity. Does special interest tourism provide a more authentic experience? Do participants of special interest tours perceive them to be more authentic? If the tourist perceives the experience to be an authentic one, is it then a quality experience?

These are areas in need of further research in special interest tourism.

Therefore, most travel to pursue a particular hobby, recreational interest, or sport, that is in some way novelty-seeking, quality-oriented and experientially-based can justifiably be included in special interest tourism. In addition to quality and experiential components, another common element of all special interest tourism is the shared social or cultural world of the travellers (see discussion in introductory chapter). This is particularly evident in very focused special interests such as particular sports, adventure travel and nature-based tourism. Although special interest tourism is not by definition a quality experience, the combined presence of an experiential dimension and a shared social world which satisfies an individual's travel motivations makes the likelihood of a quality experience greater than in conventional mass tourism.

Regarding the profile of special interest travellers, they appear to be very diverse in socio-demographic characteristics. One of the few commonalities, at least in the examples in this book, is that special interest tourists are adults, usually travelling without children. Some of the case studies have provided limited evidence that special interest travellers are better educated and from higher income strata. As with most travellers, they are also typically from Western and developed countries. It is not known whether they have similar psychographic profiles, but this seems likely, and would be a fruitful avenue for future research. Certainly they are similar in their desire for novelty, quality and experiential travel.

With respect to travel behaviour, the one aspect that seems to be consistent throughout the book is the 'seeking' behaviour. Iso-Ahola (1989) postulates that all leisure motivation can be separated into two tendencies, escaping (avoidance) and seeking (search). Special interest tourists seem to be much more concerned with seeking both personal and interpersonal rewards and opportunities rather than with escaping personal and interpersonal environments. However, research is needed concerning the relationship between special interest tourists' motives and Iso-Ahola's theory of leisure motivation.

Host Population and Environment

> An ecological, or sustainable, tourism implies that the human and natural ecosystems of an area will be able to adapt to the stresses of tourism in a way that does not threaten their continued functioning... The issue of sustainability in tourism, then, seems to come down to whether the culture will adapt and yet retain its fundamental character through a period of change or whether tourists will destroy the qualities that attracted them in the first place and in the process leave the local inhabitants worse off (Goering, 1990, p.24).

A quality tourism product from the tourist's point of view is only one side of the picture. How much potential does special interest tourism have to provide a quality experience for the host population?

It seems that different forms of special interest tourism differ considerably in their impact on both host populations and environments. Ethnic travel by its nature probably has the greatest impact, both positive and negative, on host populations.

Nature-based travel by definition probably has the greatest potential to impact the natural environment. But other types of special interest tourism such as adventure travel and heritage tourism also affect both the natural and the built environment. As discussed in the introductory chapter, the experiential nature of special interest tourism creates a greater need for intimate contact with the human and natural environment. It is often presumed that this symbiotic relationship results in positive social and environmental impacts, but further research is needed to determine if this is in fact the case.

Numerous papers and even conferences have been devoted to the theme of 'ethical', 'responsible' or 'appropriate' travel (Frommer, 1989; Gonsalves, 1987; Richter, 1987; Kutay, 1989). Efforts to make tourism both culturally and environmentally 'sustainable' have been discussed for conventional mass tourism, but only limited consideration has been given to the role of special interest tourism in achieving this objective.

The principles of an alternative form of tourism discussed by Harron and Weiler in their chapter on ethnic tourism apply equally well to other forms of special interest tourism. Clearly, there needs to be some local control in choosing to become involved in tourism, in selecting the type of tourism development, in determining the scale and rate of development, and particularly in choosing which tourists will be encouraged to visit. By choosing to cater to special interest tourists, the local population may gain control in many other aspects of tourism.

In addition to local control, the other major ingredient to achieving quality tourism from the host population's point of view seems to be the education of the tourist. This has led to the development of codes of ethics and guides, both for culturally-appropriate behaviour in other cultures as well as environmentally-sensitive behaviour (see Table 7.2; Mitchell, 1988; Community Aid Abroad, 1990). While their distribution and enforcement have been limited, the nature of special interest tourism, in particular the shared social world of its participants, lends itself to the sharing of these behavioural guidelines with tourists (see Chapters 2 and 9).

Codes of ethics only go so far; to change behaviour, we need to change attitudes. 'Real change toward a more sustainable tourism will come only when tourists change their attitudes' (Goering, 1990, p.24). Again, special interest tourism lends itself to such attitude change, as the market is relatively defined. As suggested in Chapter 2 by Kalinowski and Weiler, education regarding the need for behavioural change, as well as the appropriate behaviour itself, can be incorporated into all stages of the travel experience.

Whether special interest tourists are open to such change is a matter still to be determined. The key will be to educate the tourist that a high-quality experience is dependent on appropriate social and environmental behaviour.

The Tourism Industry

> The common goal [of tourists and hosts] must be to develop and promote new forms of tourism, which will bring the greatest possible benefit to all the participants – travellers,

> the host population *and the tourist business* – without causing intolerable ecological and social damage (Krippendorf, 1987, p.106).

Few writers have seriously considered the benefits and costs of special interest tourism from the tourism industry's perspective. The growth of alternative guidebooks and indexes (for example, Frommer, 1989; *Index of Cultural, Environmental, Educational Tourism*; *Specialty Travel Index*) would suggest that marketers are well aware of the demand for such travel experiences. However, supplying such opportunities has generally been on an *ad hoc* basis, ranging from fully independent travel to all-inclusive package tours.

One of the few writers who recognizes that alternative tourism must be sensitive to the needs of industry is Krippendorf (1987). He also holds the industry partially responsible for achieving such quality:

> I want to call on all suppliers of tourist services to acknowledge their responsibilities towards travellers, the host population and the tourist environment, to state clearly what contribution they are prepared to make to a more human tourism and what regulations they are willing to observe. I propose that they should formulate and make public a code of practice and the principles of their internal and external business conduct. Not in a few beautifully worded and vague sentences but in concrete and practicable policy statements, to which they would be answerable (Krippendorf, 1987, pp.138–89).

One example of industry's attempt to take responsibility on the environmental front is the Australian Tourism Industry Association's (1990) *Code of Environmental Practice for the Australian Tourism Industry*. Specific guidelines have yet to be developed for particular segments of the industry including tour operators, but the Code is certainly a step in the right direction.

The education and training sector of the tourism industry also has a role to play. Most tourism textbooks, in their effort to comprehensively examine all industry segments, are oriented mainly to conventional mass tourism. Some texts focus on one type of tourism such as foreign independent tours (Poynter, 1989), on one management tool such as marketing (Morrison, 1989), or on one disciplinary perspective such as geography (Pearce, 1987), anthropology (Smith, 1989), or psychology (Pearce, 1988). Perhaps the diversity in special interest travel markets does not lend itself to the preparation of texts and manuals on 'how to develop and operate special interest travel experiences'. The common elements identified above for both the tourist and the host/destination, however, suggest that there are principles and approaches that are common to all forms of special interest tourism. Some of the experiences shared by Wood (Chapter 4) and by Richins (Chapter 15) in their descriptions of special interest tour companies, along with the guidelines outlined by Harron and Weiler (Chapter 7) and Valentine (Chapter 9), provide a beginning to the development of a text or manual on providing high-quality experiences for these market segments.

The Future

The growing sophistication of travellers, resulting in part from demographic, economic and technological changes in society, has contributed to the blossoming of special interest tourism as a major component of modern tourism. Its future will be driven by the demands of these tourists and by the opportunities and limitations of the cultural and natural environments on which special interest tourism depends. If the reviews and case studies of this book are any indication, special interest tourism has an exciting and dynamic future.

References

Australian Tourism Industry Association, 1990, *Code of environmental practice for the Australian tourism industry*, Australian Tourism Industry Association, Canberra

Community Aid Abroad, 1990, *Travel wise and be welcome: A guide to responsible travel in the 90s*, Community Aid Abroad, Melbourne

Frommer, A., 1989, *The new world of travel 1989*, Prentice Hall, New York

Goering, P.G., 1990, The response to tourism in Ladakh, *Cultural Survival Quarterly* 14 (1): 20–25

Gonsalves, P.S., 1987, Alternative tourism – the evolution of a concept and establishment of a network, *Tourism Recreation Research* 12 (2): 9–12

Hall, C.M., 1989, Special interest travel: A prime force in the expansion of tourism?, 81–89 in R. Welch, ed., *Geography in action*, University of Otago, Dunedin

Index of Cultural, Environmental, Educational Tourism, ICEET, St Kilda West, Australia

Iso-Ahola, S.E., 1989, Motivations for Leisure, 247–279 in E.L. Jackson, and T.L. Burton, eds, *Understanding leisure and recreation: mapping the past, charting the future*, Venture Publishing, State College, PA

Krippendorf, J., 1987, *The holiday makers: understanding the impact of leisure and travel*, Heinemann, Oxford

Kutay, K., 1989, The new ethic in adventure travel, *Buzzworm: The Environmental Journal* 1 (4): 31–36

Mitchell, P.A.M., 1988, *The traveller's guide to good manners*, Gooday Publishers, West Sussey

Morrison, A.M., 1989, *Hospitality and travel marketing*, Delmar Publishing, Albany

Pearce, D., 1987, *Tourism today: a geographical analysis*, Longman, Essex

Pearce, P.L., 1988, *The Ulysses factor: evaluating visitors in tourist settings*, Springer-Verlag, New York

Poynter, J., 1989, *Foreign independent tours: planning, pricing, and processing*, Delmar Publishers, Albany

Read, S.E., 1980, A prime force in the expansion of tourism in the next decade: special interest travel, 193–202 in D.E. Hawkins, E.L. Shafer, J.M. Rovelstad, eds, *Tourism marketing and management issues*, George Washington University, Washington D.C.

Richter, L.K., 1987, The search for appropriate tourism, *Tourism Recreation Research* 12 (2): 5–7

Smith, V.L., ed., 1989, *Hosts and guests: the anthropology of tourism*, 2nd ed., University of Pennsylvania, Philadelphia

Specialty Travel Index: Directory of Special Interest Travel, Alpine Hansen Publishers, San Anselmo, CA

Subject Index

Author Index

Place Index